Law and the
Hospitality Industry

Law and the Hospitality Industry

SECOND EDITION

Sandi Towers-Romero
FLORIDA SOUTHWESTERN STATE COLLEGE

CAROLINA ACADEMIC PRESS
Durham, North Carolina

Library of Congress Cataloging-in-Publication Data

Names: Towers-Romero, Sandi, author.
Title: Law and the hospitality industry / by Sandi Towers-Romero.
Description: Second edition. | Durham, North Carolina : Carolina Academic
    Press, 2021. | Includes index.
Identifiers: LCCN 2021020633 (print) | LCCN 2021020634 (ebook) | ISBN
    9781531022495 (paperback) | ISBN 9781531022501 (ebook)
Subjects: LCSH: Hotels--Law and legislation--United States. | Hospitality
    industry--Law and legislation--United States. | Hotel management--Law
    and legislation--United States. | Tourism--Law and legislation--United
    States.
Classification: LCC KF2042.H6 T69 2021 (print) | LCC KF2042.H6 (ebook) |
    DDC 343.7307/891--dc23
LC record available at https://lccn.loc.gov/2021020633
LC ebook record available at https://lccn.loc.gov/2021020634

CAROLINA ACADEMIC PRESS
700 Kent Street
Durham, North Carolina 27701
(919) 489-7486
www.cap-press.com

Printed in the United States of America

To my students, my friends, my colleagues and the wonderful staff at Carolina Academic Press.

Contents

Table of Cases

Preface to the First Edition

Law and the Hospitality Industry was designed and written to give the reader an easy-to-understand view of the multifaceted world of hospitality law. Both United States and international law are highlighted in this text. Within each chapter are found chapter objectives, chapter summary, and key terms — all meant to give the reader a better understanding of the subject-matter.

Law and the Hospitality Industry was designed to be versatile — it can be used as a complete text, a reference book, or as a hospitality manager's legal handbook.

Sandi Towers-Romero

Preface to the Second Edition

I am so excited to welcome you to the completely updated *Law and the Hospitality Industry*.

New cases in the second edition include:

> *Bostock v. Clayton County, Georgia*
> *Braswell v. Colonial Pipeline Co.*
> *California, et al. vs. Texas, et al.*
> *Craig v. Boren*
> *Department of Revenue of Ky. v. Davis*
> *Fisher v. University of Texas at Austin I and II*
> *Granholm v. Heald*
> *Guy v. Baltimore*
> *Stricker v. Shor*
> *Tennessee Wine and Spirits Retailers Assn. v. Thomas, Executive Director of the Tennessee Alcoholic Beverage Commission, et al.*
> *Texas v. Azar*

Other new material in the second edition includes:

A Note on the COVID-19's Pandemic Impact on the Hospitality Industry

Chapter One:

- Complete update on the associations in the hospitality industry — their new roles and new statistics
- Updates on states having regulations over the hospitality industry
- Update on the High Speed Rail Initiative
- Update on Cruise Lines International Association (CLIA®)
- Update on Indian Gaming

Chapter Two:

- Update on franchising fees
- Update on international franchising requirements, including the new Brazilian Franchise Law

Chapter Three:

- Update on Federal Unemployment Tax Act (FUTA)
- Inclusion of *Bostock v. Clayton County, Georgia,* 590 U.S. ___ (2020), (S. Ct. June 15, 2020) the Supreme Court held that firing individuals because of their sexual orientation or transgender status violates Title VII's prohibition on discrimination because of sex. Title VII prohibits discrimination because of an "individual's ... sex." 42 U.S.C. § 2000e-2(a)(1).

Chapter Five:

- Updates on the Restatement of Torts 2nd and 3rd

Chapter Six:

- Updates on State Innkeepers' Laws

Chapter Seven:

- Update on background checks for employment
- Update on affirmative action and *Fisher v. University of Texas at Austin I,* 570 U.S. 297 (2013), the USSC stated the 5th Circuit Court of Appeals should apply strict scrutiny to determine the constitutionality of the University's race-sensitive admissions policy, and in *Fisher II,* 579 U.S. ___, 136 S. Ct. 2198, 195 L, Ed, 2d 511, (2016) the USSC held the Court of Appeals for the 5th Circuit correctly found that the University of Texas at Austin's undergraduate admission policy survived strict scrutiny.
- Update on how to qualify employees for employee exemptions as to overtime pay
- Complete update on tip credits — their use and amounts
- Update on when tip pooling is allowed
- Inclusion of updates on the Trade Adjustment Assistance Reauthorization Act 2015

Chapter Eight:

- Discussion of the Defend Trade Secrets Act of 2016 (DTSA)

Chapter Nine:

- Update on the roles of the Hotel and Motel Associations

Chapter Ten:

- Update on the FDA and defining gluten free
- Inclusion and discussion of *Tennessee Wine and Spirits Retailers Assn. v. Thomas, Executive Director of the Tennessee Alcoholic Beverage Commission, et al.,* 139 S. Ct. 2449 (2019), a case that chipped away at some of a state's control over alcohol.

Chapter Twelve:

- Update to the Alabama Workers' Compensation Law
- Update to the Affordable Care Act (ACA)
- Inclusion and discussion of *California, et al. vs. Texas, et al. and California v. Texas* as they pertain to the future of the ACA
- Update on the ACA and small businesses

Enjoy!

Sandi Towers-Romero, May 2021

A Note on the COVID-19 Pandemic's Impact on the Hospitality Industry

This book is being updated for the second edition, during the first worldwide pandemic in 100-years — COVID-19. The Spanish Flu pandemic of 1918 to 1920, affected the hospitality industry the same as today — with social distancing, lockdowns, required mask wearing, and limiting access to public places. Governments encouraged higher sanitation procedures, and yes, there was the mass distribution of flu vaccines. Just as today, there were protests against these restrictions. Some people felt they went too far, and some felt stricter measures were called for.

> It was reported in the cities of Minneapolis and St. Paul, Minnesota, that several establishments serving alcohol and food deliberately broke the Spanish Flu closing order to continue their regular business. "One saloon was discovered with the back door route open."
>
> The elevator regulations in St. Paul were particularly unpopular. "Some of the downtown hotels objected to stopping their elevators, saying that they would lose guests." This caused a change in the regulations to permit hotel elevators and those in apartment houses to operate. Many people insisted it was unhealthy for the sick to be forced to climb stairs in their impaired state, while others felt concerned people would be shut off from fresh air if they were not allowed to use their elevators. The city of St. Paul compromised and all elevators were back in use starting November 9, 1918, although only one person per 5 square feet was permitted. (www.ncbi.nlm.nih.gov/pmc/articles/PMC1997248)

Fast-forward to 2020–2021, and the hospitality industry is now following similar, albeit, more modern protocols and mandates that were imposed 100-years ago during the Spanish Flu pandemic:

- Requiring social distancing in enclosed areas
- Increased sanitation measures — from more regular and deeper cleaning procedures, to the installation of HEPA air filters in ventilation systems
- Limiting the number of guests at hospitality functions, to allow for social distancing
- Lockdowns of establishments such as restaurants and especially "saloons" — bars and nightclubs
- Mask mandates prior to entering the hospitality business or venue.

As I am writing this, there are multiple vaccines being distributed and administered around the globe. They are promising great efficacy in protecting against the COVID-19 virus. As such, I felt adding this issue to the core of the book would make the book less relevant and dated as the world hopefully reopens in the near future. But still, we need to look briefly at COVID's lasting impact on the hospitality industry.

Impact on Hospitality
- According to the American Hotel and Lodging Association, 71% of American hotels will not make it for another 6 months without federal assistance, as per projected travel demands. (www.ahla.com)
- The World Travel & Tourism Council has recently warned the COVID-19 pandemic could lead to a cut of 50 million jobs worldwide, in the travel and tourism industry. As per an Oxford economics study, Asia is expected to be the worst affected. The hospitality industry accounts for 10% of global GDP. (www. hospitalityinsights.ehl.edu)

Impact by Country
- **Fiji's** tourism total contribution to GDP: $2 billion (39.3 percent of total GDP). Jobs reliant on tourism: 117,200 (35.7 percent of all jobs). Fiji tourist arrivals fell by 99 percent in May 2020, compared with the same period 2019. With such a large chunk of its revenue usually relying on foreign visitors, the country is expecting its overall economy to decline by 21.7 percent in 2020. (www.travelpulse.com)
- **Belize's** tourism total contribution to GDP: $794 million (41.8 percent of total GDP). Jobs reliant on tourism: 61,400 (37.1 percent of all jobs). Without tourism dollars coming in, indigenous business

owners in Belize are closing up shop and reverting to their roots as farmers and fisherman to sustain themselves. (www.travelpulse.com)

- In **Thailand** 11% of the population rely on tourism for their income, that is 4.4 million people. After a record 39.8 million foreign visitors in 2019, whose spending accounted for 11.4% of gross domestic product, Thailand had looked to welcome more than 40 million tourists in 2020. But with flight bans and quarantines, the Central Bank of Thailand expects only 8 million visitors this year. (www.weforum.org)
- **Mexico** is perhaps the most vulnerable of the countries, with 15.5% of its GDP relying on the travel and tourism industry. (www.we forum.org)
- **Spain and Italy** are highly vulnerable; Spain owes 14.3% of its GDP and Italy owes 13.0% of its GDP to tourism. (www.weforum.org)
- In the **U.S.**, despite just 8.6% of GDP being associated with tourism, the travel and tourism industry represents 16.8 million jobs. (www. weforum.org)

Companies Filing for Bankruptcy Due to COVID
- **FoodFirst Global Holdings**, the parent company of restaurant chains Bravo Cucina Italiano and Brio Tuscan Grille, filed for Chapter 11 bankruptcy on April 10, 2020. (www.nbcnews.com)
- **CMX Cinemas**, a chain of movie theaters with dine-in options, filed for Chapter 11 bankruptcy on April 25, 2020. The theaters, are owned by parent company Cinemex Holdings. Cinemex was in the process of acquiring the Star Cinema Grill, a deal that was inked only six weeks prior to filing for bankruptcy. (www.nbcnews.com)
- **Hertz Corporation**, car rental services, filed for Chapter 11 bankruptcy on May 22, 2020. Hertz, also owns Dollar and Thrifty car rental brands. (www.nbcnews.com)
- French-inspired bakery and café chain **Le Pain Quotidien** filed for Chapter 11 bankruptcy on May 27, 2020. The company's U.S.-based unit, PQ New York, is selling its locations to Aurify Brands, which owns fast casual chains The Little Beet and Five Guys Burgers, among others. (www.nbcnews.com)
- **CEC Entertainment**, the parent company of kid-friendly Chuck E. Cheese restaurants, filed for Chapter 11 bankruptcy on June 24, 2020. The Texas-based company operates over 700 Chuck E. Cheese and Peter Piper's Pizza locations. (www.nbcnews.com)
- **Cirque du Soleil**, the Canadian-based acrobatics and entertainment group, filed for Chapter 15 bankruptcy on June 29, 2020. The com-

pany said their financial restructuring is due to pandemic-related cancellations and closures. (www.nbcnews.com)

- **Sizzler USA**, the operator of the casual steakhouse chain, filed for Chapter 11 bankruptcy on Sept. 21, 2020. The 62-year-old brand cited the filing as a direct result of pandemic financial strain and stated it plans to keep all of its 14 company-owned locations open. This information is according to a press release from Sizzler. Sizzler also has more than 90 franchised locations. (www.nbcnews.com)
- **Garden Fresh Restaurants**, LLC (Souplantation/Sweet Tomatoes) is liquidating all assets under their Chapter 7 Bankruptcy filing. The chain, could not survive the impact of the COVID-19 pandemic. They permanently closed all 97 restaurants and 3 distribution centers in early May 2020. It is, to-date, the largest restaurant bankruptcy and liquidation as a result of the pandemic. (www.prnewswire.com)
- **Thai Airways** officially entered its bankruptcy reorganization, filed on 27 May 2020. This bankruptcy reorganization was granted by the Central Bankruptcy Court of Thailand on 14 September, 2020. This allows the company to proceed with its recovery plans. The company expects to complete the legal steps and be fully into its reorganization process before the end of first quarter, 2021. (www.paxex.aero)

This is a short list of bankruptcy filings due to COVID-19. Not all of these filings will result in complete closures, unless so noted, but it shows the severe economic distress placed on the hospitality industry resulting from this pandemic.

Expansion of Chapter 11 Bankruptcy for Small Businesses

On February 19, 2020, the Small Business Reorganization Act (SBRA), added a new subchapter to the United States Bankruptcy Code. Commonly referred to as Subchapter V, the SBRA was enacted in an effort to reduce the cost and expense of small business bankruptcy reorganizations. Congress passed this just in time for the global COVID-19 pandemic, which is anticipated to have a devastating impact on small businesses, especially the hospitality industry. Subchapter V may be a key to their survival. The Coronavirus Aid, Relief, and Economic Security (CARES) Act, which includes the first amendment to Subchapter V, greatly expanded bankruptcy protection to small businesses. In the first full year of Subchapter V, 1643 cases have been filed nationwide. (https://news.bloomberglaw.com/)

Who Is an Eligible Debtor under Subchapter V?

To be eligible for Subchapter V, an individual or business debtor must be engaged in a commercial activity with total debts of less than $2,725,625. In response to the COVID-19 pandemic, the Coronavirus Aid, Relief and Economic Security Act ("CARES") temporarily amended SBRA to increase the debt eligibility ceiling for Subchapter V to $7.5 million until March 27, 2022. (https://www.jdsupra.com/legalnews/global-pandemic-subchapter-v-debt-4550283/)

Face Masks, Quarantines, Lockdowns

As I am writing this in May 2021, Japan has declared a 3rd state of emergency for most of the country. In India, a variant of COVID is tearing through the country, infecting millions of people. Yet, the United States has just lifted its mask mandate for people that have been fully vaccinated. And, even bigger news, the European Union will reopen its borders to fully vaccinated, non-European visitors sometime in June 2021.

Other countries worldwide, and states in the U.S. have gone in and out of partial to total lockdowns. Of course the first businesses to be shut down are those that are considered non-essential, especially places where people gather in close proximity to each other, such as restaurants, theaters, theme parks, and especially bars. Many countries have imposed quarantines on people arriving into their country.

Which country, at this time, has been the most effective in controlling COVID-19, with the imposition of restrictions and lockdowns on their citizens? The winner at this time is ... New Zealand! Life within the country has gone back to pre-COVID times. They even celebrated the 2021 New Year with the normal crowds and fireworks. Does the country still have quarantines and restrictions on incoming visitors? Absolutely! But whatever Jacinda Ardern, New Zealand's 40th prime minister is doing, all I can say is "keep up the good work."

Looking ahead, as someone who loves the hospitality industry, I am hoping the world's vaccination effort is successful and we get back to "normal." I cannot wait to get into a plane, cruise ship, hotel, dine-in restaurant, theme park, casino, or any other place we gather in the hospitality industry!

Take care and enjoy the book!

Sandi

About the Author

Sandi Towers-Romero has been involved in the hospitality industry since the age of four. She was first introduced to this wonderful industry in the Catskills of New York. For twenty-five summers, Sandi learned first-hand the ins and outs of hospitality. At first, she would help her father with his role as athletic or social director, and when she was old enough, she became a water safety instructor, social director, and camp director; did front and back office work; and even did some dining service.

She has had her own travel agency in Corona del Mar, California; done tours to Mexico, Hollywood, Universal Studios, and NBC studios in Burbank, California. Sandi had her own tour operation to Cabo San Lucas, Mexico; has done the ground work for a fast-food franchise in London, England; given tours of Solomon's Castle in Florida; and taught students to become travel agents and flight attendants at Kottner Travel Institute in Honolulu, Hawaii. She has been around the world alone, twice, traveling by plane, train, boat, ship, car, bus, "tap-tap," rickshaw, camel, and elephant.

Besides holding her JD degree, she is also a graduate of Pacific Travel School in Santa Ana, California. She currently teaches hospitality law at Florida South-Western State College at their Fort Myers, Florida campus. Sandi has also taught business and law classes at South Florida Community College, Arcadia campus; Florida Southern College, Charlotte/DeSoto campus, and the University of California, Irvine. She has authored five other books— *The Essentials of Florida Real Estate Law, Media and Entertainment Law, Those of Distant Campfires, Then There's Tomorrow,* and *Sandi and the Ladybug.*

Law and the
Hospitality Industry

Chapter One

Overview of the Hospitality Industry

Chapter Objectives

What is the nature of the hospitality industry?

Who are the participants in the industry?

Who are they regulated by?

How does the internet affect the industry?

Travel Agents

What Is the Function of a Travel Agent?

Despite the use of online booking sites for all things travel, **travel agents** are still used by many.

A travel agent is the retail purveyor of vacation packages, cruises, tours, air and train tickets, hotel bookings, and car rental services. The travel agent interacts with all hospitality venues.

If managing a bed and breakfast, a major hotel chain, or working for a cruise line in your day-to-day operations, you will be communicating with a travel agent.

Travel Agent Compensation

Travel agents work on a commission basis from travel industry partners they represent — such as cruise lines and tour operators. They receive a percentage of the package price from the travel purveyor — this is usually around 10% for a cruise, tour, or hotel; up to 35% for selling a client trip cancellation insurance.

If a travel agent books flight segments only, they receive no commission from the airline. Thus, most travel agencies are now charging a service fee if the client is only making an airline booking.

Responsibilities of a Travel Agent

Travel agents have contractual obligations to their clients for travel services they book for them. They are **fiduciaries** of their clients. Thus, a travel agent must act *in the best interest of their client*, not the cruise company, or airline, hotel, etc.

> A fiduciary relationship is founded on trust or confidence reposed by one person in the integrity and fidelity of another.

A travel agent is expected to be knowledgeable in their field — if an agent represents a cruise line as being four-star rated and it is only of one-star quality, they can be held legally responsible under the tort of **misrepresentation**. It is therefore, imperative a travel agent be diligent in doing their research prior to representing and selling a product to their customers.

> Misrepresentation is an assertion by words or conduct that is not in accord with facts.

If the client is leaving their country of residence, a travel agent must, at the time of the travel booking, advise their clients of the necessary passport and visa requirements. The client should be informed to contact their local health department or personal physician concerning the need for any health or vaccination requirements for the scheduled trip. Not to do so can lead to legal action against the travel agent for **negligence**.

> Negligence occurs if a person departs from the conduct expected of a reasonably prudent person acting under similar circumstances.

At the time of booking, the travel agent must inform the client of the possibility and the amount of any cancellation fees, revision fees, service or fuel charges, or any other fees that may be charged by the supplier of the travel service.

Trip cancellation insurance should be discussed with the client. It needs to be noted if the client has any pre-existing conditions, e.g., a heart condition. Trip cancellation insurance will not cover pre-existing conditions unless travel insurance is purchased by the client at the time of payment for the trip. Some insurers will give a fourteen-day grace period from the date of payment and still cover pre-existing conditions, but it is best to advise the client to buy travel insurance sooner rather than later.

> Travel insurance protects a client's vacation costs against adverse events such as cancellation and interruption due to medical or other listed conditions and reimburses medical expenses and evacuation of the client from the countries covered under the policy. It also covers the loss or damage to property and transit delays.

The manager of a travel agency has the responsibility of training their staff to be knowledgeable in all areas of the travel agency business.

Travel Agency Regulators and Facilitators

ARC® Airline Reporting Corporation
Verified Travel Consultants (VTC®s)

Registration and the posting of bond used to be the requirement for travel agents to sell any U.S. or non-U.S. based air, bus, or rail tickets. Without an ARC® number a travel agent could not function. In July 2007, in response to the fact most travel agencies no longer sell airline, bus, or rail tickets without their inclusion in a tour or cruise package, The Airline Reporting Corporation® introduced ARC VTC® certification. This certification addresses the needs of a significant and growing segment of travel professionals — those that can benefit significantly from ARC®'s unique systems and services but are not, or are no longer ARC®-accredited for air, bus, and rail ticketing. VTC®s enjoy a streamlined, yet stringent, accreditation process that excludes such requirements as a bond or letter of credit associated with ticketing entities and full accreditation.

VTC®s can generate revenue through service fees by assessing their clients' credit card a fee for travel services rendered; they receive weekly payment using ARC®'s **Interactive Agent Reporting (IAR®) system**®. In addition, a VTC® has access to the 6,000-plus commissionable products and services that are offered through ARC MarketPlace®.

By becoming a VTC®, home-based, independent, and storefront agencies gain credibility with their clients.[1]

International Air Transport Association (IATA®)

As the IATA® name implies, this is the regulator of international air traffic. IATA® is an international trade body, created in Havana, Cuba, on 19 April 1945. Today, IATA® represents some 290 airlines comprising 82% of scheduled international air traffic.

Why IATA® Accreditation?

Choosing to become accredited with IATA® is a wise and strategic business choice. It ensures the agency and its sales are accurately identified and recognized by industry suppliers globally. Some 60,000 IATA travel agents worldwide currently benefit from IATA® accreditation, selling US $220 billion worth of airline tickets on behalf of IATA® airline members. IATA® accreditation simplifies the business relationship between travel agents and airlines.

IATA® Agency Benefits:

- Access to IATA® airline members with a single Sales Agency Agreement which authorizes the sale of international and/or domestic tickets
- Access to IATA®'s Billing and Settlement Plan, an interface for invoicing and payment between the agent, airlines, and transport providers
- Unique identification throughout the global travel industry with the "IATA® Numeric Code"
- Use of the "IATA® Accredited Agent" logo provides visibility and credibility on premises and websites
- Agent staff eligibility for the IATA® ID Card. This card gives access to the special deals of over 1,000 suppliers (*Author's note — As a travel agent, whenever I sought discounts on airlines, hotels, etc., in my travels, the number that was asked for first was the agency's IATA® number. Without this number, a travel supplier usually would not honor any travel agency discounts.*)
- Standardized procedures to ensure fair dealings with the airlines.[2]

---

1. www.arccorp.com.
2. www.iata.org.

American Society of Travel Advisors (ASTA®)

ASTA®, short for the American Society of Travel Advisors, is the world's largest association of travel professionals. Members include travel agents and the companies whose products they sell, such as tours, cruises, hotels, car rentals, etc. ASTA® is the leading advocate for travel agents, the travel industry, and the traveling public.[3]

The Travel Institute

The Travel Institute maintains information on travel industry employment opportunities as well as advice on working as a successful agent in the travel industry. The Travel Institute was born from the Institute of Certified Travel Agents (ICTA®) founded in 1964. ICTA® was founded on the purpose of attaining excellence and professionalism in the travel industry through continuing education. ICTA®, now The Travel Institute, established a travel intensive training program which has helped travel agents become more professional. Graduates of The Travel Institute are awarded the prestigious designation of **Certified Travel Counselor (CTC®), Certified Travel Associate (CTA®), or Certified Travel Industry Executive (CTIE®)**.[4]

Are There U.S. Federal Regulations of the Travel Industry?

Although there are no U.S. federal regulations for travel service, the following states do put forth regulations on the industry.

CALIFORNIA: California Business and Professional Code Section 17554
FLORIDA: Florida Statutes Annotated, Sections 559.927(10) and (11)
HAWAII: Hawaii Revised Laws, Section 468L
ILLINOIS: Illinois Travel Promotion Consumer Protection Act 815 ILCS 420
IOWA: Iowa Code Chapter 9D
LOUISIANA: Travel agencies must pay an occupational license tax based on gross commissions
MASSACHUSETTS: Massachusetts General Laws, Chapter 93A

3. www.asta.org.
4. www.thetravelinstitute.com.

NEVADA: Requires payment into a Consumer Recovery Fund
NEW YORK: Truth in Travel Act, Article 10-A §§ 155–159a
PENNSYLVANIA: Must post a $10,000 security bond. Under broker
statutes
RHODE ISLAND: Rhode Island Revised Laws Annotated, Section
5-52-12
VIRGINIA: Virginia Statutes, Section 59.1-448 et seq.
WASHINGTON: Washington Revised Code Sections 19.138 et seq.

Travel Agency Liability Issues

1. Failure to Provide Services Promised

Travel agents have a duty to use reasonable care when providing their services. If an agency knowingly represents a hotel, tour, or other travel service has a particular amenity and it does not, the agency may be held legally accountable for these statements.

If the agent or agency recklessly guaranteed a client that an important service or amenity would be available and if it was not, the agent and agency may face liability.

There is no liability on the part of the agency or the agent if something occurs that is out of control of the agency or travel agent. Examples of such events would be weather issues, tsunamis, a cruise ship breakdown, or closure of a hotel pool for repairs. If the agent had no prior knowledge or control of the event, the agent and agency will not face legal liability.

2. Failure to Honor an Agreed Upon Price

If an agent or agency represents the amount paid by a client will be the full price for a particular vacation, hotel room, or transportation, such information must be accurate. If it is not, and the client must pay more for the service, there is potentially legal liability against the agent or agency. If such misinformation was intentional, it would be misrepresentation; if reckless it would be negligence; and for not providing agreed upon services it would be a **breach of contract**.

3. Failure to Discover and Disclose

Travel agents have a fiduciary duty to their client. The client puts trust into what the agent and agency are representing. Just as in any representation made in a fiduciary relationship, the agent or agency must have knowledge the representation is true before making such representation.

This duty can be fulfilled if the agent has **actual knowledge** of what is represented. For example, if an agent tells a client a hotel is located in a very safe neighborhood and the agent recently stayed at the hotel, or the agent or agency can research what is being represented to the client.

Making representations without knowing the accuracy of the statements can lead to legal liability on the part of the agent and agency.

Transportation

Common Carriers

When a client selects transportation for their trip, they are choosing a **common carrier**. Common carriers include airlines, cruise ships, trains, buses, and freight transportation such as FedEx® and UPS®.

A common carrier is any association or corporation engaged in the business of carrying or transporting passengers or goods or both. They offer their services to the public for compensation. All common carriers have the duty to exercise the utmost care and extraordinary diligence in any contract of carriage. A common carrier is held absolutely liable for any damage to goods or the injury or death of a passenger.

There are, however, four exceptions to the liability of a common carrier:

- An act of nature causing damage
- An act of a public enemy causing damage
- Fault or fraud by the shipper causing damage
- An inherent defect in the goods causing damage

Common carriers are legally obligated to carry all passengers or freight if they have sufficient space; the agreed price is paid; and there are no reasonable grounds to refuse to do so. A common carrier that unjustifiably refuses to carry a particular person or cargo may be sued for damages.

The individual U.S. states regulate common carriers engaged in business within their borders (**intrastate**). If a common carrier travels **interstate** (between two or more states) or travels between countries (**foreign Nations**), the federal government, under the **Commerce Clause** in the United States Constitution, regulates the activities of such carriers.

The Commerce Clause is found in **Article 1, Section 8, Clause 3**, of the Constitution. This clause empowers Congress, "to regulate Commerce with foreign Nations, and among several States, and with the Indian Tribes." The term commerce means business or commercial exchanges in all of its forms between citizens of different states (interstate), including the passage of people from one state to another for either business or pleasure.

Airlines

The airline industry has transformed from a small exclusive form of transportation in the 1940s and 1950s to the preferred mode of transportation between two destinations in the 2020s.

The contract between passengers and the airline is called the **tariff**. The tariff defines the duties and obligations of the airline to the passenger. By law, the tariff in its entirety must be available to airline passengers. For the sake of inspection, the tariff can be delivered by email or mail to the client.

Delay or Cancellation of U.S. Flights

For domestic U.S. flights, there are no U.S. federal regulations that require any compensation for a delayed or cancelled flight. Compensation is required by U.S. law only when certain passengers are "bumped" from a flight that is oversold.[5]

Tarmac Delays/U.S. Flights

Under new federal rules, U.S. airlines operating domestic flights must allow passengers to deplane after a **tarmac delay** of three hours for U.S. flights and after four hours for all international flights at U.S. airports.[6] The only exceptions allowed are for safety or security, or if air traffic control advises the pilot otherwise. Carriers are also required to provide adequate food and drinking water within two hours of being delayed on the tarmac; they must also maintain operable lavatories and, if necessary, provide medical attention.[7]

---

5. www.airconsumer.dot.gov.
6. www.dot.gov.
7. ibid.

Delay or Cancellation of Non-U.S. Domestic Flights (Flights Intra-Country Outside the U.S.)

Rules for compensation for delayed and cancelled flights will depend on the rules of that country and the rules of the airline.

Delay or Cancellation of European Union Related Flights

Unlike the U.S., the **European Union** (EU) does provide for compensation for flight delays and cancellations. In most, but not all, cases involving a delay or cancellation of a flight, a passenger is entitled to compensation under **European Parliament Regulation (EC) 261/2004** for delayed and cancelled flights. There are three levels of compensation:[8]

- In the event of long delays (two hours or more, depending on the distance of the flight), passengers must, in every case, be offered free meals and refreshments plus two free telephone calls, telex, or fax messages, or emails.
- If the time of departure is deferred until the next day, passengers must also be offered hotel accommodation and transport between the airport and the place of accommodation.
- When the delay is five hours or longer, passengers may opt for reimbursement for the full cost of the ticket together with, when relevant, a return flight to the first point of departure.

This regulation applies to all airline flights departing from an EU airport or to any airline licensed in the EU if that flight is departing from an airport outside the EU and is going to an airport in an EU member state.[9]

Delay and Cancellation of Non-EU International Flights

The most relevant international treaty concerning non-EU flights is the **Montreal Convention, 1999**. This is an international agreement signed by the U.S. and many other countries. There is no specific language in this agreement that obligates the airline to compensate passengers in the event of a flight delay

---

8. www.ec.europa.eu.
9. www.airpassengersrights.eu.

or flight cancellation. Yet, the Montreal Convention (formally known as the **Convention for the Unification of Certain Rules for International Carriage by Air**) amends provisions of the **Warsaw Convention** and gives uniformity and predictability of rules relating to the international air carriage of passengers, baggage, and cargo.[10]

Overbooking and Involuntary Bumping on U.S. Airlines

U.S. airlines are allowed to overbook flights to allow for **"no-show" passengers**. But before involuntarily bumping a passenger, the airlines are required to ask for volunteers to give up their seats in exchange for compensation.

The Department of Transportation (DOT) has not mandated the form or amount of compensation that airlines offer to volunteers. DOT does, however, require airlines to advise any volunteer whether he or she might be involuntarily bumped and, if that were to occur, the amount of compensation that would be due. Carriers can negotiate with their passengers for mutually acceptable compensation. Airlines generally offer a free trip or other transportation benefits to prospective volunteers. The airlines give employees guidelines for bargaining with passengers, and employees may select those volunteers willing to sell back their reservations for the lowest price.

If the airline is forced to do an involuntary bump, the "bumped" passenger is entitled to the following minimum compensation schedule:

DOT requires each airline to give all passengers who are bumped involuntarily a written statement describing their rights and explaining how the carrier decides who gets on an oversold flight and who doesn't. Those travelers who don't get to fly are frequently entitled to denied boarding compensation in the form of a check or cash. The amount depends on the price of their ticket and the length of the delay:

- If a passenger is bumped involuntarily and the airline arranges substitute transportation that is scheduled to get the passenger to their final destination (including later connections) within one hour of the original scheduled arrival time, there is no compensation.
- If the airline arranges substitute transportation that is scheduled to arrive between one and two hours after the original arrival time (between one and four hours on international flights), the airline must

---

10. www.jus.uio.no.

pay the passenger an amount equal to 200% of the one-way fare to the final destination that day, with a $675 maximum.

- If the substitute transportation is scheduled to get the passenger to their destination more than two hours later (four hours internationally), or if the airline does not make any substitute travel arrangements for the passenger, the compensation doubles (400% of the one-way fare, $1350 maximum).
- If the ticket does not show a fare (for example, a frequent-flyer award ticket or a ticket issued by a consolidator), denied boarding compensation is based on the lowest cash, check or credit card payment charged for a ticket in the same class of service (e.g., coach, first class) on that flight.
- The passenger always gets to keep the original ticket and use it on another flight.
- If the passenger paid for optional services on the original flight (e.g., seat selection, checked baggage) and they did not receive those services on the substitute flight or were required to pay a second time, the airline that bumped the passenger must refund those payments to the passenger.
- To be eligible for compensation, the passenger must have a confirmed reservation. A written confirmation issued by the airline or an authorized agent or reservation service qualifies the passenger in this regard, even if the airline can't find the reservation in the computer. This applies as long as the passenger didn't cancel their reservation or miss a reconfirmation deadline.
- Each airline has a check-in deadline, which is the amount of time before scheduled departure. For domestic flights, most carriers require the passenger to be at the departure gate between 10 minutes and 30 minutes before scheduled departure, but some deadlines can be an hour or longer. Check-in deadlines on international flights can be as much as three hours before the scheduled departure time. Some airlines may simply require the passenger to be at the ticket/baggage counter by this time, most, however, require that the passenger get all the way to the boarding area. Some may have deadlines at both locations. If the passenger misses the check-in deadline, the reservation may be lost, and the right to compensation may be lost as well.
- If the airline must substitute a smaller plane for the one it originally planned to use, the carrier isn't required to pay people who are bumped as a result of this substitution of equipment. In addition, on flights using aircraft with 30 to 60 passenger seats, compensation

is not required if the passenger was bumped due to safety-related aircraft weight or balance constraints.[11]

U.S. Airline Passenger Protections

Airlines and ticket agents must disclose all mandatory taxes and fees in published airfares. All baggage fees must be disclosed to the consumer when they book a flight online, and consumers must be informed where to find these fees. Information on baggage fees must be included in all e-ticket confirmations, and baggage fees must be returned if the luggage is lost by the air carrier.

Furthermore, passengers may hold a reservation without payment, or cancel a booking without penalty for 24 hours after the reservation is made as long as the reservation is made at least one week or more prior to the flight's departure date. Airlines are also required to promptly notify passengers of flight delays of over 30 minutes, as well as flight cancellations and diversions. Air carriers will generally be prohibited from increasing the price of a passenger's ticket after it is bought. The refund/reservation requirement for airlines does not apply to tickets booked through online travel agencies, travel agents, or other third-party agents. However, these agents are free to apply the same or similar procedures to provide equivalent or similar customer service.[12]

Denied Boarding Compensation in the EU

If a passenger is bumped from a flight and the flight was departing from an EU country, or the airline is registered in the EU and the flight departed outside the EU for a destination within the EU, the following rights apply:

- Reimbursement of the cost of the ticket within seven days or a return flight to the first point of departure or re-routing to the final destination
- Refreshments, meals, hotel accommodation, transport between the airport and place of accommodation, two free telephone calls, telex or fax messages, or emails
- Compensation totaling:
  o 250 Euros for all flights of 1,500 kilometers or less

---

11. www.airconsumer.dot.gov.

12. *Spirit Airlines v. U.S. Department of Transportation* No 11-1219 (D.C. Cir. 2012), www.transportation.gov.

- 400 Euros for all flights within the European Community of more than 1,500 kilometers, and for all other flights between 1,500 and 3,500 kilometers
- 600 Euros for all other flights

The UK Has Left the EU

In preparation for post Brexit, the UK Parliament passed the European Union (Withdrawal) Act 2018. This is directly applicable to EU legislation like EU261 (EU air passenger rights). EU261 is to be incorporated into UK law, creating a new type of UK legislation known as "retained EU law." EU261 will continue in the UK, for the foreseeable future. A few changes have been made to the wording of EU261 as it applies in the UK. This to ensure that it operates effectively despite the fact the UK is no longer an EU Member State. These changes were implemented by the Air Passenger Rights and Air Travel Organisers' [sic] Licensing (Amendment) (EU Exit) Regulations 2019. This brings into force what is effectively "UK261." One of the changes is the replacement of the Euro value of the compensation payable under Article 7 of EU261 with new Sterling amounts.[13]

Trains

Amtrak® (a blend of America and track) is the National Railroad Passenger Corporation.

The **National Railroad Passenger Corporation** is a government owned corporation. It was organized on May 1, 1971, to provide intercity passenger train service in the U.S. Amtrak® is headquartered at Union Station in Washington, D.C.

As a common carrier, Amtrak® is responsible for the safety of its passengers. It is held to a higher level of duty to its travelers under the doctrine of negligence.

Amtrak's® Disclaimer of Liability

Amtrak's® fares, time schedules, equipment, routing, services, and information are not guaranteed and are provided "as is" without any warranties of any

---

13. www.airpassengerrights.eu.

kind, either express or implied. Amtrak® reserves the right to change its policies without notice.

Amtrak® further specifically disclaims liability for any inconvenience, expense, or damages, incidental, consequential, punitive, lost profits, lost business or otherwise, resulting from errors in its timetable, shortages of equipment, or due to delayed trains, except when such a delay causes a passenger to miss an Amtrak® train guaranteed connection. If a guaranteed Amtrak® train connection is missed, Amtrak® will provide a passenger with alternate transportation on Amtrak®, another carrier, or provide overnight hotel accommodations, at Amtrak's® sole discretion, but only when such circumstances resulted from the actions of Amtrak® and this shall constitute Amtrak's® sole liability and a passenger's sole and exclusive remedy.

Amtrak® also disclaims any liability for the products and/or services of Amtrak's® advertisers, business partners, sponsors, suppliers, licensors, and agents to the extent permissible under the law, and Amtrak® shall only be responsible for the rail transportation services that it provides.[14]

High Speed Rail Initiative and the Budget

The Obama administration, in 2011, proposed $53 billion dollars for the construction of **high-speed rail** in the United States. Vice President Biden stated, at that time, the United States, which "taught the world" about transportation in the 19th and 20th centuries, has seen its vast network of roads, rails, and bridges fall pitifully below global standards.

So what happened with the High Speed Rail Initiative?

Much good did come out of the initiative, but virtually none of it was high-speed rail. In short, there simply wasn't enough money for these enormously expensive projects. It was woefully underfunded, but the Federal Railroad Administration, states, and Amtrak® have used the money for other infrastructure projects—such as intercity passenger train projects.[15]

Buses

Many times, in the hospitality industry, a bus will need to be used. They may be used either as the sole means of transportation between two points, or as the land transportation of choice for a tour operation.

---

14. www.amtrak.com.
15. www. railroads.dot.gov.

The following descriptions give more insight of what the passenger can look forward to when using a bus for transportation:

Economy buses are school-type buses — they, have bench seating and have no restrooms.

Deluxe motor coaches usually seat 48 passengers, have DVD players, sound systems, and restroom facilities.

Executive motor coaches are custom-made. Most have bedrooms, showers, meeting space and advanced telecommunication facilities. These types of buses are for smaller capacity — five to fifteen people.

Double-decker buses are specialty buses used for tours. Some of the most famous are in London, England.

Buses, like any common carrier transportation, are held to common carrier liability requirements as noted above.

Car Rentals

Car rental companies are not common carriers, since they are in the business of leasing/renting cars, not carrying passengers.

These companies are regulated by the state in which they do business.

This sizable industry is the backbone of American travel and business markets, given the country's reliance on road travel. Like most large industries, the auto rental sector faces regulations aimed at consumer protections. Aside from having their cars licensed and insured, states vary considerably in their legislation. However, there are a few categories of concerns that multiple states and cities commonly address.

Price Disclosure

Numerous jurisdictions require car rental companies to disclose the total cost of renting a car — post taxes and fees — in their advertising and bookings. The City of New York, for example, mandates that, when advertising, car rental companies list in print of a prescribed size the breakdown of additional fees beyond the advertised rate and the final estimated total for rental. California does not require these things to be disclosed in advertising, but the rental car company's websites and other travel booking sites must disclose the total rental cost.

GPS Monitoring

As **GPS** technology became more affordable, car rental companies began installing tracking devices in their fleets to help them locate lost, stolen, or missing vehicles. However, some companies began tracking customer movements and charging them for "wear and tear" if they exceeded the speed limit for more than two minutes or if they went out of the states covered by their rental agreements. Lawsuits for invasion of privacy led to the end of this practice, and legislation to prevent such tracking quickly followed.

Taxes

Many car rental companies have a difficult time keeping prices as competitive as they would like. One reason advertised prices don't match the final invoice is that many states, counties, cities, and airports add car rental taxes which car companies have to collect. For example, on top of its standard sales tax, the state of Washington asks rental car companies to collect an additional 5.9 percent, and counties are permitted to impose a 1 percent rental car rate, so in certain counties the rate is 6.9 percent.[16]

Liability

Most states hold rental car companies partially liable for accidents, injuries, and wrongful deaths caused by renters driving their cars. States consider it the rental car company's responsibility to screen drivers responsibly, and properly maintain their vehicles.

Lodging

The concept of mass lodging traces its roots to the beginnings of the Holiday Inn® chain. Kemmons Wilson initially came up with the idea after a family road trip to Washington, D.C. On that trip, he was disappointed by the quality and consistency provided by the roadside motels or boarding houses of the time.

---

16. https://dor.wa.gov/education/industry-guides/auto-dealers/rental-car-tax#.

The name Holiday Inn® was given to the original hotel by his architect Eddie Bluestein as a joke, in reference to the Bing Crosby movie. The first Holiday Inn® opened in 1952, on Summer Avenue in Memphis, the main highway to Nashville. The motel was demolished in the early 1990s, but there is a plaque commemorating the site as the first in the hotel's history.

Today there are a variety of hotels and lodging. They range from the luxurious, to the more modest **bed and breakfast**, to **timeshares**, and **campgrounds**.

> A bed and breakfast is a type of lodging that is smaller than a hotel and may be in a private residence that is licensed to accept guests.
>
> A timeshare is a form of shared property ownership, in which rights vest in several owners to use the property for a specified period each year, usually in one-week intervals.
>
> Campgrounds are places to set up camp. Some are more elaborate with swimming pools and clubhouses. Some are merely places to set up a tent or a recreational vehicle.

Cruise Lines

A **cruise ship** is another form of lodging—one that moves on a body of water. Prior to the use of airplanes to cross the oceans, the cruise ship was actually a form of transportation from one place to another. Now, although cruise lines do offer transatlantic or transpacific crossings (called **repositioning cruises**), they are not merely transportation anymore. They offer clients lodging, activities, and entertainment.

Cruise Lines International Association (CLIA®)

Cruise Lines International Association (CLIA®) is the world's largest cruise association and is dedicated to the promotion and growth of the cruise industry. CLIA® is composed of more than 60 of the world's major cruise lines and serves as a non-governmental consultative organization to the **International Maritime Organization** (IMO), an agency of the United Nations. CLIA® was originally formed in 1975, in North America. The genesis of CLIA® was in response to a need for an association to promote the special benefits of cruising, and in 2006, merged with the **International Council of Cruise Lines** (ICCL), a sister entity created in 1990. CLIA's® mission is to promote policies and practices that foster a safe, secure, and healthy cruise ship environment; educate and train its travel agent members; and promote and explain the value, desirability and affordability of a cruise holiday. More than 20,000 travel agencies are affiliated with CLIA® around the world and display the CLIA® seal—identifying them as authorities for selling cruise holidays.[17]

World's Largest Cruise Ships

In 2020, the world's largest cruise ships were:

Vessel	Cruise Line	Pass.	Year Built
Symphony of the Seas	Royal Caribbean®	5,500	2018
Harmony of the Seas	Royal Caribbean®	5,400	2016
Allure of the Seas	Royal Caribbean®	5,400	2010
Oasis of the Seas	Royal Caribbean®	5,400	2009[18]

Admiralty Law

Admiralty law (also referred to as **maritime law**) is a distinct body of law which governs maritime legal issues. It is a body of *domestic law* governing maritime activities, and *private international law* governing the relationships between private entities which operate vessels on the oceans. It deals with matters including marine commerce, marine navigation, shipping, sailors, and the transportation of passengers and goods by sea. Admiralty law also covers many commercial activities that are land based or occurring on land, but that are maritime in character, e.g. transportation on or to a maritime dock. Although each legal jurisdiction usually has its own enacted legislation governing maritime matters, admiralty law is characterized by a significant amount of international law developed in recent decades, including numerous treaties between nations.

Admiralty law is distinguished from the **Law of the Sea**, which is a body of *public international law* dealing with navigational rights, ocean mineral rights (for example, access to undersea oil deposits), jurisdiction over coastal waters, and international law governing relationships between nations.

Jurisdiction on the Sea

To determine which legal jurisdiction a ship is subject to, first look at where the ship is located. If a ship is docked or sailing on internal waters of a particular country, then the country's laws where the ship is, apply.

---

17. www.cruising.org.
18. www.marineinsight.com.

Territorial waters of a country vary from three miles to twelve miles (nineteen kilometers) from its coastline. (At one time, Ecuador attempted to claim 200 miles from its coastline as territorial waters.) Countries also have **contiguous zones** extending twelve to twenty-four miles (nineteen to thirty-nine kilometers) from the coastline. In these contiguous zones, a country has legal privileges — such as the right to board ships suspected of carrying drugs. If a ship is on the high seas in an area considered international waters, then it is subject to the laws of the country where it is registered, e.g., if a ship is registered in the Bahamas and the ship is in international waters, the laws of the Bahamas apply to all that occurs onboard.

The **Federal Maritime Commission (FMC)** has limited jurisdiction over cruise vessels and operators. Primarily, the Commission ensures that cruise line operators who are embarking passengers from a United States port have evidence of financial responsibility to indemnify passengers in the event of nonperformance (e.g., the cruise does not sail). Passengers are not covered by the Commission's financial responsibility program if they did not embark from a United States port. Relations between the cruise lines and their customers, however, are contractual matters governed by the terms of the passenger ticket.

As to the legal issues associated with cruising, aside from the jurisdictional one, a cruise ship needs to be treated like a floating hotel. Guest safety, security, and liability issues must be handled the same as they would be in a land-based hotel with a slight twist — cruise ships are also subject to the above-mentioned maritime laws.[19]

Tour Operators

Although travel agents and tour operators work together closely, they are different entities in the hospitality business.

The definition of a **tour operator** is:

A company that assembles the various elements of a tour.

A tour operator will usually purchase travel services in bulk from a company or individual providing the service and then sells these services to the individual traveler — either directly to the traveler or via a travel agency that represents a client.

---

19. www.fmc.gov.

A tour operator purchases the travel service at a discount, marks the service up, and this mark-up then represents the tour operators' profit margin. This is different from a travel agent that makes their money in commissions from the sale of travel, which may include a tour.

A travel agency may wear both hats of being the tour operator and the travel agency that sells their own tour products to the client. In that case, they would get the profits from negotiating a price for the tour from the tour vendor and the commission for selling the tour to the client.

The legal difference between a tour operator and a travel agent is that the tour operator is the **principal**, not the **agent**. Thus, the tour operator is directly responsible for the services they are selling. As a principal, the tour operator is liable for any failure to provide services promised. The travel agent, on the other hand, as an agent, has greater legal protections unless they knew or should have known at the time of booking, the tour service could not be provided as was represented to the client.

> A principal is the person who gives authority to another, called an agent, to act on his or her behalf.

Regulations of Tour Operators

European Package Travel Directive

As the name suggests, this regulation applies to the sale of a package to a consumer. A package is a booking that involves two or more travel elements, for example, a flight, a tour, and a hotel; or a hotel, tour, and car hire. Any booking for a single item, for example, a flight only booking, is not covered by the Package Travel Directive. The Directive makes the following financial demands on a travel business for package sales: The company selling the package to a consumer must have guarantees in place that should the seller, or any of its suppliers' cease to trade, the customer gets a refund on the holiday they purchased. If the customer is on vacation at the time of the default, then the seller must guarantee customer repatriation. The travel business must provide a guarantee that, in the event of the travel company getting into financial difficulties, the customer is guaranteed their holiday, their cash, or safe passage home. This guarantee must be backed by a third party, or in the alternative, a bond may be purchased to guarantee customer payment.[20]

---

20. www.eur-lex europa.eu.

South Africa Tour Operator Regulations under the Operation License Board

There are 4 major requirements for a **South Africa Tour Operator**:

- In order to carry fare-paying passengers (i.e., tourists), a vehicle must be registered with the Operation License Board which will issue an operating license. Applicants are normally required to specify that they will be carrying tourists and also to specify the intended routes.
- A driver of tourists must have a Professional Driving Permit (PrDP). This is issued by the Traffic department based on a normal driving license and the applicant is subject to a medical examination and a check for any criminal convictions. There is a cost for a PrDP.
- Any operator providing a guided tour is required to use a tourist guide who is qualified & DEAT/FGASA accredited. It is illegal to guide a tour without the necessary qualifications.
- Passenger Liability Insurance coverage: SATSA (Southern Africa Tourism Services Association) recommends a minimum of R7 million (Rand) for a vehicle carrying seven passengers.[21]

The United States Tour Operators Association (USTOA®)

The United States Tour Operators Association (USTOA®) is a professional association representing the tour operator industry. It is composed of companies whose tours and packages encompass the globe and who conduct business in the U.S.

USTOA® was founded in 1972, by a small group of California tour operators concerned about tour operator bankruptcies. These founding members recognized the need for a unified voice to protect the traveling public, as well as to represent the interests of tour operators. In 1975, USTOA® became a national organization with headquarters in New York.

To become an Active Member of USTOA®, a tour operator is required to have a total of eighteen references from a variety of industry sources and financial institutions and must meet specific minimums in terms of tour passengers and/or dollar volume. The company must also be in business at least three years under the same management in the U.S. and must carry a minimum of $1,000,000 professional liability insurance.

---

21. www.satsa.com.

A member must adhere to the USTOA's® code of ethics which pledges to encourage and maintain the highest standards of professionalism, integrity, and service in the tour operation business.[22]

Besides these entities monitoring tour operators, states regulate tour operators as well—especially in the area of financial stability. State statutes are in place to assure the tour operator can provide the services which they have contracted with the client. If they cannot provide such a service, they must have the financial capability to repay the client for services not received. Every state has general consumer disclosure and fraud statutes, and refund policy requirements, some specifically addressing travel services companies.

The following states have specific laws for the regulation, registration, licensing, or bonding of sellers of travel:

- California
- Florida
- Hawaii
- Illinois
- Iowa
- Louisiana
- Massachusetts
- Michigan
- Nevada
- New York
- Pennsylvania
- Virginia
- Washington (State)

Of these states, there are currently six states which require registration as a seller of travel regardless of where the agency is located: California, Florida, Hawaii, Iowa, Nevada, and Washington.

Washington and Florida have additional regulations regarding independent agents and outside sales agents. Travel clubs also must adhere to additional requirements in California and Virginia. Some states require submission of certificates and disclosure language as part of their seller of travel application.

While regulations vary from state to state, every license issuing state requires registration, fees and compliance with some financial security regulation or statute. Some states offer options to meet the financial security requirements

---

22. www.ustoa.com.

by allowing the sellers of travel to provide: a letter of credit; a certificate of deposit; or by maintaining a bond or trust account.

The National Tour Association (NTA®)

A source of legal information for tour operators is the **National Tour Association (NTA®)**. The NTA® is the leading association for professionals serving travelers to, from and within North America. Since its founding in 1951, the association has served a broad and diverse membership and helped them expand market reach with innovative business tools, strategic relationships, and collaboration within the industry. NTA's® 700 buyer members are tour operators and travel planners who package travel products domestically and around the world. NTA's® seller membership represents products in all 50 U.S. states, each Canadian Province, and more than 40 other countries. NTA® seller members represent — 500 destinations, and 1,100 tour suppliers.[23]

Liability Issues with Tour Operators

- *Non-Payment for Services* — In the hospitality business when working with tour operators, for example as a hotel or eating establishment, the hotel or restaurant needs to get paid for services booked by the tour operator. It is customary in the hospitality business for the tour operator to pay the supplier of services or goods in advance. Why? The tour operator received payment from the client before the trip, so now needs to pay for these services before the client uses them. If, as a hospitality manager, payment is not made "up-front" it is very difficult if not impossible to collect it later. It is almost impossible to track down a tour operator in a foreign country and sue them for payment. Put in the contract that payment is due within a certain number of days prior to the guests' arrival.
- *Services not delivered* — A tour operator usually relies on others to supply the services they are selling. Thus, it is up to the tour operator to be sure that they are dealing with reliable vendors of tour services. It is up to the business booking the tour to make sure the tour operator is contracting with reliable vendors. It is important to check with na-

---

23. www.ntaonline.com.

tional and overseas tour agencies and regulators as to the reliability of the tour operator. Not checking on the tour operator can lead to suits against a travel agency for negligence, misrepresentation, or other torts. **Breach of contract** is another cause of action against the travel agency, since there is a contractual agreement between the agency and the client as soon as the client books and pays for a trip. (Torts and contract law will be discussed in depth in future chapters.)

Breach of contract is failing to perform any term of a contract without a legitimate legal excuse. The contract may be either written or oral. A breach may include not finishing a job, failure to make payment in full or on time, failure to deliver all the goods, or substituting inferior or significantly different goods than those contracted for.

- *Liability for Injuries*— If the tour operator is negligent in choosing a provider of travel services and a client is injured while using the services, the tour operator may be sued for their recklessness in their choice of travel service provider. An injured client's attorney will bring all parties into court— the travel agent, tour operator, the provider of the services, and even the manufacturer of an item if that item can be shown to have contributed to the injury— all will be **defendants** in the case.

A defendant is a person against whom an action or claim is brought in a court of law.

- *Adhesion contracts*— Avoid doing business with a tour operator that attempts to use an **adhesion contract**.

An adhesion contract is a legally binding agreement between two parties, in which one side has all the bargaining power and uses it to write the contract primarily to his or her advantage. It is when the court deems the contract to be one of "take-it-or-leave-it."

Be cautious of the use of **boilerplate** on the back of a tour operator's invoice. They may be charging excessive cancellation or change fees.

Boilerplate is the use of uniform language in legal documents that has a definite, unvarying meaning. It denotes the words have not been individually fashioned to address the legal issue presented.

If a tour operator presents a contract that is one-sided, and the courts deem it as such, the contract will be deemed an **unenforceable contract**, since it is an adhesion contract. It is imperative that contracts be considered by the courts to be fair to all parties involved.

An unenforceable contract is a valid contract that cannot be fully enforced due to some technical defect.

Food Services

It is required by law that food served to a customer must be safe and wholesome. In the United States, this is mandated by the **Uniform Commercial Code (UCC)**.

The Uniform Commercial Code is a comprehensive code addressing most aspects of commercial law.

Under the UCC there is an implied warranty that the food is **merchantable**. That means the food or beverages served at an eating or drinking establishment must not contain **food borne illnesses** or contain objects that could cause injury.

The courts in the U.S. have always held that if an object found in food or beverage is foreign—it is not supposed to be in the food or beverage—the food service business would have violated the UCCs implied warranty of merchantability *(UCC §2-314)*.

If the object found is natural to the product—such as fish bones in a fish, or pits in cherries, then the implied warranty of merchantability would not be violated. Thus, the patron of the business would not recover for any injury sustained while eating or drinking the product, since the object found in the food is a normal occurrence. It is up to the patron to exercise caution while consuming the food product.

For example, if a patron of a restaurant orders Cherries Jubilee and upon biting down on one of the cherries breaks a tooth on a forgotten pit, it would be unlikely the patron could collect damages. A cherry pit is a natural item found in cherries.

However, if the same patron ordering the same product bites down and breaks a tooth on a ring that accidentally fell into the cherries, it would be a violation of merchantability of the food, since rings are not a natural part of a cherry.

An alternative legal theory to the UCCs would be what a patron reasonably expects to find in their food or beverage. A ring in Cherries Jubilee, although exciting to find, especially if it is valuable, is not what one could reasonably expect in one's dessert.

On either the violation of implied warranty of merchantability or reasonable expectation theory, if something is found in a patrons' food either on the premises of the business or elsewhere and it is not a natural part of the product, the business establishment could face a suit for negligence.

Attractions and Entertainment

Often overlooked in the area of hospitality are amusement parks and other attractions such as zoos, museums, water parks, and aquariums. Yet these entertainments are usually the reason guests visit a particular destination. For example, Disney World®, Universal®, and other attractions are the main reasons visitors come and stay in Orlando, Florida. It is the goal of such attractions to deliver memorable experiences, and these attractions must maintain safe and comfortable environments.

The **International Association of Amusement Parks and Attractions, IAAPA**® is an organization amusement venues can join for ideas on how best to keep their guests returning repeatedly. This organization's mission is:

> "… to serve the membership by promoting safe operations, global development, professional growth, and commercial success of the amusement parks and attractions industry."

The IAAPA® is an international organization located in the U.S., Canada, Europe, Middle East, Africa, Asia/Pacific, Caribbean, and Latin America. It is for professionals in the attraction industry. IAAPA® provides for its 6,000 members', from over 100 countries, industry-specific training; counsel to promote safety and protect attraction and amusement park interests; timely industry information; and press and public relations support.[24]

Liability of Amusement Venues

Safety and Amusement Parks

An amusement park must demonstrate they have exhibited an appropriate amount of care in the maintenance of the activity — whether it is a roller coaster, Ferris wheel, aquarium exhibit, or water slide. If the park cannot demonstrate the use of reasonable care, then the issue of negligence arises.

Behavior of Park Guests

If an amusement park guest behaves inappropriately, the amusement park must remove the offending guest. If they do not, then they can be held liable

---

24. www.iaapa.org.

in tort or even criminally if the badly behaving guest accosts another guest or employee. The guest that is causing the problem can be evicted on the grounds of **trespass**.

Trespass is an unlawful intrusion that interferes with one's person or property.

Expectations of Guests

When a guest enters an amusement park, they expect the rides to function safely; the rides or amusements will be available to use; restrooms will be available, clean, and functioning; food and beverage facilities will be clean and safe; and the property itself will be clean and safe.

Part of the expectation of a guest is that the employees are well-trained and knowledgeable about the amusements and safety concerns surrounding them. It is the responsibility of the management of the park or facility to adequately train employees.

If any of these expectations are not met, there can be tort or even criminal liability, depending on the severity of the problems encountered.

Gaming

Although many do not think of gaming as part of the hospitality business, it is, and it plays an integral role. There are federal and state regulations for gaming. Federally the Justice Department, Treasury Department, FBI, IRS, U.S. Marshals, Secret Service, and the U.S. Attorney General's office have control over gaming in the United States. Also, the Department of Interior and the Bureau of Indian Affairs have a say in Indian Tribal gaming. The **National Indian Gaming Commission (NIGC)** further regulates gaming on Indian reservations.

As an independent federal regulatory agency, the National Indian Gaming Commission (Commission) was established pursuant to the **Indian Gaming Regulatory Act of 1988** (Act) codified at 25 U.S.C. §2701. The Commission comprises a Chairman and two Commissioners, each of whom serves on a full-time basis for a three-year term. The Chairman is appointed by the President and must be confirmed by the Senate. The Secretary of the Interior appoints the other two Commissioners. Under the Act, at least two of the three Commissioners must be enrolled members of a federally recognized Indian tribe, and no more than two members may be of the same political party.

The Commission maintains its headquarters in Washington, D.C., with regional offices located in Portland, Oregon; Sacramento, California; Phoenix,

Arizona; St. Paul, Minnesota; Rapid City, South Dakota: Tulsa, Oklahoma; Oklahoma City, Oklahoma; and Washington, D.C.

The Commission's primary mission is to regulate gaming activities on Indian lands for the purpose of shielding Indian tribes from organized crime and other corrupting influences, to ensure that Indian tribes are the primary beneficiaries of gaming revenue; and to assure that gaming is conducted fairly and honestly by both operators and players.

To achieve these goals, the Commission is authorized to conduct investigations; undertake enforcement actions, including the issuance of notices of violation, assessment of civil fines, and/or issuance of closure orders; conduct background investigations; conduct audits; and review and approve Tribal gaming ordinances.

In general, the Commission does not specifically approve the opening of every Indian casino or gaming facility. However, before a tribe may operate a gaming facility, the NIGC must have reviewed and approved a tribe's gaming ordinance. A tribe must also license every gaming facility. In addition, the land upon which the gaming operation will be located, must be Indian land for gaming purposes. If a tribe wishes to have management by a third party, the Commission must review and approve the management contract.

> Indian gaming must occur on "Indian lands," as defined by IGRA. Indian lands include land within the boundaries of a reservation as well as land held in trust or restricted status by the United States on behalf of a tribe or an individual Indian, over which a tribe has jurisdiction and exercises governmental power. IGRA generally prohibits Indian gaming on lands acquired after October 17, 1988. However, there are certain exceptions to this prohibition. See 25 U.S.C. §2719. If a tribe is uncertain as to whether the land on which they intend to game qualifies as "Indian lands," it should seek an advisory opinion from the NIGC prior to initiating gaming. Furthermore, tribes should notify the NIGC whenever they plan to open a new facility so that the NIGC may assure that the operation will be located on Indian lands.
>
> In 1988, Congress passed the Indian Gaming Regulatory Act (IGRA) which provided a regulatory framework for Indian gaming. The Act established three classes of gaming with a different regulatory scheme for each. IGRA offered states a voice in determining the scope and the extent of tribal gaming by providing that the state in question must permit some form of gaming. The Act requires Tribal-State compacts for Class III gaming (casino gaming). Regulatory authority over Class II gaming (bingo, pull tabs, and certain card games) was left to

the tribes. Class I gaming is defined as traditional Indian gaming and social gaming for minimum prizes. Regulatory authority over Class I gaming is vested in tribal governments. IGRA further provided for general regulatory oversight at the federal level and created the National Indian Gaming Commission (NIGC) as the primary responsible federal agency.

As of this writing, these are the states with Indian gaming:

Alabama, Alaska, Arizona, Arkansas, California, Colorado, Connecticut, Florida, Idaho, Indiana, Iowa, Kansas, Louisiana, Michigan, Minnesota, Mississippi, Montana, Nebraska, Nevada, New Mexico, New York, North Carolina, North Dakota, Oklahoma, Oregon, South Dakota, Texas, Virginia, Washington, Wisconsin, Wyoming[25]

Internet Gambling

The Unlawful Internet Gambling Enforcement Act of 2006, § Section 5363 bans and § 5366 criminalizes the acceptance of funds from bettors by operators of most online gambling websites. The operators affected are those who:

Are engaged in the business of betting or wagering and knowingly accept proceeds from credit cards, electronic fund transfers and checks in connection with the participation of a bettor in unlawful internet gambling, which is the sponsorship of online gambling that violates any other federal or state anti-gambling law.

Mere participation in online betting or wagering is not banned or criminalized by the Act.

Section 5364 requires financial institutions to adopt procedures and policies designed to block the flow of prohibited funding to the operators of the affected online gambling websites.

Section 5365 gives Federal and State Attorneys General the power to seek civil remedies to help enforce the other provisions of the Act. The remedies include ordering an internet service provider to remove access to the website of an operator who violates § 5363 or other websites that contain hyperlinks to such sites. Such remedies may only be sought on websites that are hosted by a particular internet service provider.

The Department of Justice has allowed states to legalize some form of online gambling. Where is online gambling legal in the U.S.? For online casino gam-

---

25. www.nigc.gov.

bling, you can gamble online in New Jersey, Delaware, and Pennsylvania. For online poker, you can legally play online in New Jersey, Nevada, Delaware and Pennsylvania.[26]

The Economic Impact of the Hospitality Industry

The hospitality industry employs millions of people worldwide. Tourism provides huge benefits for federal, state, and local governments in the form of taxes (e.g., bed, excise, sales, income, and property taxes).[27]

In 2019, domestic and international travelers spent $1.1 trillion ($1,127 billion) in the U.S. This spending directly supported 9 million jobs, and generated $277 billion in payroll income and $180 billion in tax revenues for federal, state, and local governments. Domestic travelers alone spent $972 billion, and international travelers spent $155 billion in the U.S.

Foodservices and lodging are the top two spending categories by domestic and international travelers. In 2019, travelers spent $279 billion on foodservices, including restaurant/grocery and drinking places, which accounted for 25% of total traveler spending in the United States. Making up 22% of the total — $242 billion was traveler spending on lodging, including hotels/motels/B&Bs, vacation homes and campgrounds.[28]

The Internet and Travel Planning

Unlike the days before the web, when travel agents were the preferred means of booking travel, now the primary tools for travel planning are online travel agency websites, search engines, company websites, and destination websites. **Online travel planners** have allowed the potential traveler to view numerous places and prices before the final booking of a trip. The internet has also led to decreases in the extent to which travelers make calls, especially to a travel agency or airline, state and local tourism office, car rental agency, or hotel.[29]

---

26. www.doj.gov.
27. www.ustravel.org.
28. ibid.
29. ibid.

Who Is Liable When Using an Online Travel Planner?

When online travel planners are used to book hospitality services, many times it is difficult to determine who are the parties to the booking. The traveler is not a problem to determine. The problems occur at the other end of the booking—the website. Is it the Marriott® that the traveler is making the reservation with, or is it Expedia® or Hotels.com®? If AAA® is used by the traveler and AAA® books online is AAA® the intermediary in all of this? Who does the traveler contact or even sue if there is a problem?

The answer many times is, everyone involved. If the traveler has made the booking through AAA®, and AAA® has booked the Marriott®, both need to be brought to court in a controversy.

Jurisdiction on the Web

So we have decided all the parties need to be brought into court, but does the traveler have **jurisdiction** over them? Without jurisdiction over the parties the traveler cannot sue them.

Jurisdiction is the legal authority to hear and determine causes of action.

If AAA® is in Florida and Marriott® offices are in Maryland, where is the case tried? Usually, when the traveler receives their documents there will be a contract involved and that contract will detail what laws should govern in case of a controversy. There may even be an **arbitration clause** inserted in the contract.

Arbitration is the submission of a dispute to an unbiased third person designated by the parties to the controversy, the parties agree in advance to comply with the arbitrator's decision.

The arbitration clause will also state what law will prevail in case of a dispute between the parties, e.g., should it be Florida or Maryland law?

Data Security and the Web

Consumers who travel have a right to privacy and a right to be assured that their private information and financial details are kept safe. This is applicable at a travel location such as a hotel or restaurant, and especially is true on the web. It is imperative that any financial information collected be done on an encrypted page—one that is not subject to hacking.

If a hospitality business is taking information on the internet, including email addresses, this information cannot be shared with any other person or company not pertinent to the booking. Sharing such information can lead to litigation and liability.

Data Delay during Booking on the Web

Unless a hospitality business's inventory is directly connected to the internet source that is making the booking this can and will cause legal problems for that business.

Let's take an example of Annie's Bed and Breakfast. Annie's is using an internet booking site to book her rooms. Let's say that this booking site, when it makes a booking, does not directly pull a room from her inventory for the date of the booking. Instead, it must fax Annie the information. During the time it takes to fax this information, Annie may have booked that room and so she is now overbooked. She now is facing potential legal issues if she cannot supply the room to the internet booking guest.

If a hospitality business cannot pay the high price of being part of a **Global Distribution System (GDS)** and thus be interfaced with an internet booking agency, there must be a clear understanding with the internet booking agent who is responsible for potential over-bookings.

A (GDS) is a computerized network system owned or operated by a company that enables transactions between travel industry service providers, mainly airlines, hotels, car rental companies, and travel agencies. The GDS uses *real-time inventory* (e.g., number of hotel rooms available, number of flight seats available, or number of cars available) to service providers.

The major global distribution systems are Amadeus, Galileo, Sabre, and Worldspan. They are owned and operated as joint ventures by airlines, car rental companies, and hotel groups. Sometimes they are referred to as automated reservation systems (ARS) or computerized reservation systems (CRS).[30]

Online Advertising

The **Federal Trade Commission (FTC)** regulates advertising on and off the web. If an ad misleads a reasonably-acting consumer, that consumer makes a decision based on the **material** facts in that ad, and later, the consumer finds what was represented in the advertisement is not true, this is called **deceptive advertising**.

---

30. www.businessdictionary.com.

Deceptive advertising is "Any advertising or promotion that misrepresents the nature, characteristics, qualities or geographic origin of goods, services or commercial activities." (Lanham Act, 15 U.S.C.A. § 1125(a)) Material facts are those that are important, significant, or essential to a reasonable person in deciding whether to engage or not to engage in a particular transaction.

To avoid deceptive advertising on or off the web, the advertiser (hospitality business) must be sure:

1. All statements and **claims** are true. A claim refers to any provable statements made. If an advertiser states a fact, it must be able to be proved truthful, or it is deceptive advertising. If an advertiser is merely stating an opinion, this can be considered **puffery** by the courts. This will not lead to a ruling for a deceptive advertisement, since opinions are not provable, only facts are. Be very cautious in stating "opinions" since if there is a provable fact hidden in the puffery, deceptive advertising can again reappear.

2. Are the prices accurate? If there are additional charges, e.g., fuel surcharges, baggage fees, taxes, or single supplements, these must be listed, or it will be deemed deceptive.

3. Be clear on what is being promised. If the ad says full breakfast, it better not be orange juice and a cracker. Are there charges associated with what is offered? If it is required to tip when receiving the "free" breakfast this must be noted in the advertisement.

4. Do not use the word "discount" or "sale" unless the advertiser can show that higher price sales have been made recently. Also, if a discount amount is listed, e.g., 50%, that must be an accurate figure.

5. Place disclosures on the same screen or near the same screen as the claims made.

6. If hyperlinks are used for disclosures, make sure these hyperlinks are easy to find and use.

7. Do not distract the reader of the ad from the disclosures.

8. If the website is lengthy, repeat the disclosures as necessary.

9. If using another business's marks, logos, or business names in the advertisement make sure permission has been obtained to use these forms of **intellectual property**. This also applies to the use of photos and images that your business did not create directly.[31]

---

31. www.ftc.gov.

Intellectual property rights are rights protecting the products of human intelligence and creation, such as copyrights, patents, trademarks, and service marks.

Chapter Summary

The hospitality industry is a multi-faceted one — involving travel agents, transportation services, lodging, tour operators, food services, attractions, and entertainment. The laws that apply include contract law, tort law, statutory law, domestic and international laws. It is essential, as a hospitality business owner or manager, that one has a basic understanding of what law may be applicable to a specific situation. This knowledge is important, not only as an aid to train employees to be aware of what is required of them and how to prevent legal issues, but also for the owner or manager to know what to do in case of a dispute or injury. It is imperative the hospitality owner or manager understand the applicable laws if their attorney needs to be consulted. This will facilitate better communication with the attorney on the legal issues and processes involved.

Key Terms

Travel agents

Fiduciaries

Misrepresentation

Negligence

Airline Reporting Corporation Verified Travel Consultants

Interactive Agent Reporting System

International Air Transport Association

American Society of Travel Advisors

Certified Travel Counselor

Certified Travel Associate

Certified Travel Industry Executive

Actual knowledge

Transportation

Common carrier

Intrastate

Interstate

Foreign Nations

Commerce Clause

Airlines

Tariff

Tarmac delay

European Union

European Parliament Regulation

Montreal Convention 1999

Convention for the Unification of Certain Rules for International Carriage by Air

Warsaw Convention

Overbooking

Involuntary bumping

No-show passengers

Denied boarding

Amtrak

National Railroad Passenger Corporation

High-speed rail

Buses

Economy buses

Deluxe motor coach

Executive motor coach

Double-decker buses

Car rentals

GPS

Lodging

Bed and breakfast

Timeshares

Campgrounds

Cruise lines

Repositioning cruises

Cruise Lines International Association

International Maritime Organization

International Council of Cruise Lines

Admiralty Law/maritime law

Law of the Sea

Contiguous zones

Federal Maritime Commission

Tour operators

Principal

Agent

European Package Travel Directive

South Africa Tour Operator

U.S. Tour Operators Association

National Tour Association

Breach of contract

Defendants

Adhesion contract

Boilerplate

Unenforceable contract

Food services

Uniform Commercial Code

Merchantable

Food borne illnesses

Attractions/entertainment

International Association of Amusement Parks and Attractions

Trespass

Gaming

National Indian Gaming Commission

Indian Gaming Regulatory Act 1988

Internet gambling

Unlawful Internet Gambling Enforcement Act 2006

Online travel planners

Jurisdiction

Arbitration clause

Global Distribution System

Federal Trade Commission

Material facts

Deceptive advertising

Claims

Puffery

Intellectual property

Chapter Two

Business Structures

Chapter Objectives

What business structure is best for a hospitality business?

What are the advantages and the disadvantages of franchising?

What are management contracts?

What is agency?

Sole Proprietorship

Sole proprietorship is the easiest and simplest business form one can use to operate a business. The sole proprietorship is not a legal entity. It is a person (in some states it can be a married couple) who owns the business and is personally responsible for its debts.

A sole proprietorship can operate under the name of its owner or it can do business under a **fictitious name**. The fictitious name is simply a trade name—it does not create a legal entity separate from the sole proprietor owner. If the owner of the business decides to use a fictitious name for the business such as A&E Printing, this name needs to be registered with the state where the business is operating; this is to protect creditors of that business and allows the owner to open a business banking account. The sole proprietor will also need to secure any needed local licenses. Once that is done, the sole proprietor is ready for business.

Since it is only the owner involved in the managing and running of the business, securing financing can be difficult. Many sole proprietors borrow money from friends or relatives to get the business started, or they may use a credit card to fund the enterprise. If the business owner has sufficient collateral, they may be able to get a loan from a bank backed by a guarantee from the **Small Business Administration (SBA)**.

> The SBA does not loan money directly to small business owners. When a business owner applies for a SBA-backed loan at their local bank or credit union, they are asking the SBA to provide a guarantee that the loan will be repaid as promised.[1]

A major disadvantage in operating a sole proprietorship is that the owner is personally liable for all the business's debts. If a sole proprietor business runs into financial trouble, or if there are suits against the business, lawsuits will be brought against the business owner. If such suits are successful, the owner will have to pay the business debts with his or her own money and assets. Thus, the sole proprietor could face losing not only the business but also their savings and even their home.

Because a sole proprietorship is indistinguishable from its owner, sole proprietorship taxation is quite simple. The income earned by a sole proprietorship is income earned by its owner. A sole proprietor reports the sole proprietorship income and/or losses and expenses by filling out and filing a **Schedule C**. Then the **adjusted net income** (or loss) from the Schedule C is transferred to the owner's personal tax return. This aspect is attractive because business losses suffered may offset income earned from other sources, thus giving the owner an actual tax deduction from any other income reported.

> Adjusted net income is the amount of money the owner will make (or lose) from the business — the bottom line.

General Partnership

General partnerships consist of two or more managing partners (this can be a married couple if they sign a partnership agreement). All the general partners are responsible for running the business. They all share the assets, profits, and liabilities (losses) of the business.

For the protection of the parties, a general partnership agreement must be in writing. It is best to have a business attorney and a certified public accountant review the contract to be assured all the legal and financial aspects

---

1. www.sba.gov.

of the partnership are noted and agreed to in the partnership agreement. Again, as in the sole proprietorship, if operating under a fictitious business name (a **DBA — Doing Business As**) this name will have to be registered with the state before the business owners can open a bank account or apply for credit.

> DBA is an abbreviation for "doing business as." Certain jurisdictions may also use the terms fictitious business name, trade name, or assumed name. DBA registration is necessary if a business operates under a name other than the full names of the owners.

Each of the individual general partners is taxed on his or her personal income tax return, which means they must include the business's income on their income tax returns. Each partner can also deduct losses from the business on his or her own individual tax return. This **pass-through tax** treatment is one of the most beneficial advantages of forming a partnership. With pass-through tax treatment, filing is relatively easy. There is no taxation on the business itself; all income, deductions, and credits "pass through" to the individual partners and are reported on their individual tax returns. This is the same as in the sole proprietorship. The only difference in the general partnership is that the profits or losses are divided among the partners as per the partnership agreement.

Another benefit of general partnerships is their simplicity and flexibility. General partnerships are usually less expensive to form and require less paperwork and formalities than **corporations**, **limited partnerships**, or **limited liability companies**. General partnerships can choose a centralized management structure, like a corporation, or a completely decentralized structure, where every partner is actively involved in the management of the business.

Other advantages of a general partnership are that the partners can combine resources and share the financial commitment. This differs from a sole proprietorship, where the one owner must meet the total financial obligations of the business.

The disadvantage of general partnerships, just as with the sole proprietorship, is the aspect of owner liability. General partners are personally **jointly and severally liable** for all the business debts and liabilities. Each partner is also liable for the debts incurred by the actions of other partners. One partner can bankrupt the business if they sign obligations for the partnership that are financially detrimental. Because of this potential personal liability, general partnerships are limited in their ability to raise money and attract investors.

> Joint and several liability occurs when two or more people (e.g., general partners) owe money. This could be to a bank, another business, or in a court judgment against them. The creditor party may

collect the entire amount from any one of the partners or from any and all of the partners in various amounts until the amount is paid in full. In other words, if any of the partners do not have enough money or assets to pay an equal share of the amount owed, the other partners must make up the difference.

Limited Partnership

Limited partnerships entail one or more general partners and one or more limited partners. The general partners participate in management and have 100 percent of the liability for partnership obligations. Limited partners cannot participate in management and have no liability for partnership obligations beyond their **capital contributions** (money they invested in the company) — they are limited in scope. This protection from liability for the limited partners disappears if they begin to manage the business operations. They then become general partners. As limited partners, they receive a share of the profits as is agreed to in the limited partnership contract. Limited partnerships must be in writing.

Many partnerships are formed as limited partnerships because the limited liability aspect is attractive to **passive investors** — investors that want to participate in a business but do not want to manage it. A limited partnership is advantageous to general partners, since they can raise money without involving outside investors in the management of the business.

A limited partnership also enjoys the advantages of pass-through tax treatment. A limited partnership is taxed like a general partnership in that the profits and losses pass through to the general and limited partners, who then include their allocated income or losses on their personal tax returns.

C Corporations

The corporations most people think of are large well known businesses — those with familiar names. These are **openly traded C corporations**.

Openly traded corporations are those that offer stock for sale to the general public via one of the major stock exchanges.
Closed corporations do not make public offerings of their stock. They are smaller corporate entities.

Corporations are different from other forms of businesses in the sense that they are an independent legal entity. Corporations are viewed as a legal "person" in the view of tax laws. Corporations can enter contracts, initiate lawsuits, and be sued.

A C corporation's profits are taxed separately from its owners under **subchapter C of the Internal Revenue Code**. A C corporation must pay corporate taxes, and shareholders must pay taxes on dividends they receive. This is called **double taxation**, one of the few drawbacks of a C corporation.

Double taxation is the taxing of the same earnings at two levels.

A shareholder will also have to pay **capital gains** if they sell their shares and make a profit on the sale of their stock.

A C corporation is owned by shareholders, who must elect a **board of directors** that make business decisions and oversee policies. A C corporation is usually required to report its financial operations to the attorney general in the state or states in which it is doing business. Because a corporation is treated as an independent entity, a C corporation does not cease to exist when its owners or shareholders change or die. Legally, it is said to live in "perpetuity."

Benefits of a C Corporation

- As opposed to a sole proprietor or a partnership, corporations are usually at a lower risk of being audited by the IRS.
- The owner/shareholders of a C corporation have a limited liability towards business debts.
- A C corporation can be used to split the corporate profit amongst the owners and the corporation. This can result in overall tax savings. The tax rate for a corporation is usually less than that for an individual, especially for the first $50,000 of taxable income.
- In a C corporation, there can be an unlimited number of stockholders. This allows the corporation to sell shares to a large number of investors, which allows for more funds to be raised for projects.
- Foreign nationals have a right to own or invest in a C corporation. There is no limitation on the types of investors. This allows a greater number of diverse investors to participate in the business.

The owner (majority shareholder) of a C corporation has the option of issuing different "classes" of stocks to different shareholders. This helps attract different groups of investors as **common stocks** and **preferred stocks** both have their own distinct advantages that may appeal to different types of investors.

> Common stockholders exercise control by electing a board of directors and voting on corporate policy. However, common stockholders are on the bottom of the priority ladder in the event of corporate liquidation. Common shareholders have rights to a company's assets only after bondholders, preferred shareholders, and other debt holders have been paid in full.
>
> Preferred stock is ownership in a corporation that has a higher claim on the assets and earnings of the corporation than common stock. Preferred stock generally has a dividend that must be paid before dividends to common stockholders are paid. Preferred shareholders usually do not have voting rights in the affairs of the corporation.

Running a C Corporation

Setting up and running a C corporation is significantly more complex than setting up a sole proprietorship or partnership. A C corporation must be established with state authorities and must abide by corporate laws in the state where it is incorporated. Corporations are registered with the secretary of state's office in the state in which they are doing business.

To form a C corporation, most states will require the registration of the corporate business name. In some states, such a Florida, mere filing of the corporation registers the corporate name as well. In all states, a business will need to file a **certificate of incorporation** or **articles of incorporation** and pay a filing fee. A corporation also needs to draft and file **corporate bylaws**.

> Articles of incorporation and certificate of incorporation are legal documents that are filed with the state to create a corporation.
>
> Bylaws are the rules of a corporation established by the board of directors during the process of starting a corporation.

Other required formalities a C corporation must follow are:

- Formal issue of stocks to the initial shareholders
- Regular meetings of directors, and the shareholders
- Upkeep and update of business records and transactions of a corporation separate from those of its owners
- Adequate investment of money (capitalization) in the corporation

The advantage of C corporations, compared to sole proprietorships and partnerships, discussed above, is that its owners (**shareholders/stockholders**) have limited liability. They are not personally liable for debts incurred by the corporation.

> Shareholder/stockholders are the individuals that own stock in a corporation.

Yet, there are certain circumstances when the limited liability of a corporation can be negated. This is called "**piercing the corporate veil**."

> The corporate veil creates a separate, legally recognized corporate entity and shields the owners/shareholders from personal liability for corporate debts.

A corporation can lose its limited liability if:

- The corporation directly injures someone.
- The corporation fails to deposit taxes that have been deducted from corporate employee wages.
- The corporation is involved in intentional fraud or other illegal actions that result in loss to the corporation or someone else.
- The courts rule that a corporation ceases to exist.

S Corporations

An **S corporation** is a special structure of business ownership. In this form of corporation, the business is able to avoid the double taxation experienced in a C corporation. This is accomplished through **Subchapter S of the Internal Revenue Code**. S corporations are not required to pay corporate income tax on the profits of the company. All profits/losses are passed on directly to the shareholders of the company. The shareholders file individual tax returns and pay income tax on whatever share of profits/losses they receive from the business. If the business has more than one shareholder, the business must file an informational tax return to provide details of the corporate income of each shareholder.

By electing to become an S corporation, a small business can take advantage of the same limited liability of a C corporation and still have the tax advantages of the sole proprietorship or partnership form of business. These provisions have been placed in the Internal Revenue Code to promote small businesses and relieve them from the financial burden of double taxation.

Most S corporations are **closely held**. Many have only one shareholder who also serves as the only corporate officer and the only corporate director (if this is allowed under state law where they are incorporated). Originally, the S corporation was designed to allow small business owners, who operated as sole proprietors, gain the limited liability protection of corporate status with a pass-through tax device. Recently, the limited liability company (LLC) is also serving that role (the LLC will be discussed next).

> A closely held corporation is one whose most (but not all) issued shares are held by a family or a small group of investors.

The IRS and the S Corporation

To qualify for S corporation status, the corporation must meet the following requirements:

- Be a domestic corporation
- Have only allowable shareholders
  - ◦ including individuals, certain trusts, and estates and
  - ◦ may not include partnerships, corporations, or non-resident alien (foreign) shareholders
- Have no more than 100 shareholders
- Have one class of stock
- Not be an ineligible corporation, i.e., certain financial institutions, insurance companies, and domestic international sales corporations

In order to become an S corporation, the corporation must submit Form 2553-Election by a Small Business Corporation signed by all the shareholders, and submit it to the Internal Revenue Service.

Advantages of an S Corporation

The advantages of an S corporation are:

- No federal corporate tax — no double taxation
- Pass through of profits and losses to individual shareholders — so they can take losses from personal taxes
- Liability protection to owners — again subject to the piercing the corporate veil rules listed under the C corporation

Disadvantages of an S Corporation

The disadvantages of an S corporation are:

- Limited to 100 shareholders (75 if formed before 2004)
- Can only have domestic investors
- Shareholders pay taxes on all corporate profits in the year they are earned — even if the profits are not distributed to them
- Usually have to operate on a calendar year, not a fiscal year[2]

Limited Liability Companies — LLCs

Owners of an LLC are called members. Since most states do not restrict ownership, members may include individuals, corporations, other LLCs, and foreign entities. There is no maximum number of members, and most states permit "single member" — one owner LLCs. Under the IRS Code, an LLC can choose to be taxed as a sole proprietorship if it is a one member LLC. If there are multiple LLC members, they can choose to be taxed as a partnership or corporation.

The LLC structure is not recognized by federal law, and therefore their filing status — how they choose to be taxed — is determined by the Entity Classification Rules. Form 8832 is used for this purpose. Pursuant to the entity classification rules, LLCs with multiple owners that do not elect to be taxed as a corporation will be taxed as a partnership.[3]

Since an LLC is not recognized by federal law, these business entities are governed and must be filed with the state where they do business. The exact requirements for setting up an LLC vary slightly from state to state, but setting up an LLC is a relatively simple process that can usually be done in an hour or less, depending on the complexity of the organizational structure chosen. Sole proprietorship form would be the simplest set-up of an LLC, and the corporate structure LLC would be more complex.

The duration of the LLC is usually determined in the LLC's organizational papers that are filed with the state. The time period for the LLC can be extended if desired by a vote of the members.

The primary characteristic an LLC shares with a corporation is the aspect of limited liability. It is important to understand that limited liability does not imply that owners are always fully protected from personal liabilities. Courts

---

2. www.irs.gov.
3. ibid.

can and sometimes will pierce the veil of a corporation (as discussed above) or that of an LLC. This usually occurs if there has been some type of fraud involved in running the business.

Advantages of an LLC

The primary characteristic an LLC shares with a partnership is the availability, if the members choose, of pass-through income taxation.

LLCs offer greater flexibility in ownership and ease of operation than an S corporation. There are no restrictions on who is a member of an LLC. An LLC is simpler to operate because it is not subject to the formalities by which S corporations must abide—there is no requirement to have regular meetings.

An LLC can be member-managed, meaning that the owners run the company; or it can be manager-managed, with responsibility delegated to managers who may or may not be owners in the LLC.

The owners of an LLC can distribute profits in the manner they see fit.

Let's say, for example, two people own an LLC. One member contributed $40,000 for capital. The other member only contributed $10,000 but this member performs 90% of the work (sweat equity). The two members then decide that, in the interest of fairness, they will each share the profits 50/50. As an LLC that can be done; with an S corporation, this could not be done. The shareholder contributing only $10,000, could only take 20% of the profits, while the shareholder contributing $40,000, would take the other 80%.

Disadvantages of an LLC

The disadvantages to an LLC are:

- LLCs are more expensive to create than a partnership or sole proprietorship.
- LLCs may be subject to a state franchise tax, e.g., California imposes a franchise tax on LLCs.
- LLCs cannot issue shares of stock to raise revenue. Revenue must come from the members themselves. This last point is one to consider if the reason for choosing a business structure is to raise revenue.

Owner-Operators

In the United States and Canada, an owner-operator is a small business that is owned, run, and managed by the same person.

Advantages of Owner-Operator Structure

The advantages of being an owner-operator are:

- There are no specific educational requirements, unless one is going into a business that has specific educational needs.
- The owner-operator makes all the decisions for the business.

Disadvantages of Owner-Operator Structure

The disadvantages of being an owner-operator are:

- The owner-operator has all the responsibilities of running the business.
- The owner-operator is the main money investor in the business.
- The owner-operator is subject to all liabilities of the business.

It is suggested if an owner-operator structure is chosen, start as a sole-proprietor and become an LLC as soon as possible to attempt to protect one's personal assets and keep company expenses separate from personal expenses.

Franchising

Franchising is when one business purchases another firm's successful business model. There is the **franchisor** — the one selling the concept, and the **franchisee** — the one purchasing. For the franchisor, selling franchises is an alternative to building "chain stores" to distribute goods and avoid investment and liability incurred by having a chain of stores.

The success of the franchisor translates into greater possible success for the franchisee, e.g., McDonald's®. The franchisee gains by buying into this success and has an advantage over a competing business by not having to create a business from the ground up.

Businesses for which franchising works best have one or several of the following characteristics:

- Have a good track record of profitability
- Are easily duplicated
- Have detailed systems, processes and procedures
- Have a unique or unusual concept
- Have broad geographic appeal
- Are relatively easy to operate
- Are relatively inexpensive to operate

Some examples of franchise costs are:

> Subway® — $116,000–263,000 plus $15,000 franchise fee[4]
> McDonald's® — $1,314,500 to $2,306,500 for a new restaurant plus
> $45,000 franchise fee, with a $500,000 non-borrowed down payment[5]
> Hampton Inns and Suites by Hilton® — $7–17 million plus $75,000
> application franchise fee[6]

What the franchisee is buying is the right to use the franchisor's trademark (their brand), other intellectual property such as copyrights and licensing rights, training, and advisory services. There may be national or international advertising done of the brand name, but the franchisee will have to pay a monthly fee to cover these ads. Although the prices paid for franchising seem high, they are not. Purchasing a well-known franchise almost always guarantees success for the franchisee.

Franchises usually last for a fixed period of time — this is detailed in the franchise contract. The time periods usually run from 5–30 years. If the franchisee wants to renew, this will be governed by the contract entered into with the franchisor. If the franchisee cancels the franchise early, for their own reasons, there will be serious monetary damages to be paid to the franchisor. A franchisee does not own the franchise — it is a temporary business investment.

Franchise fees paid by the franchisee to the franchisor are based on "gross" revenues of the franchise, not "net" revenues (profits). A franchise disclosure document will list possible revenues and profits, but it will not show profitability of the franchise since there is no legal requirement to establish

---

4. www.subway.com.
5. www.mcdonalds.com.
6. www.hamptonfranchise.com.

this amount. It is imperative a franchisee seek advice from their accountant for input into what possible net amount could be made from the franchise.

Franchises usually will protect a specific territory to assure the franchisee success. If the franchisor has oversold franchises in a particular area, this will dilute the chances of success for their franchisees.

What the Franchisor Wants

- The one selling the franchise needs to protect their trademark, control the umbrella business, and secure any trade secrets.
- The franchise needs to carry the franchisors' signs, logos, trademark, architectural and decorating design. The uniforms of the staff must follow franchise standards, and the service given the patrons needs to follow the franchisors' manuals and training sessions.
- The franchisor may require the franchisee to buy equipment and supplies from the franchisor. This could include uniforms, signs, food, and paper products.

What the Franchisee Wants

- Franchisees want a marketing and business plan from the franchisor that assures success. The fees the franchisee pays for this must be fully disclosed, and there should be no hidden fees.
- It is imperative that start-up costs and working capital needed by the franchisee be known to the franchisee before signing the franchise contract.
- The franchisee wants assurances in writing that they have the rights to the territory purchased, as long as the franchisee lives up to the requirements of the franchise contract.
- The franchisee must be protected by the franchisor for any trademark infringements by third parties.
- Training periods must be sufficient to train the franchisee to operate the business successfully. This can be done by manuals, in-person training, or corporate universities, e.g., McDonald's® "Hamburger University®."

Franchise contracts tend to be one-sided in favor of the franchisor. The franchisor is usually protected from lawsuits because the franchisee signs a contract that requires them to acknowledge that they are buying the franchise knowing there is risk, and they have not been promised success or profits by the franchisor. Most franchise agreements require franchisees to waive their legal rights under federal and state law, and these agreements usually pick the legal forum where a lawsuit will be heard.

> In the hospitality industry in 1932, Howard Deering Johnson was the first modern restaurant franchise—Howard Johnson®. This was a new idea—independent operators could use the Howard Johnson® name, food, supplies, logo, and building design in exchange for a franchise fee. The 1950s saw a boom in franchise chains in conjunction with the development of the U.S. Interstate Highway System.

In the U.S., the **Federal Trade Commission (FTC)** has oversight of franchising. This oversight is via the **FTC Franchise Rule**. For franchises the FTC requires the franchisee be furnished a **Franchise Disclosure Document** (FDD) by the franchisor at least fourteen days before any money changes hands or a franchise agreement is signed. The FDD is very detailed. The **Uniform Franchise Offering Circular** (UFOC) lists the elements of a FDD. The FDD will include data on the names, addresses, and telephone numbers of the franchisees in the area. These current franchisees can be contacted and consulted prior to the individual seeking a franchise beginning negotiations with the franchisor. If there are state requirements as to franchising, the state disclosure requirements must be in compliance with the FTC rules.

Under the FTC franchise rules, there is no private right of action against franchisors in violation of the FDD, but many states will allow a right of action if the franchisee can prove fraud on the part of the franchisor. States will be the primary collectors of data on franchising in their respective state and will enforce state franchise laws for franchises located within their jurisdiction.[7]

International Franchise Laws

Internationally, China, Australia, Europe, Brazil, and India are some of the countries and regions that have franchise laws in place.

Australia

In Australia, franchising is regulated by the **Franchising Code of Conduct**. This Code requires franchisors to give to a perspective franchisee a disclosure

---

7. www.ftc.gov.

document, a copy of the Franchising Code, and a copy of the franchise agreement at least fourteen days before the franchise agreement is entered.[8]

Brazil

The country of Brazil has one of the largest numbers of franchises outside of the U.S.

The new **Brazilian Franchise Law** as of January 2020, defines a franchise as a system in which the franchisor *licenses* to the franchisee, for a payment, the right to use a trademark/patent along with the right to distribute products or services on an exclusive or semi-exclusive basis.

The **Franchising Disclosure Document** ("FDD," *Circular de Oferta de Franquia* in Portuguese) requires substantially more detail than under the previous law. The FDD must be written in Portuguese, with "objective and accessible" language, and must contain:

- A summarized history of the franchise business
- Full details about the franchisor and its related entities, together with their Brazilian company tax number (*Cadastro das Pessoas Jurídicas*, "CNPJ")
- Balance sheets and financial statements relating to the two previous tax years
- A list of the court cases relating to the franchise "that challenge the system or that may compromise the operation of the franchise" in Brazil and that have listed the master franchisor, its controlling entities, the sub-franchisor and the holders of the trademarks and other related intellectual property rights
- A detailed description of the franchise, and a general description of the business and the activities that will be performed by the franchisee
- The joining or franchising fee
- A profile of the ideal franchisee as it refers to prior experience, level of education and other characteristics that the franchisee must have or may preferably have
- The requirements relating to the franchisee's direct involvement in the operation and management of the business
- Details about the total estimated initial investment required for the acquisition, deployment and start of operations of the franchise
- Details about the estimated value of the installations, equipment and initial stock and payment terms for these

---

8. www.austlii.edu.au.

- A list containing the name, address and telephone numbers of all existing franchisees, sub-franchisees or sub-franchisors, and all those that have terminated the franchise relationship in the previous 24 months
- Details about the territorial policy (including if the franchisee has exclusivity or a right of first refusal over the territory and if the franchisee can make sales or provide services outside of the territory or export them, and the rules about territorial competition between franchisor-owned businesses and franchisees in the territory)
- Details about the franchisee's obligation to purchase any goods, services, or raw materials required for the deployment, operation, or management of the franchise from franchisor-approved suppliers (including a complete list of these supplies)
- What will be offered to the franchisee and the terms and conditions applicable to support, franchise network supervision, services, technological innovation, franchisee and employee training (including duration, content and costs), franchise manuals, assistance in the analysis and choice of location where the franchise will be located, and layout and architectural standards for the franchise (including physical location of equipment, list of equipment and architectural drawings)
- Details about the trademark and other intellectual property rights relating to the franchise that will be used by the franchisee
- Details about how the product, process, or management know-how and confidential information relating to industry, commerce, finance, and business will be dealt with upon termination and whether the franchisee will be allowed to compete with the franchise
- A full a copy of the standard franchise agreement (and preliminary contract, if any) to be entered into with the proposed franchisee
- Assignment and succession rules (if any)
- Events that will trigger penalties, fines or payment of damages and their respective amounts
- Information on the existence of minimum purchase quotas by the franchisee from the franchisor or those designated by the franchisor, and the possibility and conditions for refusal of the products or services required by the franchisor
- Whether a board or association of franchisees exists and, if so, the attributions, powers and mechanisms of representation before the franchisor, and details about the powers over management and supervision over fund allocations

- Indication of the rules limiting competition between the franchisor and the franchisees, and among the franchisees, during the term of the franchise agreement, and details of the territorial scope, the term of the restriction and the penalties for non-compliance
- The franchise contract's term and renewal conditions (if any)
- Ongoing fees "as well as other amounts" to be paid to the franchisor or to third parties indicated by the franchisor, "detailing the respective formulas and what the fee is being paid for or for what [the funds] are to be used" (the ongoing fee for the franchise "system," the rent for equipment or lease payments for the location of the business, the marketing fee and the minimum insurance must be stated)
- State that the franchisor can make a profit from subleasing the premises to the franchisee (only required if the franchisee subleases the business premises from the franchisor and the franchisor makes a profit from that arrangement).

The FDD must be delivered to the prospective franchisee at least 10 days before the earlier of:

- The signing of the franchising agreement (or preliminary contract, if any), or
- The franchisee pays any fee to the franchisor or any entity related to the franchisor.[9]

China

China has the most franchises in the world, but the scale of their operations is relatively small. KFC® was the most significant foreign entry in 1987.

In 2007, a new and revised Chinese franchise law came into effect. This law is applicable if there are any transactions involving the use of a trademark and payments for its use.

Under this law, the franchisor must meet a list of requirements for registration, among which are:

- They must supply a standard franchise agreement, a work manual for the franchisee, and satisfy Chinese working capital requirements
- The franchisor must have a track-record of operations, and ample ability to supply materials

---

9. www.lawsofbrazil.com/2020/01/03/the-new-brazilian-franchising-law.

- Have the ability to train Chinese personnel and provide them with long-term operational guidance
- The franchisor will be liable for actions of its suppliers
- There are monetary and other penalties that apply for franchisor infractions of the regulations

Relationship Laws

- The franchisor must have had two company-owned units (in China or elsewhere) for at least one year
- The franchise agreement must provide for a "cooling-off" period
- The franchise agreement must have a minimum three-year term

Registration Laws

Franchisors must register with the Chinese government agencies (MOFCOM, Ministry of Commerce, People's Republic of China, at the central government level) within 15 days after signing the first franchise agreement.

Franchisor disclosures must be made thirty days in advance of entering any franchise agreement and must contain:

- Details of the franchisor's experience in the franchised business
- Identification of the franchisor's principal officers
- Any litigation that was pursued against the franchisor during the past five years
- Full details about all franchise fees
- The amount of a franchisee's initial investment
- A list of the goods or services the franchisor can supply, and the terms of supply
- The training franchisees will receive
- Information about the franchise trademarks, including registration, usage, and litigation
- Demonstration of the franchisor's capabilities to provide training and guidance
- Statistics about existing units, including number, locations, and operational results, and the percentage of franchises that have been terminated
- An audited financial report and tax information

Further aspects of the Chinese franchise law are:

- The franchisee's business and other information will remain confidential indefinitely after termination or expiration of the franchise agreement
- If the franchisee has paid a deposit to the franchisor, it must be refunded on termination of the franchise agreement
- Upon termination, the franchisee is prohibited from continuing to use the franchisor's marks.[10]

Europe

The **European Union** has not adopted a uniform franchise disclosure policy. Six of the European countries in the Union have adopted pre-sale of a franchise disclosure obligations. They are France, Spain, Lithuania, Romania, Italy, and Sweden. In these formal disclosure countries there must be contract summaries provided highlighting:

- The object of the contract
- The rights and obligations of the parties
- The financial conditions of the franchisor
- The term of the contract
- The requirement to hire an attorney to enter and finalize a franchise agreement.[11]

India

Franchise agreements in India aren't governed by any franchise-specific legislation but by various applicable statutory enactments of the country. A few of them are the Indian Contract Act 1872; the Consumer Protection Act, 1986; the Trade Marks Act, 1999; the Copyright Act, 1957; the Patents Act, 1970; the Design Act, 2000; the Specific Relief Act, 1963; the Foreign Exchange Management Act, 1999; the Transfer of Property Act, 1882; the Indian Stamp Act, 1899; the Income Tax Act, 1961; the Arbitration and Conciliation Act, 1996; and the Information Technology Act, 2000.[12]

---

10. www.franchise.org/international/china; www.mofcom.gov.cn.
11. www.lexology.com.
12. www.indiafilings.com.

Management Contracts

When running a business, a management company may be employed to help manage the enterprise. The company providing these services may be an outside firm or even a unit within the business itself. Many corporations will have management divisions within their corporate structure, or an LLC may have a management company as one of its members.

The management company performs the necessary managerial functions in return for an agreed upon fee. These management contracts can involve such functions as the technical operation of a production facility; management of personnel; accounting services; marketing services and marketing training; and property management. Or, the management company may run the entire business.

Agency

In the hospitality industry it will sometimes be necessary to appoint an **agent** to perform certain acts for the business. This could be a realtor, a sales person, or a contract negotiator. This creates an agency relationship.

The purpose of an agency is to allow the **principal** (the one appointing an agent) to authorize another to carry out certain duties; either specific duties or general transactions. Agency relationships can be informal, but it is best to get all the specifics, obligations, and duties of both principal and agent in a written contract signed by both parties.

Who Can Be a Principal?

Any person who has the legal capacity to perform the act required can be a principal. Once the individual is deemed to be a principal, they may empower an agent to carry out that act or task. Persons, corporations, partnerships, not-for-profit organizations, and government agencies may all be principals and appoint agents.

Who Can Be an Agent?

Any individual capable of comprehending the act to be undertaken is qualified to serve as an agent. There is no legal capacity requirement for an individual to be appointed as an agent (unless there are licensure requirements, e.g., real estate).

What Is the Basis of the Agency Relationship?

Inherent in the principal-agent relationship is the understanding that the agent will act for and on behalf of the principal. The agent assumes an obligation of loyalty to the principal that he/she will follow the principal's instructions and will neither intentionally nor negligently act improperly in the performance of the act. An agent cannot take personal advantage of the business opportunities the agency position uncovers. A principal, in turn, reposes trust and confidence in the agent. These obligations bring forth a **fiduciary relationship** of trust and confidence between the principal and agent.

What Are the Obligations of the Agent to the Principal?

An agent must obey reasonable instructions given by the principal. The agent must not do acts that have not been expressly or impliedly authorized by the principal. The agent must use reasonable care and skill in performing the duties. Most importantly, the agent must be loyal to the principal. The agent must refrain from putting themselves in a position that would ordinarily encourage a conflict between the agent's own interests and those of the principal. The agent must keep the principal informed of all facts that materially affect the agency relationship.

An agent is liable to indemnify a principal for loss or damage resulting from their acts, if they go beyond the scope of the agency.

What Are the Obligations of the Principal to the Agent?

A principal owes certain contractual duties to their agent. In conjunction with the duties of an agent to serve a principal loyally and obediently, a principal's primary duties to their agent include:

- To compensate the agent as agreed
- To indemnify and protect the agent against claims, liabilities, and expenses incurred in the discharge of the agency duties assigned by the principal

Because of the fiduciary relationship, a principal owes their agent a duty of good faith and fair dealing. However, a principal can be relieved of contractual obligations by an agent's breach of the agency contract, or if the agent oversteps the principal's instructions under the agency agreement—they then have acted **outside the scope** of their actual authority.

If an agent acts **within the scope** of their actual authority, then the principal is liable to indemnify the agent for any payments made by the agent on behalf of the principal during the course of the relationship, irrespective of whether the expenditure was expressly authorized or merely necessary in promoting the principal's business.[13]

Chapter Summary

The business structure chosen by a hospitality enterprise is a critical choice. The organizational form selected will be based on the personality of the owners; where the creators of the venture expect to obtain financing and capitalization, and what the entrepreneurs' tolerance for legal and personal economic risk is. Whether a sole proprietorship, general or limited partnership, S corporation, C corporation, LLC, or franchise is chosen makes a significant difference in the potential success of the undertaking.

The use of management contracts and agents will be other important decisions made by the business. Does the firm want or need others to perform specific functions and duties in the running of the enterprise? Will the delegation of tasks and the use of others to manage or represent the undertaking make the entire organization run more smoothly? If the answer to these questions is yes, then an agent or management company should be considered.

Key Terms

Sole proprietorship	Adjusted net income
Fictitious name	General partnerships
Small Business Administration	DBA—Doing Business As
Schedule C	Pass-through tax

---

13. Restatement 3rd of Agency, § 8.02 et seq.

Corporations
Limited partnerships
Limited liability companies
Jointly and severally liable
General partners
Limited partners
Capital contributions
Passive investors
Openly traded C corporations
Closed corporations
Subchapter C of the Internal Revenue Code
Double taxation
Capital gains
Board of directors
Common stocks
Preferred stocks
Certificate of incorporation
Articles of incorporation
Corporate bylaws
Shareholders/stockholders
Piercing the corporate veil
S corporation

Subchapter S of the Internal Revenue Code
Closely held
Owner-operators
Franchisor
Franchisee
Federal Trade Commission
FTC Franchise Rule
Franchise Disclosure Document
Uniform Franchise Offering Circular
Franchising Code of Conduct
Brazilian Franchise Law
Franchise Disclosure Document (Brazil)
European Union
Management contracts
Agency
Agent
Principal
Fiduciary relationship
Outside the scope
Within the scope

Chapter Three

The Legal System and the Hospitality Industry

Chapter Objectives

What is the structure of the federal court system?

What types of cases does the federal court system hear?

How is the federal court system different from the state court system?

What types of cases do state courts hear?

What is Alternative Dispute Resolution?

Which federal agencies affect the hospitality industry?

Which state agencies affect the hospitality industry?

How do local agencies affect the hospitality industry?

The Court System

Federal Courts

In the U.S., there are **federal courts** and **state courts**. Every state offers both venues, and each court, whether state or federal, has specific jurisdictional requirements for a case to be heard in a specific court.

For example, state courts handle cases involving:

- Divorce and child custody matters
- Probate and inheritance issues

- Real estate questions
- Juvenile matters
- Most criminal cases, contract disputes, traffic violations, and personal injury cases
- State constitutional issues

While federal courts hear cases involving:

- The constitutionality of a law
- Cases involving the laws and treaties of the U.S., such as federal crimes
- Cases where the parties are ambassadors and public ministers
- Disputes between two or more states
- Disputes involving citizens of two or more states, or a citizen of the U.S. against a citizen of another country
- Admiralty law
- Tax law
- Bankruptcy cases

Before a federal court can hear a case, or "exercise its jurisdiction," certain conditions must be met. Under the U.S. Constitution, federal courts exercise only "judicial" powers. This means that federal judges may interpret the law only through the resolution of actual legal disputes, referred to in Article III of the Constitution as "**Cases or Controversies**." A court cannot attempt to correct a problem or answer a hypothetical legal question on its own initiative.

Assuming there is an actual case or controversy, the **plaintiff**, in a federal lawsuit, must have legal "**standing**" to ask the court for a decision.

Standing means the plaintiff must have been aggrieved or legally harmed by the **defendant**.
A plaintiff is the party that institutes a civil suit in a court.
A defendant is the party in a civil suit denying their liability to the plaintiff.

The case must also present a category of dispute that the law in question was designed to address, and it must be a complaint that the court has the power to remedy, the federal court must have **jurisdiction** over the case.

Jurisdiction is the power, right, or authority to interpret and apply the law to the particular case.

The court must be authorized, under the U.S. Constitution or federal law, to hear the case and grant appropriate relief to the plaintiff, e.g., a Constitutional law issue, a "**federal question**," or a case between citizens of different states or between a citizen of the U.S. and a citizen of another country, called **diversity of citizenship** cases.

Examples of some "federal question" cases include a claim by an individual for entitlement to money under a federal government program such as Social Security, a claim by the government that someone has violated federal laws, or a challenge to actions taken by a federal agency.

Cases involving the "diversity of citizenship" of the litigants allow the federal courts to have jurisdiction under Art. III § 2 of the U.S. Constitution. This granting of federal jurisdiction ensures fairness to out-of-state or out-of-country litigants.

An important limit to diversity jurisdiction is that only cases involving more than $75,000 in potential damages may be filed in a federal court. Claims below that amount may only be pursued in state court.

In any diversity jurisdiction case, regardless of the amount of money involved, the case can always be heard in a state court rather than a federal court. The plaintiff in the case makes the federal versus state court decision. This decision is usually made based on input from the plaintiff's attorney. Many times the plaintiff's attorney will base his/her decision on their comfort of trying a case in the federal court system.

In a diversity case, the federal court must apply the law of the state in which it sits, *Braswell v. Colonial Pipeline Co.*, 395 F. Supp. 3d 641 (2019). However, if a case is transferred from one court to another, the transferor court's state laws will apply, *Stricker v. Shor*, Case No. 17-cv-03491-HSG (N.D. Cal. Apr. 11, 2018). For example, if a federal court began to hear the case in California but transfers the case to Michigan, California law will be used. The transferee court is "obligated to apply the state law that would have been applied if there had been no change of venue."

Finally, for a federal court to have jurisdiction in the case, the issue presented in the case cannot be "**moot**," that is, it must present an ongoing problem for the court to resolve.[1]

> Moot means that it is an issue not currently a controversy able to be decided, typically because it was resolved or otherwise removed from the court's purview.

The federal courts, thus, are courts of "**limited jurisdiction**" because they may only decide certain types of cases as provided by Congress or as identified in the U.S. Constitution.

---

1. www.uscourts.gov.

U.S. District Court

The **U.S. district courts** are the general trial courts of the federal court system. Within limits set by Congress and the U.S. Constitution, the district courts have jurisdiction to hear nearly all categories of federal cases, including both civil and criminal matters. (Only crimes that break a law of the U.S. government will be prosecuted in the federal courts.)

There is at least one district court in each state, and the District of Columbia. Each district includes a U.S. bankruptcy court as a unit of the district court. Four territories of the United States have U.S. district courts that hear federal cases, including bankruptcy cases: Puerto Rico, the Virgin Islands, Guam, and the Northern Mariana Islands.[2]

Bankruptcy Courts

Each of the 94 federal judicial districts handles bankruptcy matters. Bankruptcy laws protect troubled businesses and provide for orderly distributions to business creditors through reorganization or liquidation. These procedures are covered under Title 11 of the United States Code (the **Bankruptcy Code**). The vast majority of cases are filed under the three main chapters of the Bankruptcy Code, which are **Chapter 7, Chapter 11,** and **Chapter 13** (Chapter 13 is for individuals or sole proprietors only, corporations cannot be Chapter 13 debtors).

Chapter 11

In a bankruptcy case, Chapter 11 may be used by a corporation, sole proprietorship, or partnership. Since a corporation exists separately from its owners/stockholders — the, Chapter 11 bankruptcy case of a corporation (corporation as debtor) does not put the personal assets of the owner/stockholders at risk. The owners/stockholders will only be subject to the loss of the value of their investment in the company if the company eventually is liquidated under a Chapter 7 bankruptcy.

A sole proprietorship (owner as debtor), on the other hand, does not have an identity separate and distinct from its owner(s). Accordingly, a Chapter 11 bankruptcy case involving a sole proprietorship includes both the business and personal assets of the owners-debtors.

In a partnership bankruptcy case, under Chapter 11, (partnership as debtor), the partners' personal assets may, in some cases, be used to pay cred-

---

2. ibid.

itors. Then the partners themselves may be forced to file for individual bankruptcy protection.

A bankrupt company, the "debtor," can use Chapter 11 of the Bankruptcy Code to "reorganize" its business and try to become profitable again. Management continues to run the day-to-day business operations, but all significant business decisions must be approved by a bankruptcy court.

Chapter 13

Any individual, even if self-employed or operating an unincorporated business, is eligible for Chapter 13 relief as long as the individual's unsecured debts are less than $419,275 and secured debts are less than $1,257,850, 11 U.S.C. § 109(e). These amounts are adjusted periodically to reflect changes in the consumer price index.

If a sole proprietor files under Chapter 13, this will not be a reorganization of the business as it would be if they filed under Chapter 11. Rather, Chapter 13 filings result only in the structuring of a re-payment plan to the sole proprietors' creditors.

Chapter 7

In Chapter 7 bankruptcy, the company stops all operations and goes completely out of business. A trustee is appointed to "liquidate" (sell) the company's assets and the money is used to pay off the debt, which may include debts to creditors and investors (stockholders).[3]

U.S. Courts of Appeals

There are 13 appellate courts that sit below the U.S. Supreme Court, and they are called the U.S. courts of appeals. The 94 U.S. judicial districts are organized into twelve regional circuits, each of which has a United States court of appeals. A U.S. court of appeals hears appeals from the district courts located within its circuit, as well as appeals from decisions of federal administrative agencies. The appellate court's task is to determine whether or not the law was applied correctly in the trial court.

In addition, the U.S. Court of Appeals for the Federal Circuit (the thirteenth U.S. Court of Appeals) has nationwide jurisdiction to hear appeals in specialized cases, such as those involving patent laws and cases decided by the Court of International Trade, and the Court of Federal Claims.[4]

---

3. www.sec.gov; www.uscourts.gov.
4. www.uscourts.gov.

U.S. Supreme Court

The U.S. Supreme Court, at its discretion, and within certain guidelines established by Congress, each year hears a limited number of the cases it is asked to decide. Those cases may begin in the federal or state courts, and they usually involve important questions about the Constitution or federal law.

The Supreme Court consists of the chief justice of the United States and such number of associate justices as may be fixed by Congress. The number of associate justices is currently fixed at eight (28 U.S.C. § 1). Power to nominate the justices is vested in the President of the United States, and appointments are made with the advice and consent of the Senate. Article III, § 1, of the U.S. Constitution further provides that "[t]he Judges, both of the supreme and inferior Courts, shall hold their Offices during good Behaviour [*sic*], and shall, at stated Times, receive for their Services, a Compensation, which shall not be diminished during their Continuance in Office."

The term of the Court begins, by law, on the first Monday in October and lasts until the first Monday in October of the next year, but decisions are made by the justices from October to July. Approximately 7,000–8,000 petitions are filed with the Court in the course of a term; only a fraction of them will be heard by the justices.

Writ of Certiorari

It is important to note that review in the U.S. Supreme Court is by means of a ***writ of certiorari***, since review of a case by the U.S. Supreme Court is not a matter of right, but of judicial discretion. The primary concern of the U.S. Supreme Court is not to correct errors in lower court decisions, but to decide cases presenting issues of importance beyond the particular facts and parties involved. The Court grants and hears arguments in only about one percent of the cases filed each Supreme Court term. The vast majority of petitions are simply denied by the Court without comment or explanation. The denial of a petition for a *writ of certiorari* only signifies the Court has chosen not to accept the case for review and does not express the Court's view of the merits of the case.[5]

---

5. www.supremecourt.gov.

Difference between Federal and State Courts

The U.S. Constitution is the supreme law of the land in the United States. It creates a federal system of government in which power is shared between the federal government and the state governments. Due to federalism, both the federal government and each of the state governments have their own court systems.

It is important to remember that federal law is the supreme law of the land. A federal court's ruling will prevail over a state's court rulings, with the United States Supreme Court having the final word on any U.S. Constitutional issues.

In the court systems, whether they are federal or state, the lower courts deal with issues of fact — what the factual accounts are in the case. These courts are referred to as the "triers of fact."

The appeals courts, whether federal or state, deal only with issues of law. For example, if an objection was incorrectly sustained or overruled, or if an incorrect interpretation of the law was given to the jury by the judge — these are issues of law. An appeals court will never look back to the facts of the case unless the appeals court feels there were egregious errors committed by the lower court.

Alternative Dispute Resolution

Alternative Dispute Resolution (ADR) typically refers to processes and techniques of resolving disputes that fall outside of the judicial process (formal litigation — court). Courts are increasingly requiring some parties to utilize ADR of some type, most often mediation, before permitting the parties' cases to be heard. There are generally four categories of ADR. These are **mediation, arbitration, negotiation and collaborative law. Conciliation** is sometimes included as a fifth category.

All ADR procedures, except negotiation, include the presence of a neutral person capable of providing an unbiased opinion, who acts as a facilitator or decision maker.

> Mediation is the attempt to settle a legal dispute through active participation of a third party (mediator) who works to find points of agreement and make those in conflict agree on a fair result. Mediation differs from arbitration, in which the third party (arbitrator) acts much like a judge, but in an informal, out-of-court setting. The mediator does not actively participate in the discussion.

STRUCTURE OF U.S. COURTS	
The Federal Court System	The State Court System
• Article III of the Constitution invests the judicial power of the United States in the federal court system. Article III, §1 specifically creates the U.S. Supreme Court and gives Congress the authority to create the lower federal courts.	• The constitution and laws of each state establish the state courts. A court of last resort, often known as a supreme court, is usually the highest court in a state. Some states also have an intermediate court of appeals. Below these appeals courts are the state trial courts. Some are referred to as circuit or district courts.
• Congress has used its power to establish the 13 U.S. courts of appeals, the 94 U.S. district courts, the U.S. Court of Claims, the U.S. Court of International Trade, and the U.S. bankruptcy courts.	• States also have courts that handle specific legal matters, e.g., probate court (wills and estates); juvenile court; family court; etc.
• Parties dissatisfied with a decision of a U.S. district court, the U.S. Court of Claims, and/or the U.S. Court of International Trade may appeal to a U.S. court of appeals.	• Parties dissatisfied with the decision of the state trial court may take their cases to the intermediate court of appeals.
• A party may ask the U.S. Supreme Court to review a decision of a U.S. court of appeals, but the U.S. Supreme Court usually is under no obligation to do so. The U.S. Supreme Court is the final arbiter of federal constitutional questions.	• Parties have the option to ask the highest state court to hear the case.
	• Only certain state court cases are eligible for review by the U.S. Supreme Court, e.g., U.S. Constitution issues.

SELECTION OF JUDGES	
The Federal Court System	The State Court System
(Article III, §1 of the Constitution) Federal judges are nominated by the President and confirmed by the Senate. They hold office during good behavior, typically, for life. Through congressional impeachment proceedings, federal judges may be removed from office for misbehavior.	**• State court judges are selected in a variety of ways, including** ◦ election ◦ appointment for a given number of years ◦ appointment for life ◦ a combination of these methods e.g., appointment followed by election

TYPES OF CASES HEARD	
The Federal Court System	The State Court System
• Cases dealing with the constitutionality of a law • Cases involving the laws and treaties of the U.S. • Cases involving ambassadors and public ministers • Disputes between two or more states • Admiralty law • Bankruptcy • *Habeas corpus* ∘ (*Habeas corpus* is a writ requiring an arrested person to be brought before a judge.)	State Cases • Most criminal cases • Probate (involving wills and estates) • Most contract cases • Tort cases (personal injuries) • Family law (marriages, divorces, adoptions), etc. State courts are the final deciders of state laws and state constitution questions. Their interpretations of federal law or the U.S. Constitution may be appealed to the U.S. Supreme Court.*

* www.uscourts.gov.

Arbitration is the process by which the parties in a dispute submit their differences to the judgment of an impartial person or group appointed by mutual consent or statutory provision.

Negotiation is a give-and-take discussion or conference in an attempt to reach an agreement or settle a dispute.

Collaborative law, in the context of divorce proceedings, is designed for the attorneys for both of the parties to assist the parties to resolve conflict using cooperative strategies rather than adversarial techniques and litigation.

Conciliation is the process of adjusting or settling disputes in a friendly manner through extra judicial means. Conciliation means bringing two opposing sides together to reach a compromise in an attempt to avoid taking a case to trial.

The **American Arbitration Association**® (AAA) provides services to individuals and organizations who wish to resolve conflicts out of court. The AAA's role in the dispute resolution process is to administer cases from filing to closing. The AAA provides administrative services in the U.S., as well as abroad through its **International Centre for Dispute Resolution**® (ICDR). The AAA's and ICDR's administrative services include assisting with the appointment of mediators and arbitrators, setting hearings, and providing users with information on dispute resolution options, including settlement through mediation.

The **Better Business Bureau**® (BBB) works with the individual and the business to reach a solution to a problem. The dispute resolution process is an alternative to going to court. It's informal and user-friendly, and it helps resolve thousands of complaints each year. BBBs offer several methods to resolve disputes. In conciliation, the BBB collects factual information from both parties in a dispute, it encourages open communication, and facilitates discussions leading to a resolution. In mediation, the BBB will provide a professionally trained mediator to talk with the parties and guide them in working out their own mutually-agreeable solutions. If conciliation and/or mediation efforts are not successful, arbitration may be the next step. The parties state their views at an arbitration hearing, offer evidence and let an impartial arbitrator make a decision that ends the dispute.[6]

Governmental Entities

Federal

Internal Revenue Service (IRS)

The **Internal Revenue Service** (IRS) is a bureau of the U.S. Department of the Treasury.

The IRS Mission

The IRS is to provide America's taxpayers top quality services by helping them understand and meet their tax responsibilities and enforce the law with integrity and fairness to all.

This mission statement describes the IRS's role and the public's expectations about how the IRS should perform that role:

- In the U.S., Congress passes tax laws and requires taxpayers to comply.
- The taxpayer's role is to understand and meet his or her tax obligations.
- The IRS's role is to help the large majority of compliant taxpayers with the tax law, while ensuring that the minority, who are unwilling to comply, pay their fair share.

---

6. www.adr.org; www.bbb.org.

In the hospitality industry, the IRS puts forth information and pamphlets instructing the hospitality manager how to address the issues of:

- Employee tips
- Meals and/or lodging given to employees and how to address these in reference to employee wage reporting
- Withholding and other tax considerations that apply to the hospitality industry[7]

Occupational Safety and Health Administration (OSHA)

The **Occupational Safety and Health Administration** (OSHA) was created in 1970, to ensure safe and healthy working conditions for working men and women. OSHA sets and enforces standards in the workplace and provides training, outreach, and assistance to employers and employees to facilitate safe conditions.

OSHA is part of the U.S. Department of Labor. It covers employers and employees either directly through federal OSHA or through an OSHA-approved state program. State programs must meet or exceed federal OSHA standards for workplace safety and health. Remember, federal law is supreme and a state law can only make a federal law more stringent, not less stringent.

Under §8 of the OSHA Act — OSHA has the right to inspect and investigate the workplace during regular working hours and other reasonable times.

They can and will examine:

- Equipment, including structures, machines, apparatus, or other devises
- Materials used
- OSHA will privately question owners, employers, employees, operators, or agents in reference to workplace conditions or injuries

Under §9 of the OSHA Act, if upon inspection or investigation, it is believed the employer has violated the Act, a citation against the employer will be issued. The citation will be in writing and "... shall describe with particularity the nature of the violation, including a reference to the provisions of the Act, standards, rules, regulations, or orders alleged to have been violated. In addition, the citation shall fix a reasonable time for the abatement of the violation."

The citations will be prominently posted at or near each place a violation has occurred.

---

7. www.irs.gov.

Penalties for violation of the OSHA Act under § 17:

- If it is deemed the violation is willful, a civil penalty of not less than $9,753.00, or more than $136,532.00, can be imposed against the employer for each violation.
- If a citation is issued for a non-serious violation of the Act, the civil penalty can be up to $13,653.00 for each violation.
- Any employer who fails to correct a cited violation within the period permitted for its correction may be assessed a civil penalty of no more than $13,653.00 for each day during which such violation continues.
- If an employer willfully violates any standard, rule, or order of the Act and the violation causes death to an employee, upon conviction of the crime, the employer shall be punished by a fine of not more than $500,000.00, and/or imprisonment for not more than six months. If the conviction for the employee's death comes after a first conviction for a violation of the OSHA Act the punishment shall be imprisonment for not more than one year.
- If any person gives advance notice of any OSHA inspection without authority from OSHA, the punishment will be a fine of, not more than $1,000.00, and/or imprisonment for not more than six months.
- If anyone knowingly makes any false statements or representations in regard to the Act, the punishment will be a fine of, not more than $10,000.00, and/or imprisonment of not more than six months.[8]

In the hospitality industry, it is imperative that the employer/owner/manager of the property have an adequate knowledge of OSHA requirements and adhere to them diligently. As noted above, the consequences of not providing a safe working environment can be costly.

Environmental Protection Agency

The **Environmental Protection Agency (EPA)**, developed in 1970, is part of the federal government and is charged with protecting human health and the environment. The EPA writes and enforces regulations based on laws passed by Congress that oversee the quality of air, water, land, and hazardous materials.

---

8. www.osha.gov.

Compliance and enforcement is how the EPA ensures that governments, businesses and industries understand and follow U.S. environmental laws and regulations.

Enforcement under the EPA

- To protect human health and the environment, the EPA can require those that are responsible for a hazardous waste site to clean it up or reimburse the EPA for cleanup.
- If there are willful and deliberate violations of environmental laws or regulations in violation of the U.S. criminal code, the EPA will investigate and assist in the criminal prosecution of such crimes.

CERCLA

The **Comprehensive Environmental Response, Compensation, and Liability Act** (CERCLA), commonly known as the Superfund, was enacted by Congress on December 11, 1980. This law created a tax on the chemical and petroleum industries and provided broad federal authority to respond directly to releases or threatened releases of hazardous substances that may endanger public health or the environment.

What CERCLA accomplishes:

- CERCLA provides for liability of persons responsible for releases of hazardous waste at hazardous substances sites.
- Establishes a trust fund to provide for cleanup when no responsible party could be identified.[9]

In the hospitality industry, the concern with CERCLA is if a business property is being purchased. It is imperative that the buyer of the property consult with an attorney that specializes in environmental and contract law to protect them from potential financial disaster if hazardous materials are found on the property purchased. Under CERCLA, the entire line of owners of that property, including the new purchaser is financially liable for the cleanup of hazardous waste.

Food and Drug Administration (FDA)

The **Food and Drug Administration** (FDA) is responsible for protecting public health by ensuring the safety, efficacy, and security of human and vet-

---

9. www.epa.gov.

erinary drugs, biological products, medical devices, our nation's food supply, cosmetics, and products that emit radiation.

The FDA is also responsible for advancing public health by helping to speed innovations that make medicines more effective, safer, and more affordable, and by helping the public get the accurate, science-based information they need to use medicines and foods to maintain and improve their health. They also have the responsibility of regulating manufacturing, marketing, and distribution of tobacco products.

The FDA plays a significant role in the nation's counterterrorism capability. They fulfill this responsibility by ensuring the security of the food supply and by fostering development of medical products to respond to deliberate and naturally emerging public health threats.

The area where the FDA directly affects the hospitality industry is in relation to how food, served in restaurants, is represented on the menu. For example, if a restaurant is making a nutritional claim, this claim must be accurate and be reflective of FDA guidelines. Under the **Nutritional Labeling and Education Act** (NLEA) of 1990, restaurants that make nutritional claims for their food must adhere to the law.

The Act requires all nutrient content claims (i.e., "high fiber," "low fat," etc.) and any other health claims be consistent with agency regulations.

- High fiber means an item has at least five grams of fiber per serving
- Low fat means an item has three grams of fat or less per serving
- Low sodium means an item contains 140 mg or less of sodium per serving
- Low cholesterol means an item contains 20 mg or less of cholesterol per serving

Since 2006, it has been much easier for people who are allergic to certain foods to avoid packaged products that contain them. This is because the FDA requires the labels of most packaged foods, marketed in the U.S., to disclose, in simple-to-understand terms, if they are made with or in a facility that uses a "major food allergen." Eight foods, and ingredients containing their proteins, are defined as major food allergens. These eight foods account for 90 percent of all food allergies. They are:

- Milk
- Eggs
- Fish, such as bass, flounder, or cod
- Shellfish, such as crab, lobster, or shrimp
- Tree nuts, such as almonds, pecans, or walnuts

- Wheat
- Peanuts
- Soybeans[10]

Equal Employment Opportunity Commission (EEOC)

The U.S. **Equal Employment Opportunity Commission** is responsible for enforcing federal laws that make it illegal to discriminate against a job applicant or an employee because of the person's race, color, religion, sex (including pregnancy), national origin, age (40 or older), disability, transgender status, sexual orientation, or genetic information.

> In *Bostock v. Clayton County, Georgia,* 590 U.S. ___ (2020), (S. Ct. June 15, 2020) the Supreme Court held that firing individuals because of their sexual orientation or transgender status violates Title VII's prohibition on discrimination because of sex. Title VII prohibits discrimination because of an "individual's ... sex." 42 U.S.C. § 2000e-2(a)(1).

Most employers with at least fifteen employees are covered by EEOC laws (20 employees in age discrimination cases). Most labor unions and employment agencies are also covered.

The laws apply to all types of work situations, including hiring, firing, promotions, harassment, training, wages, and benefits.

Authority and Role of the EEOC

The EEOC has the authority to investigate charges of discrimination against employers who are covered by the law. Their role in an investigation is to fairly and accurately assess the allegations in the charge and then make a finding. If they find that discrimination has occurred, they will try to settle the charge. If they aren't successful, they have the authority to file a lawsuit to protect the rights of individuals and the interests of the public.

The EEOC also works to prevent discrimination before it occurs through outreach, education and technical assistance programs.[11]

---

10. www.fda.gov.
11. www.eeoc.gov.

Bureau of Alcohol, Tobacco, Firearms and Explosives (ATF)

The **Bureau of Alcohol, Tobacco, Firearms and Explosives** is a law enforcement agency housed within the United States Department of Justice. The ATF protects communities from violent criminals; criminal organizations; the illegal use and trafficking of firearms; the illegal use and storage of explosives; acts of arson and bombings; acts of terrorism; and the illegal diversion of alcohol and tobacco products.

The ATF partners with communities, industries, law enforcement, and public safety agencies to safeguard the public served, through information sharing, training, research, and the use of technology.

In the hospitality industry, the ATF, along with **The Alcohol and Tobacco Tax and Trade Bureau (TTB)**, are involved with:

- The administering of the federal liquor tax
- Regulation of the non-use of previously used liquor bottles (this also prohibits the sale of such bottles)
- The requirement that vendors of alcohol must keep receipts for all liquor products purchased
- How to properly dispose of liquor bottles.[12]

Department of Labor

The **Department of Labor** fosters, promotes, and develops the welfare of wage earners, job seekers, and retirees in the United States. It improves working conditions, advances opportunities for profitable employment, and assures work-related benefits and rights.

The Department of Labor enforces the **Fair Labor Standards Act** (FLSA) which sets basic minimum wage and overtime pay standards. These standards are enforced by the Department of Labor's wage and hour division.

Workers who are covered by the FLSA are entitled to a minimum wage of not less than $7.25 per hour, effective July 24, 2009. (As of this writing, there is a strong movement in the U.S. for a rise in the federal minimum wage.) Overtime pay at a rate of not less than one and one-half times the regular rate of pay is required after 40 hours of work in a workweek. Certain exemptions apply to specific types of businesses or specific types of work.[13]

---

12. www.atf.gov; www.ttb.gov.
13. www.dol.gov.

Family and Medical Leave Act

The **Family and Medical Leave Act of 1993** (FMLA) provides a entitlement of up to twelve weeks of job-protected, unpaid leave during any twelve-month period to eligible, covered employees for the following reasons:

- Birth and care of the eligible employee's child, or placement for adoption or foster care of a child with an employee
- To bond with a child (leave must be taken within one year of the child's birth or placement)
- Care of an immediate family member (spouse, child, parent) who has a serious health condition
- Care of the employee's own serious health condition.

It also requires that employee's group health benefits be maintained during the leave.

On January 28, 2008, President Bush signed into law H.R. 4986, the **National Defense Authorization Act** for FY 2008 (NDAA), Pub. L. 110-181. It has been amended twice.

Now the NDAA and FMLA provide:

- Military caregiver leave which helps families of covered service members (current service members and certain veterans) with a serious injury or illness by providing up to 26 workweeks of FMLA job-protected leave in a single 12-month period to certain eligible family members to care for the covered service members; and
- Qualifying exigency leave, which helps families of military members in the regular armed forces, as well as the National Guard and Reserves, manage their affairs when the military members are going to be or have been deployed to a foreign country by providing up to 12 workweeks of FMLA job-protected leave in the applicable 12-month leave period to certain eligible family members.[14]

As of January 1, 2021, California, Hawaii, Massachusetts, New Jersey, New York, Rhode Island, Washington, and Washington, DC (DC) all have mandated paid leave for an employee's own health condition. Except for Hawaii, these jurisdictions also require paid family leave for bonding with a new child, caring for a seriously ill or injured family member, and certain other reasons for the employee's leave.

---

14. ibid.

Due to the COVID-19 pandemic, the Families First Coronavirus Response Act (FFCRA), the statute providing for paid family leave and paid sick leave for employees with COVID-19 issues who work for employers with fewer than 500 employees, was implemented in the United States. In 2020, all employers with fewer than 500 employees were required to provide FFCRA paid leave to employees covered by the Act.

As of January 1, 2021, FFCRA paid leave became optional. So, covered employers are not required to participate in these programs, But, if the employer opts into these and continues to pay his employees, under the American Rescue Plan Act (ARPA) the time period for the tax credit benefit for employers that voluntarily offer the paid leave was extended until September 30, 2021.[15]

Immigration and Nationality Act

The **Immigration and Nationality Act** (INA) of 1990, applies to employers seeking to hire non immigrant aliens as workers in specialty occupations under H-1B visas. An H-1B visa establishes the beneficiary of the visa is coming to the United States temporarily to work in a specialty occupation, and the employer demonstrates the beneficiary is qualified to perform services in a specialty occupation.

The INA sets forth the conditions for the temporary and permanent employment of aliens in the United States and includes provisions that address employment eligibility and employment verification.[16]

Consolidated Omnibus Budget Reconciliation Act

The **Consolidated Omnibus Budget Reconciliation Act** (COBRA) gives workers who lose their job and their job's health benefits the right to choose to continue group health benefits provided by their former job's group health plan. COBRA covers the loss of health benefits for such reasons as:

- The voluntary or involuntary loss of a job
- Reduction in the number of hours worked
- Transition between jobs
- Death, divorce, and other life events

This is for a limited period of time (usually for eighteen months—the maximum will be up to three years if the employee becomes disabled or is

---

15. ibid.
16. www.uscis.gov.

caring for a member of the Armed Forces). Qualified individuals may be required to pay the entire premium for coverage, up to 102 percent of the cost to the plan.[17]

Department of Justice (DOJ)

The **Department of Justice** exists to enforce the law and defend the interests of the United States according to the law; to ensure public safety against threats foreign and domestic; to provide federal leadership in preventing and controlling crime; to seek just punishment for those guilty of unlawful behavior; and to ensure fair and impartial administration of justice for all Americans.

I-9 forms and the DOJ

All U.S. employers must complete and retain a Form I-9 for each individual they hire for employment in the United States. This includes citizens and noncitizens. **U.S. Citizenship and Immigration Services (USCIS), in the Department of Homeland Security** (DHS), publishes the Form I-9 and accompanying instructions. Some employers also use E-Verify, an electronic system that compares a worker's Form I-9 information with government databases to verify employment eligibility.

Form I-9 must be kept by the employer for three years after the date of hire or for one year after employment is terminated, whichever is later. The form must be available for inspection by authorized U.S. Government officials (e.g., Department of Homeland Security, Department of Labor, and Department of Justice).

On the form, the employer must examine the employment eligibility and identity document(s) an employee presents to determine whether they are entitled to work in the U.S. and whether the document(s) reasonably appear to be genuine and relate to the individual. The employer must record the document information on the Form I-9.[18]

State Regulators

Besides federal regulators, states have their own agencies that will have an impact on the hospitality industry.

---

17. www.dol.gov.
18. www.uscis.gov.

Employment Security

Unemployment compensation is money received from the United States and a state by a worker who has become unemployed through no fault of their own. Unemployment insurance is a federal-state program jointly financed through federal and state employer payroll taxes (federal and state UI taxes).

The **Federal Unemployment Tax Act (FUTA)**, along with state unemployment systems, provides for payments of unemployment compensation to workers who have lost their jobs. Generally, employers must pay both state and federal unemployment taxes if:

- They pay wages to employees totaling $1,500 or more in any quarter of a calendar year, or
- They had at least one employee during any day of a week during 20 weeks in a calendar year, regardless of whether the weeks were consecutive. However, some state laws differ from federal law.

FUTA authorizes the IRS to collect an annual federal employer tax to fund state workforce agencies. Under FUTA, only the employer pays, not the employee. FUTA covers the costs of administering the **Unemployment Insurance and Job Service** programs in all states.

Wages paid to U.S. citizens employed outside the United States are generally subject to FUTA tax if the employer is an "American employer."

The term "American employer" means a person who is:

- An individual who is a resident of the United States.
- A partnership, if two-thirds or more of the partners are residents of the United States.
- A trust, if all the trustees are residents of the United States.
- A corporation organized under the laws of the United States or of any state or the District of Columbia.[19]

To qualify for unemployment insurance, an employee must file weekly or biweekly claims, and respond to questions concerning continued eligibility. The employee must report any earnings from work done during the unemployed week(s). Any job offers or refusal of work during the week must be reported.

---

19. www.irs.gov.

These claims are usually filed by mail, online, or telephone; each state provides filing instructions.

- In general, benefits are based on a percentage of an individual's earnings over a recent 52-week period — up to a state maximum amount.
- Benefits can be paid for a maximum of 26 weeks in most states. (Although, during times of economic downturns, duration of benefit payments has been extended.)[20]
- Benefits are subject to federal income taxes and must be reported on the individual's tax return.[21]

Workers' Compensation

Workers' compensation is a form of insurance that provides wage replacement and medical benefits for employees who are injured in the course and scope of employment. Workers' compensation is provided by the employer, so there is a mandatory relinquishment of the employee's right to sue his or her employer for the tort of negligence.

Workers' compensation is administered on a state-by-state basis, with a state governing board overseeing varying public/private combinations of workers' compensation systems. (In Texas, unlike other states, private employers can choose to carry workers' compensation insurance coverage, but it is not required in most cases.)

Alcohol and Beverage Control

The ratification of the **Twenty-first Amendment** on December 5, 1933, gave the right to the states to control the sale of alcohol within the states' borders. This control of the sale of liquor extends to counties and towns as well.

A state's **Alcohol and Beverage Control** Commission will be responsible for controlling alcohol as follows:

- Liquor license issuance
- Permitted hours of sale
- Methods of alcohol business operations

---

20. www.cbpp.org.
21. www.oui.doleta.gov.

- Method of reporting alcohol sales for tax purposes
- Revocation of a liquor license

Revocation of a liquor license can result from an establishment serving liquor and consistently allowing:

- Disorderly conduct and fighting on the premises
- Prostitution or the solicitation of prostitution
- Drug and narcotic sales
- Unlawful adult entertainment, e.g., nude dancing
- A failure to maintain required liquor sales records
- Sale of alcohol to minors

Violations of state law, with regard to the sale of alcohol, can result in civil fines and/or criminal sanctions.

In *South Dakota v. Dole*, 483 U.S. 203 (1987), the U.S. Supreme Court upheld the withholding of federal highway funds to South Dakota. This withholding of highway funds was implemented because beer with an alcohol level below a specified percentage could be lawfully sold to adults under the age of 21. In a 7–2 majority opinion by Chief Justice Rehnquist, the Court held the withholding of highway funding by the federal government is not coercion that invades state sovereignty. The Twenty-first Amendment could not constitute an "independent constitutional bar" to the spending power granted to Congress under Article I, § 8, clause 1 of the Constitution.

Dram Shop Acts

Dram shop acts refer to the liability of taverns, liquor stores, and other liquor selling commercial establishments when they sell liquor to an intoxicated person or minor. If a commercial business sells alcohol to such an individual and that person then injures a third party due to their intoxication, the alcohol selling commercial business will potentially face liability for the third party's injuries.

The majority of states allow for recovery when the defendant knew (or should have known) the customer was intoxicated. Some states have attempted to address this problem through more exacting tests. Missouri's revised dram shop law requires proof that the party demonstrates "significantly uncoordinated physical action or significant physical dysfunction." In Texas, a patron must be so obviously intoxicated that he/she presents a clear danger to himself/herself and others.

On the other hand, in Massachusetts, the state's highest court has held that a bar could be sued where a patron exhibiting "drunk, loud and vulgar" behavior was determined to be "visibly intoxicated."[22]

Attorney General

The **attorney general** of a state is the states' chief legal officer. A hospitality business may receive letters from this state office with regard to new or existing state laws and regulations.

Department of Revenue

The state's **department of revenue's** sole function is to collect taxes. Whether these are taxes on occupancy (bed), liquor, cigarettes, or gambling. There will be specific forms and deadlines that the hospitality business will need to adhere to in their dealings with this agency.

Health Department

As a hospitality manager, the **health department** will be your best friend or your worst enemy. This branch of the state government is responsible for the inspection and licensing of facilities, including restaurants, hotels, cruise ships, water parks, etc.

Duties of the health department include assuring:

- Food and beverage cleanliness and food and beverage preparation requirements are followed.
- Food storage standards are complied with.
- Food handling employees are following mandated health procedures.
- The proper washing and care of food equipment, dishes, and utensils are followed.
- There is the proper washing and care of towels and bedding prior to providing these items to guests.
- Water standards for swimming pools, showers, sinks, cleaning, and dishwashing are maintained.
- Standards for water and sewage disposal are followed.
- Smoking regulations are followed.
- Posters are displayed to employees in methods to help choking or heart attack victims.

---

22. www.moga.mo.gov; www.statutes.legis.state.tx.us; www.malegislature.gov.

Depending on the state, if health violations are found, there can be fines or even jail time for the employees, managers, or even owners of the hospitality business. If the violations are egregious enough, the entire facility may be shut down.

Even worse, if the media discloses these health violations, this would be a crippling blow to the business's goodwill and reputation.

Department of Transportation

The state's **department of transportation** (DOT) is responsible for all forms of transportation within the state, such as state highways and state roads. This department will be contacting the hospitality business if the business is creating a traffic hazard, traffic congestion, or the driveway is interfering with normal traffic flow.

If there is a need for a traffic light to be placed in front of a business to allow for a safer traffic flow, the department of transportation will be one of the agencies that will need to be contacted. Or, if there is an issue of the speed limit on the roads adjacent to the business, the state DOT is the agency to contact.

Local (Town, City, County) Regulators

Health and Sanitation

Not only are there state health department inspectors, there are local **health and sanitation** inspectors as well. They will see if the facility is following town, city, or county regulations.

They inspect:

- How food and beverages are being prepared and served
- They will make sure food service workers possess the needed certifications
- They establish restroom standards
- They check to make sure safe water standards are maintained

Building and Zoning

The **building and zoning** department will be one of the major agencies a hospitality business will deal with as they develop and expand their business.

Building and zoning regulates:

- The issuance of building permits.
- Building inspections before, during, and after construction.

- Lighting, ventilation, restroom, elevator, and public area standards.
- Land use in various neighborhoods and violations of zoning.
- Permits for sidewalks.
- Permits for al fresco dining.
- Placement and construction of signage.

Building or zoning violations committed by the hospitality business will result in monetary fines. If the violations are blatant, these transgressions can lead to the closure of the business or even jail time for the owner or manager if someone is injured due to code violations.

Historic Preservation

Depending on where the hospitality business is located, there may be requirements for a specific form of architecture for the building; there may be limitations on razing a building and building a new one, or there may be requirements to maintain the landscaping of the business in a certain way — this is called **historic preservation**. These regulations are implemented by the locality to preserve the historical integrity of the area.

Although these regulations may seem picayune, they actually increase the value of the property since they maintain the historical ambience that the visitor to the area is seeking or expecting. For example, one would not want to see a glass encased high rise building in the middle of historic downtown Williamsburg, Virginia, or a parking lot in the historic district of Savannah, Georgia.

Fire Departments

Each locality has its own **fire department**, whether it is a volunteer or paid for service. The fire department helps the hospitality manager assure the safety of their guests. A good fire department will limit the potential liability a hospitality business owes to their guests.

The fire department will:

- See the fire codes are followed.
- With the assistance of the building and zoning department, be sure construction plans are in line with fire codes.
- Assure proper sprinklers, smoke detectors, ventilation systems, and emergency lighting is in place and operational.
- Check fire extinguishers for placement and operability.
- Check grease traps in commercial kitchens to assure they are in compliance with fire safety codes of cleanliness and ventilation.

- Maintain and monitor maximum room capacities in public gathering areas and assure signs as to maximum capacity are properly displayed.
- Regulate the use of pyrotechnics during holidays and celebrations.

Police

The **police** will assist the hospitality business:

- Patrolling the property for individuals potentially trespassing.
- Enforcing local liquor laws.
- Enforcing parking restrictions.
- Helping maintain a safe environment for guests.

Tax Assessor/Collector

Each county or sometimes a locality has a **tax assessor/collector**. This office determines the value of the land and the buildings upon it. Based on this valuation, the amount of property taxes will be determined. There also may be added to the tax bill surcharges for fire, sanitation, police, or other fees that have been approved by local governmental officials.

In the hospitality industry, there may be local occupancy taxes. These will be in addition to the occupancy "bed" taxes the state collects. Each locality varies as to the assessment of these taxes, but most have implemented them to assure an increased revenue stream.

Chapter Summary

The court system is divided into federal and state courts, each with their own jurisdiction over specific cases. An alternative to going to court is to use Alternative Dispute Resolution. This could be mediation, arbitration, negotiation, collaborative law, or conciliation.

There are Federal Government regulatory agencies that affect the hospitality industry such as the IRS, OSHA, EPA, FDA, EEOC, ATF, and DOL.

States' regulations over the hospitality industry include unemployment insurance, workers' compensation insurance, alcohol and beverage control, department of revenue, health department, and department of transportation.

Local agencies that are involved with the hospitality industry are health and sanitation, building and zoning, historic preservation, the fire department, the police, and the tax assessor.

Key Terms

Federal courts
State courts
Cases or Controversies
Plaintiff
Standing
Defendant
Jurisdiction
Federal question
Diversity of citizenship
Moot
Limited jurisdiction
U.S. district courts
Bankruptcy courts
Bankruptcy Code
Chapter 7
Chapter 11
Chapter 13
U.S. court of appeals
U.S. Supreme Court
Writ of Certiorari
Habeas corpus
Alternative Dispute Resolution
Mediation
Arbitration
Negotiation
Collaborative law
Conciliation
American Arbitration Association
International Centre for Dispute
    Resolution
Better Business Bureau
Internal Revenue Service
Occupational Safety and Health
    Administration
Environmental Protection Agency

Comprehensive Environmental Re-
    sponse, Compensation, and Li-
    ability Act
Food and Drug Administration
Nutritional Labeling and Educa-
    tion Act
Equal Employment Opportunity
    Commission
Bureau of Alcohol, Tobacco,
    Firearms and Explosives
The Alcohol and Tobacco Tax and
    Trade Bureau
Department of Labor
Fair Labor Standards Act
Family and Medical Leave Act
National Defense Authorization Act
Immigration and Nationality Act
Consolidated Omnibus Budget Rec-
    onciliation Act
Department of Justice
U.S. Citizenship and Immigration
    Services (USCIS)
Department of Homeland Security
Unemployment compensation
Federal Unemployment Tax Act
Unemployment Insurance and Job
    Service
Workers' compensation
Twenty-first Amendment
Alcohol and Beverage Control
Dram shop acts
Attorney general
Department of revenue
Health department
Department of transportation

Health and sanitation   Fire department
Building and zoning   Police
Historic preservation   Tax assessor/collector

Chapter Four

Contracts

Chapter Objectives

What are the essential elements of a contract?

When does a breach of contract occur?

What is the statute of limitations?

What are the remedies for contract breach?

How can contract breach be avoided?

How can the hospitality industry address the issue of capacity?

How does the UCC affect contract law in the hospitality industry?

The hospitality industry relies on **contracts** extensively, whether they are verbal, e.g., a restaurant reservation, or written, e.g., a complicated airline tariff. The key to a valid contract is attention to detail and meeting all the contractual elements required.

Essential Elements of a Contract

The essential elements of a contract are:

1. There has to be an **offer** to sell by the seller and an **acceptance** by the buyer. The acceptance must match the offer, or it becomes a counteroffer. There must be a "**meeting of the minds**," or "**mutual assent**."

2. The parties in a contract must have **contractual capacity** — they may not be under 18. If they are, the contract is **voidable** at the option of the minor. The parties may not be *adjudged* mentally incompetent. If they are, the contract is **void**. Even if they are mentally incompetent (not adjudged) the contract is voidable, as in the case of a minor.
3. There must be **legality of the subject matter**. For example, if a property is sold to be a "crack house" the contract will be void. The sale of crack is not legal.
4. There must be **consideration** given — something that is a legal detriment to the parties. There are two types of consideration — *valuable*, wherein something in terms of money is exchanged, or *good* consideration, such as love and affection. Although love and affection cannot be measured by money, nonetheless they are considered consideration and thus make the contract binding.
5. Certain contracts must be in *writing* to be enforceable in a court of law:
   • Under the Uniform Commercial Code any contract over $500.00[1]

Also, under the **Statute of Frauds**, a contract must be in writing, to be enforceable in a court of law if:

• By its terms, the contract cannot be completed within one year of its signing
• It is a contract promising to answer for the debts of another
• It is with regard to real property — this includes leases for land or buildings
• It is in consideration of marriage — where there is a promise to give the prospective spouse something of value for getting married

Contracts do not have to have any particular format to be enforceable, as long as all of the above essential contractual elements are present.

The Statute of Frauds was implemented to prevent fraud and perjury in contracts.
A void contract means the contract can never be a valid contract no matter what is done.
A voidable contract means the contract can be avoided by the party lacking the capacity to sign it.

---

1. Article 2 §2-201 UCC Formal Requirements; Statute of Frauds.

A contract that is not enforceable, an **unenforceable contract**, is one in which one of the elements of the contract is missing, such as not being put into writing. Once the contract is put into written form, then the contract is again enforceable.

Unilateral and Bilateral Contracts

A **bilateral contract** is one in which both the party making the offer (the offeror) and the party accepting the offer (the offeree) make *mutual promises* to each other. This form of contract, once agreed to, obligates both parties to perform. In the hospitality industry, a room reservation would be a bilateral contract. The hospitality manager is promising to have a room and the guest promises to pay for the room.

A **unilateral contract** is one in which only one party makes a promise and the other party accepts by performing. For example, in property contracts the person offering the property may allow another person to take an **option** on the property — the **optionor** (the one holding the property for another's action) agrees not to sell the property to anyone else during the option period. The **optionee** pays some consideration for the granting of the option, but the optionee is not obligated to buy the real estate. The option allows the optionee to consider buying, while preventing a sale to anyone else. Since only one person is making the promise — the optionor (by promising not to sell) — this is a unilateral contract. If the optionee decides to exercise the option, then both parties have made a promise, and this in turn creates a bilateral contract — a promise for a promise.

Why is it important to understand when a contract is unilateral or bilateral? For example, in a unilateral contract, if a hospitality manager calls a lawn service to mow the lawn, and the lawn service does not show up, this would *not* be a breach of contract. The lawn service never promised to mow the lawn. Only their act of showing up would create the contract.

Now, in the same scenario, if the lawn service, when called by the manager, promised to mow the lawn, this then created a bilateral contract since there are mutual promises on both sides. In this case, if the lawn service does not show up to mow the lawn, this is a breach of contract because they promised to perform. The act of making promises by both parties obligates the lawn service and the hospitality manager to complete the contract.

Termination of Contract Rights

Breach of Contract

A **breach of contract** is when one party fails to perform and there is no legal reason for the nonperformance. In case of breach, the non-breaching party has the right to seek legal remedies (discussed below). For example, if a hotel orders food from a supplier, and the supplier does not deliver and has no legal reason for not supplying the food, this can be treated as a breach of contract.

Impossibility of Performance

Impossibility of performance is when an event, *beyond the control of the parties*, occurs — one that will make the contract *impossible* to perform. Examples would be the burning down of the hotel that is being sold, or the death of the parties in the contract. (Unless, in the contract, it has been stated the parties' heirs or assigns have the legal right to honor the agreement.)

Mutual Rescission

Mutual rescission occurs when the parties in a contract agree to terminate their duties in the agreement. For example, a supplier of linens contacts the hotel and says he/she will not deliver the linens and the hotel manager agrees to this non-delivery.

Operation of Law

Termination of a contract by **operation of law** can occur if the subject matter of the contract becomes unlawful. The contract is then void. For example, when liquor became unlawful during Prohibition, any contracts for alcohol would have been terminated by operation of law.

Statute of Limitations

The **statute of limitations** is a federal or state law that limits the time within which a legal proceeding may be brought. These statutes apply to civil, contract, and criminal actions. These laws are designed to prevent fraudulent and stale claims from being brought after evidence in the case may have been lost; after the facts have been forgotten, or after the death or disappearance of witnesses.

The defense of statute of limitations is asserted by the defendant to defeat an action brought against him or her. The defendant must **plead** this defense upon answering the plaintiff's complaint. If the defendant does not so plead, this defense is waived and will not be allowed to be used in subsequent proceedings.

Pleadings are the statements, allegations, and counter allegations made by plaintiff and defendant, or prosecutor and accused, in a legal proceeding.

The Uniform Commercial Code's view of the statute of limitations, under Article 2 — Contract for Sale, states if there is a breach of contract, a case must be commenced within four years (this time period cannot be extended). The UCC also states if there is agreement between the parties, and it is so noted in the original contract, the parties may shorten this time to not less than one year.

UCC §2-725. Statute of Limitations in Contracts for Sale
An action for breach of any contract for sale must be commenced within four years after the cause of action has accrued. By the original agreement the parties may reduce the period of limitation to not less than one year but may not extend it.

Thus, in the hospitality industry, if a contract comes under Article 2 of the UCC, it may be of benefit to the parties to the contract to shorten the four-year statute of limitations time period. This will facilitate business transactions by relieving the anxiety of the threat of suit for contract breach.

Contract Remedies for Breach

In a perfect world, all contracts would be fully performed, and there would be no need to seek legal recourse for contract breach. Unfortunately, though, no one lives in a perfect world.

There are four legal **remedies** for contract breach:

1. **Specific performance** is sought if either party to the contract wants the other party to perform on the contract. For example, if a piece of land is part of a contract, each piece of land is unique, and as such, if the seller refuses to convey the real estate, money alone will not be sufficient to compensate the buyer for their loss. In this case, the buyer can seek relief in the **court of equity** for specific perform-ance. The buyer does not want their money back; what they want is the land. A court of equity is unlike a law court. A law court can only award money damages, the court of equity can require a party to perform on their promise. The court of equity can force the seller to convey the land in question.

2. **Liquidated damages** is a sum certain stated in the contract to compensate the non-breaching party in case of contract breach. For example, if the owner of a bed and breakfast leases their property to someone else to run, and then the person leasing the bed and breakfast allows the business to deteriorate, the original owner will have to return to get the business going again. Thus, the original owner will need to be compensated for this breach. If there is a liquidated damages clause in the lease contract, the original owner can collect these pre-set damages. As long as the liquidated damages fairly represent the potential "actual" damages that may be incurred by the breach, the courts will usually uphold the award of such damages. Liquidated damages will not be upheld if the court deems the amount would be a penalty to the breaching party.[2] In the above mentioned scenario, in regard to the bed and breakfast, liquidated damages could be set high and still not be considered a penalty, since the original owners may have moved away from the area and would have to return to begin running the business again.

3. **Compensatory damages** are the remedy of choice if there are economic losses due to breach of contract. Then the non-breaching party can sue, in a court of law, for the amount of damages resulting from the contract breach.

4. Suit for **rescission and restitution** is another relief sought in a court of equity. Rescission sets aside the existing contract and restores the parties to their positions prior to entering into the contract. It is the cancellation of a contract. Restitution occurs when any money paid by one party to the other, with regard to the rescinded contract, is returned.

Avoiding Breach of Contract

In the hospitality industry, some ways to prevent a breach of contract are to:

• Put the contract in writing. Especially if it is required by law (see above as to when a contract needs to be in writing), or if the terms of the agreement are extremely complicated.

---

2. (12 A.L.R. 4th 891, 899).

- Read a contract thoroughly before signing it. Or, better yet, have an attorney read it before signing.
- Do not sign anything you do not have the authority to sign. If you are an agent working for a principal, e.g., a general manager for the Marriott®; do you, as an agent, have the legal capacity to sign the document?
- Keep copies of all contract documents. If the contract was formed verbally and it is still enforceable, keep notes on all negotiations, dates, and agreements made between the parties.
- Use **good faith** (an honest belief the contract can be honored) in all contract negotiations. Be realistic in negotiations. If it can't be done, don't promise it will be.
- Note all contract deadlines for performance. Make all these deadlines reasonable for all the parties.
- Always work with reliable third parties. Check out all the contractors and vendors before doing business with them. Talk to others in the hospitality industry to get their experiences with these entities. If there is a history of chronic problems, do not do business with them, no matter what the price. This will be more of a headache than it is worth.
- Address the issue of possible damages if there is a contract breach. Put this in writing or take notes on what is being promised if the other party cannot perform.
- Let employees know what needs to be done to perform on any contracts. Will there be a need for special accommodations to make the contract work? For example, if a hotel accommodates flight crews, do they get to cash their payroll checks, while regular guests cannot? To complete a contract, will employees have to work overtime or carry out duties they usually do not do?
- Resolve any contract ambiguities as quickly as possible. Do this in a fair and ethical manner. It may sound good to take someone to court, but litigation is costly and time consuming. Is it worth losing the restaurant's goodwill for the cost of a dinner?

Reservations as Contracts

In the hospitality industry, when a reservation is made, either verbally or in writing, this is considered a contract. There is a meeting of the minds, consideration (since both parties are making promises to perform), there is the presumption there is capacity on the part of the parties, and there is the legality of the subject matter.

Because of this, it is best to have some sort of guarantee that the guest will honor their side of the contract. For example, take a credit card number if it is a hotel, airline, or ticket reservation. This protects both parties. The guest will be assured a room, seat, or ticket will be available when they arrive, and the hospitality operator will be assured they will be paid for their services.

If a credit card is taken for pre-payment, cancellation policies must be detailed completely to the guest. Explain the room, airline seat, or ticket will be held for them and their credit card will be billed whether or not they pick-up the tickets or occupy the room. Information can be given verbally, but it is best to have a standard email sent to the guest. This email must be sent to each guest every time a reservation or a ticket is booked. This shows a pattern of behavior of the hospitality business. This is protection for the business against the no-show guest protesting the charges to their credit card company, and it is evidence the guest was informed of the business's cancellation policies. This protects the business against credit card **chargebacks**.

> A chargeback is when a credit card company withdraws money for a transaction from a merchant's (hospitality business) account and then deposits this money back into the customer's account.

Cancellation policies must be very detailed regarding when, how, or even if a cancellation will result in any type of refund of money, or if the reservation can be changed with or without penalty. If a penalty attaches to any changes in reservation, this must be explained. The cancellation policy must disclose the **venue** where disputes over cancellations or changes in reservations will be held and whether or not **Alternative Dispute Resolution** will be used.

> Venue is where the trial or resolution will be held.
> Alternative Dispute Resolution is resolving a dispute outside of a courtroom.

If one owns a restaurant, reservations usually are made over the phone. The restaurant owner will want to protect themselves against no-shows by getting a phone number from the customer. By doing so, the customer will feel more obligated to honor the reservation made. If the restaurant wishes, they can call to see if the customer is coming, or if the reservation needs to be cancelled or changed.

Estimating Guest/Traveler/Capacity/Arrivals

Airlines have always **overbooked** flights to protect themselves against the usual ten percent of passengers that never make it to the gate; restaurants usually overbook by fifteen percent to protect their bottom lines; and hotels, like airlines, overbook by ten percent.

> Overbooking is the process of taking more reservations than the hospitality business has the ability to honor.

Why do these industries do this? They overbook to maximize their profits. To have empty rooms, airline seats, or restaurant tables means losing revenue. Yet if a hospitality business overbooks, and there is a guaranteed reservation that is not honored, this is a breach of contract.

If a hospitality business is overbooked and everyone that made reservations shows up, the first thing a manager must do is establish which reservations are guaranteed and which are not. If there is a confirmed reservation and a credit card has been given to secure the service, these agreements must be honored.

If the reservation is not guaranteed by a credit card or some form of payment and if the guest does not arrive, it is best not to try to penalize the guest for not showing up; doing so leads to a loss of **goodwill**. On the other hand, if a guest arrives with a confirmed but not guaranteed reservation and their hotel room has already been rented, although there is no legal obligation to do so, hospitality managers should try to find a comparable hotel in the vicinity for the guest.

> Goodwill arises from the reputation of a business and its relations with their customers. It is a valuable, salable asset for the business.

If a restaurant has overbooked and all the people that made reservations show up; try to accommodate them. It is a good policy for a restaurant to inform a guest that there may be a short wait for a table even with a reservation. This will alleviate tensions when a reservation cannot be honored immediately.

If a customer is bumped from an airline flight because of overbooking there are specific laws with regard to what needs to be done. See Chapter One for a discussion of delayed or cancelled flights, "bumping," and overbooking of flights and the legal requirements surrounding this.

Uniform Commercial Code

The **Uniform Commercial Code** (UCC) is a set of suggested laws relating to commercial transactions. With the growth of the Interstate Highway System in the 1950s and the subsequent growth of **interstate business** (business between the states), there was a need for more uniformity in the laws between the states. This brought about the UCC. In September 1951, a final draft of the UCC was completed and approved by the **American Law Institute** (ALI) and the **National Conference of Commissioners on Uniform State Laws** (NC-CUSL), and then by the **House of Delegates of the American Bar Association**. After some additional amendments and changes, the official edition, with explanatory comments, was published in 1952. Pennsylvania was the first state to adopt the UCC, followed by Massachusetts. By 1967, the District of Columbia and all the states, except for Louisiana, have adopted the UCC in whole or in part. Louisiana eventually adopted all the articles in the UCC except Articles 2 (sale of goods) and 2A (leases of goods). Louisiana follows civil law, i.e., the laws of the Roman Empire (since Louisiana follows French tradition), and Articles 2 and 2A do not comply with the civil law concept.

In the hospitality industry, the Articles to be most concerned with are:

Article 2/Sales of Goods

Article 2 does not apply to services, it only applies to goods. What is the difference? Goods are material items, while services are tasks done by people. What about a restaurant? Is that goods or services? Well, most people go to a restaurant for food, a good, and the service is extra. So this is a good and the sale of the food is controlled under Article 2. What about a spa? Well, here people go for massage etc., not for the products, so this is a service and not covered by Article 2 of the UCC. What if there is a mixture of goods and services? To determine which prevails, look at the main reason the guest is going to that particular hospitality business.

Warranties under the UCC

UCC Article 2 outlines certain **warranties** included as part of the sale.

When people use the word "warranty," they are typically referring to a specific kind of warranty that the UCC calls an "**express warranty**." Express warranties are affirmative promises about the quality and features of the goods being sold. Claiming a watch is "waterproof to 250 feet," or that a car gets "35 mpg on the highway," are all examples of express warranties. But express warranties under the UCC include more than just affirmative statements. They also include descriptions of the goods being sold or samples shown to the buyer. If the potential diner is shown a picture of a dinner, the actual dinner needs to be very similar to the picture. By posting this picture, this is an express warranty of the meal to be served.[3]

---

3. Article 2 §2-313 UCC Express Warranties by Affirmation, Promise, Description, Sample.

In addition to express warranties, the UCC creates a second kind of warranty, called an "**implied warranty**." As the name suggests, an implied warranty is made regardless of whether or not it is specifically mentioned. The implied warranties created by the UCC ended the old rule of *caveat emptor*— "*Let the buyer beware*." Implied warranties allow buyers to purchase goods and be confident that they meet certain minimum standards. The two implied warranties the UCC creates are the implied warranty of "**merchantability**" of the goods being sold,[4] and the implied warranty that the goods are "**fit for a particular purpose**."[5]

Under the UCC's definition of "merchantability," goods must be at least of average quality, properly packaged and labeled, and fit for the ordinary purposes they are intended to serve. For example, food served in a restaurant must be fit for human consumption.

The application of the implied warranty of merchantability is limited to a seller of "goods of that kind," meaning the kind of goods the seller usually sells in the marketplace. A seller does not make an implied warranty of merchantability when he/she sells goods of a kind that he/she does not normally sell. For example, a clothing store selling shirts and suits impliedly warrants that the shirts and suits are merchantable because shirts and suits are the kind of goods a clothing store typically sells. On the other hand, if the store sells coffee one day, this coffee is not subject to an implied warranty of merchantability because clothing stores generally do not sell coffee. Of course, if the seller makes an express warranty regarding the coffee, they will be held to any such warranty, but none will be implied unless the goods being sold are goods of a kind the seller normally sells.

The implied warranty of fitness for a particular purpose applies if the seller knows or has reason to know that the buyer will be using the goods he or she is buying for a certain purpose. If the seller knows the purpose for which the goods are to be used, the seller impliedly warrants that the goods being sold are suitable for that specific purpose.

For example, a car salesman may sell a car that is perfectly suitable for everyday driving, and therefore is merchantable. But if the car salesman knows the buyer wants to use the car as a race car, the car salesman also impliedly warrants that the car is suitable for racing.

The rationale behind the implied warranty of fitness for a particular purpose is that buyers typically rely on the seller's skill and expertise to help them find

---

4. Article 2 §2-314 UCC Implied Warranty: Merchantability; Usage of Trade.
5. Article 2 §2-315 UCC Implied Warranty: Fitness for Particular Purpose.

the specific goods that meet their specific needs. A buyer who goes to an appliance store may know he/she wants a refrigerator, but he/she relies on the appliance salesperson to find the specific refrigerator that fits the house, is big enough for the family, and meets any other specific requirements he/she might have. Accordingly, it is unfair for a seller to sell something they know will not do the job and later tells the buyer it is not his or her fault it did not work.

In the hospitality business, implied warranties of fitness for a particular purpose will be applicable to restaurants when a restaurant knows a diner is relying on the restaurant's expertise in serving a particular item; for example, gluten-free food, low-fat food, or sugar-free food. The customer relies on the expertise of the restaurant to prepare such food, to accommodate their dietary needs. If the restaurant does not serve such food, they are in breach of the implied warranty that the goods (foods) are fit for a particular purpose.

Because warranties typically only become an issue when a buyer is dissatisfied, a prudent seller tries to limit the scope of the warranties he or she makes. The UCC specifically allows sellers to disclaim both express and implied warranties on goods they sell, within certain limits. For example, a restaurant could not disclaim the implied warranty of merchantability of their food — otherwise the food would not be fit to eat. But the restaurant may disclaim the express warranty of a picture representing the food that is being served by stating, "The food served may not look exactly like the picture on the menu."

The UCC does not provide many specific rules regarding how warranties are disclaimed. In keeping with the idea, the purpose of the UCC is to make business transactions easier, the UCC provides that attempts to disclaim warranties should be construed reasonably and enforced unless doing so is unreasonable under the circumstances. Generally, a seller who wants to disclaim UCC warranties must do so specifically. A general statement that there are "no warranties, express or implied" is usually ineffective. An express warranty must be expressly disclaimed.

A disclaimer that disclaims the implied warranty of merchantability must specifically mention the word "merchantability" in the disclaimer. A seller may disclaim all implied warranties by stating that the good is being sold "**as is**," "with all faults," or by stating some other phrase that makes it plain to the buyer there are no implied warranties.[6]

The UCC also requires all disclaimers of implied warranties to be in writing. However, a warranty disclaimer hidden in the fine print of a three-page sales contract will not be enforced because the *UCC also requires a disclaimer be*

---

6. Article 2 §2-316 UCC Exclusion or Modification of Warranties.

conspicuous. A section of a contract is conspicuous if it clearly stands out from the rest of the contract and draws the eye of the reader. Common ways to make contract provisions conspicuous is to put them in bold type, different colored type, larger type, or in all capitals. Many disclaimers combine several of these elements, e.g., disclaiming implied warranties in bold red capitals when the rest of the contract is in regular black type.[7]

However, there are outer limits to what even the best-drafted disclaimer of warranties can accomplish. Unless all warranties have been effectively disclaimed, a buyer usually must have some meaningful remedy if the goods they receive are defective or not what was represented by the hospitality business. Additionally, most states have consumer protection statutes for transactions involving the purchase of consumer goods. These statutes often provide the buyer with remedies other than those provided by the UCC, and often provide that a consumer's rights under the statute cannot be abridged by means of a disclaimer.

Article 2A/Leases of Personal Property

A **lease** is a transfer of the right to possession and use of goods for a specified period of time. **UCC Article 2A** is a set of laws relating to personal property leasing. Article 2A made many changes in the existing law which benefited both lessors and lessees. These changes essentially standardized state law so that the lessor would be unable to select favorable quirks in the law of their home state.

Under Article 2A, a lease could be a **lease of goods**. These are leases made by a lessor that is regularly engaged in the business of leasing or selling such goods. For example, a hospitality business (lessee) may need to lease a large tent for a special function, or a specific piece of equipment for a week.

Under Article 2A it could be a **finance lease**. A finance lease involves three or more parties: the lessee (the hospitality business), the lessor (this is usually a bank that buys the equipment for the hospitality business and then charges the lessee lease rent), and the equipment supplier(s).[8]

A finance lease would be used when the lessee (the hospitality business) selects the equipment and negotiates particularized modifications with the equipment supplier. The lessor (usually a bank) then purchases the selected equipment and leases it to the lessee. Traditionally, lessors involved in "lease

---

7. Article 2 § 2-103 UCC Definitions and Index of Definitions.
8. Article 2A § 2A-103UCC Definitions and Index of Definitions.

financings" have been thought of as passive lessors—these transactions are functionally the equivalent of an extension of credit.[9]

An example of a finance lease would be if a hospitality business needed a new air conditioning system that costs $5 million. The hospitality business would rather not directly purchase this system, so they go to their bank and arrange a finance lease. This is advantageous to the business since they do not have to have a large outlay of cash immediately and it is advantageous to the bank since they will make money on the lease payments to them. But remember, given the limited function of the lessor (the supplier of the money to buy the equipment), the lessee must rely entirely on the supplier for representations, covenants, and warranties. Thus, if that air conditioning unit breaks down, the hospitality business should not call the bank, because they are not responsible for fixing it. The supplier of the air conditioning unit must honor any warranties that were given.

Article 9/Secured Transactions

UCC Article 9 covers the creation of security interests in goods.

To create a valid security interest under Article 9, the creditor or supplier of goods (usually a provider of inventory or equipment to a hospitality business) must:

1. Extend credit to the hospitality business.
2. Receive a security agreement signed by the debtor or buyer of the goods (the hospitality business).
3. **Perfect the security agreement** by filing a **UCC-1 Financing Statement**.[10] A UCC-1 Financing Statement is prepared, signed, and filed with a state agency, such as the secretary of state, in the state where the debtor (the hospitality business) is located. This process is called "perfecting the security interest" in the property. This type of loan is then a **secured loan**.[11]
4. Filing the UCC-1, besides securing the loan, also gives the creditor priority in payment over other non-perfected creditors or creditors who have filed but have done a defective filing. (A filing of the UCC-

---

9. *Nath v. Nat. Equipment Leasing Corp., 439 A.2d 633 (Pa. 1981)* (noting that this type of lessor "is not in the business of selling or marketing merchandise [but rather, it is in] the business of circulating funds").

10. www.gsccca.org.

11. Article 9 § 9-302 UCC When Filing Is Required to Perfect Security Interest.

1 is defective if the information in the statement is seriously mis-
leading or the filing is made in the wrong state office; then the filing
fails to perfect the security interest.) The priority in collection of the
debt is extremely important to a creditor (supplier of the goods) in
case the hospitality business goes into bankruptcy.

Another method of perfecting the security agreement would be if the creditor
(supplier of the goods) actually held on to the items until they are paid off.
Here, the hospitality business would seek credit for an expensive item and
rather than receiving it immediately, would make an agreed amount of payments to the creditor prior to receiving the merchandise. The advantage here
would be, the hospitality business would be assured of getting the products
and have the ability to pay them off. The advantage to the creditor would be
to never have to worry about getting the items back if the hospitality business
failed and did not make their payments on the goods. Why would a business
want to enter such form of secured transaction? This version of business "lay-
away" would be valuable to the hospitality business if the item was expensive
and difficult to obtain or if there was significant inflation occurring where the
hospitality business is located. In countries with hyper-inflation, each day that
passes items become more and more expensive.[12]

Chapter Summary

For a contract to be enforceable, there are specific requirements that must
be adhered to. If these requirements are not met, the contract may be voidable,
void, or merely unenforceable until the contract requirements are complied
with. Contracts can be terminated if there is a breach, if there is impossibility
of performance by one or both of the parties, if there is mutual rescission by
both parties, and by operation of law. Remedies for contract breach or termination can be obtained in a court of law or a court of equity. It is in the business's best interest to avoid breaching a contract.

The Uniform Commercial Code Article 2 addresses contracts for the sale
of goods and warranties for those goods. Article 2A addresses leases including
finance leases of goods. Article 9 concerns itself with the creation of security
interests in goods purchased on credit.

---

12. www.sba.gov.

Key Terms

Contracts
Offer
Acceptance
Meeting of the minds
Mutual assent
Contractual capacity
Voidable
Void
Legality of the subject matter
Consideration
Statute of Frauds
Unenforceable contract
Bilateral contract
Unilateral contract
Option
Optionor
Optionee
Breach of contract
Impossibility of performance
Mutual rescission
Operation of law
Statute of limitations
Plead
Remedies
Specific performance
Court of equity
Liquidated damages
Compensatory damages
Rescission and restitution
Breach of contract

Good faith
Chargebacks
Venue
Alternative Dispute Resolution
Overbooked
Goodwill
Uniform Commercial Code
Interstate business
American Law Institute
National Conference of Commis-
    sioners on Uniform State Laws
House of Delegates of the American
    Bar Association
UCC Article 2
Warranties
Express warranty
Implied warranty
Caveat emptor
Merchantability
Fit for a particular purpose
As is
Lease
UCC Article 2A
Lease of goods
Finance lease
UCC Article 9
Perfect the security agreement
UCC-1 Financing Statement
Secured loan

Chapter Five

Torts/Crimes

Chapter Objectives

What is an intentional tort?

What is negligence?

What are the elements of negligence?

Define a reasonable person.

Define causation.

What are the defenses to negligence?

What is strict liability?

What are the damages that can be awarded in a tort case?

What types of crimes are committed against a hospitality business?

A **crime** is a wrong arising from a violation of a **public duty**. A **tort** is a wrong arising from the violation of a **private duty**. However, a crime can also constitute a tort. For example, assault is a tort, but it is also a crime. A person who is assaulted may bring criminal charges against the assailant and may also sue the assailant for damages under tort law. An employee's theft of his employer's property, which was entrusted to the employee, constitutes the crime of embezzlement as well as the tort of conversion.

In the hospitality industry, usually the most prevalent area of liability will be under the tort of **negligence** (to be discussed at length in this chapter). It is rare for a hospitality manager to encounter many intentional torts or crimes being committed by either employees or guests. Yet it is important to learn the terminology and what constitutes these offenses in the event one is confronted by them.

Intentional Torts/Crimes

Assault and Battery

Assault and **battery** are two separate offenses. When they are used in one expression they may be defined as any unlawful and unpermitted touching of another. Assault is an act that creates an *apprehension* in another of an imminent, harmful, or offensive contact. The act consists of a threat of harm accompanied by an *apparent, present ability to carry out the threat.*[1] Battery is a *harmful or offensive touching* of another.[2]

The main distinction between the two offenses is the existence or nonexistence of touching or contact. While contact is an essential element of battery, there must be an absence of contact for assault.

Assault and battery are offenses in both criminal and tort law; therefore, they can give rise to criminal or civil liability. In criminal law, an assault may additionally be defined as any attempt to commit a battery.

Intent is an essential element of both offenses in crimes and tort. Generally, it is only necessary for the defendant to have the *intent to do the act* that causes the harm. In other words, the act must be done *voluntarily*. For example, if someone flails out while they are sleeping and then makes contact with someone this would not be assault or battery. This was not a voluntary act. There was no intent to do the act.[3]

Defamation

Defamation is any intentional false communication, either written or spoken, that harms a person's reputation; decreases the respect, regard, or confidence in which a person is held; or induces disparaging, hostile, or disagreeable opinions or feelings against a person.[4]

Defamation may be a criminal or civil charge. It encompasses both written statements, known as **libel**, and spoken statements, called **slander**.

---

1. Restatement (2d) of Torts §§ 21–34.
2. Restatement (2d) of Torts §§ 13–20.
3. *Garratt v. Dailey*, 279 P.2d 1091 (Wash. 1955).
4. Restatement (2d) of Torts § 558.

Invasion of Privacy

The courts recognize four categories of **invasion of privacy**:

- **Intrusion** upon one's physical solitude or seclusion
- **Public disclosure of private facts**
- **False light** in the public eye
- **Appropriation** — Use of a person's name, likeness or identity for trade or advertising purposes without consent[5]

Intrusion occurs when **one intentionally intrudes, physically or otherwise, upon the solitude or seclusion of another or intrudes into his or her private affairs or concerns.**[6]

The tort of public disclosure of private facts entails three elements:

- The disclosure of private facts must be a public disclosure.
- The facts disclosed must be private facts, and not public ones.
- The matter made public must be one which would be offensive and objectionable to a reasonable person of ordinary sensibilities.[7]

Public disclosure of private facts occurs when a person gives publicity to a matter that concerns the private life of another, a matter that would be highly offensive to a reasonable person and that is not of legitimate public concern. A communication to a single person or to a small group of people is not actionable since the publicity element requires communication with the public at large or to so many people that the matter is substantially certain to become one of public knowledge.[8]

For a fact to be private, plaintiffs must demonstrate they actually expected a disclosed fact to remain private. Society would recognize this expectation of privacy as reasonable, and be willing to respect it.

Public disclosure of private facts is a tort, but a crime may have been committed in getting the information, e.g., trespassing on someone's land.

Liability under false light requires public disclosure of some falsity or fiction concerning a plaintiff.[9]

In the hospitality industry, it is important not to divulge private information obtained from or about one's guests. Although a guest may be willing to give

---

5. Restatement (2d) of Torts §652.
6. Restatement (2d) of Torts§652B.
7. Restatement (2d) of Torts §652D.
8. Restatement (2d) of Torts §652.
9. Restatement (2d) of Torts §577.

an innkeeper or restaurateur needed information about a reservation or booking, such as who checked into a hotel, or who ate with whom, this is not information that should be made public by the hospitality business.

It is also considered a tort for a business to use the name or likeness of a famous individual for commercial advantage, also called appropriation of name or likeness. All individuals are vested with an exclusive property right in their identity. No person, business, or other entity may appropriate an individual's name or likeness without permission. Despite the existence of this tort, businesses occasionally associate their products with popular celebrities without first obtaining the celebrity's consent. A business that falsely suggests that a celebrity has sponsored or endorsed one of its products will be held liable for money damages equal to the economic gain derived from the wrongful appropriation of the celebrity's likeness.[10]

Disparagement

The tort of **disparagement** is an interference with business or economic relations. Disparagement is the publication of derogatory information about a person's title to his or her property; to his or her business in general, or anything else made for the purpose of discouraging people from dealing with the individual. Generally, the aspersions are cast upon the quality of what the person has to sell, or the person's business itself. In this tort it is imperative to prove there were damages. No damages, no tort.[11]

Disparagement may turn into a crime if there is **fraud**. Fraud is commonly understood as dishonesty calculated for advantage.

False Advertising/Unfair Competition

Advertising need not be entirely false to be actionable under the tort of **false advertising** or **unfair competition**, so long as it is sufficiently inaccurate to mislead or deceive consumers in a manner that inflicts injury on a competitor. In general, businesses are prohibited from placing ads that either unfairly disparage the goods or services of a competitor or unfairly inflate the value of their own goods and services. False advertising deprives consumers of the opportunity to make intelligent comparisons between rival products. It also drives up costs for consumers who must spend additional resources in examining and sampling products.

---

10. Restatement (2d) of Torts § 652C.
11. Salmond, Torts § 149 (1st Ed. 1907).

Both federal and state laws regulate deceptive advertising. The **Lanham Trademark Act**[12] regulates false advertising at the federal level. Many states have adopted the **Uniform Deceptive Trade Practices Act**,[13] which prohibits three specific types of representations:

- False representations that goods or services have certain characteristics, ingredients, uses, benefits, or quantities
- False representations that goods or services are new or original
- False representations that goods or services are of a particular grade, standard, or quality

Advertisements that are only partially accurate may give rise to liability if they are likely to confuse prospective consumers. Ambiguous representations may require clarification to prevent the imposition of liability. For example, a business that accuses a hospitality competitor of being "unreliable" may be required to clarify that description with additional information if consumer confusion is likely to result.[14]

In the hospitality industry, it is imperative that any *factual information* given to prospective guests be as accurate as possible, e.g., pictures of the property, rate information, and information represented on the menu in a restaurant.

If only representing opinions, statements that are not factual only business hyperbole (**puffing**), these statements would not be actionable as deceptive advertising since "mere opinions" are subjective and thus not provable in one way or the other.

False Imprisonment

False imprisonment is the unlawful confinement of one individual against his or her will by another individual in such a manner as to violate the confined individual's right to be free from restraint of movement, and the individual has no reasonable means of escape.

To recover damages for false imprisonment, an individual must be confined to a substantial degree, with her or his freedom of movement totally restrained. Interfering with or obstructing an individual's freedom to go where she or he wishes does not constitute false imprisonment. For example, if Bob enters a room, and Anne prevents him from leaving through one exit but does not pre

---

12. Lanham Trademark Act (15 USC).
13. Restatement (2d) of Torts § 549.
14. Restatement (2d) of Torts § 538 A.

vent him from leaving the way he came in, then Bob would not have been falsely imprisoned.[15]

An individual whose conduct constitutes the tort of false imprisonment may also be charged with committing the crime of **kidnapping**. Kidnapping is the taking of a person from one place to another against his or her will, or the confining of a person in a controlled space.[16]

In the hospitality industry, if a guest is somehow locked in a room without any means of reasonable escape, then false imprisonment or even kidnapping can be charged. This could happen if there were some sort of emergency situation that eliminated any form of reasonable egress on the part of the guest. An example of this would be if a cruise ship sank due to the fault of the captain. Guaranteed, in the lawsuits to follow, false imprisonment would be one of the causes of action pled by the plaintiffs.

Intentional Infliction of Emotional Distress

The tort of **intentional infliction of emotional distress** has four elements:

- The defendant must act intentionally or recklessly
- The defendant's conduct must be extreme and outrageous
- The conduct must be the cause
- Of severe emotional distress

Although case law does not provide us with a precise definition of "extreme and outrageous," the test usually adopted for actionable conduct is that the conduct must be "so outrageous in character, and so extreme in degree, as to go beyond all possible bounds of decency, and to be regarded as atrocious, and utterly intolerable in a civilized community."[17]

This tort would be pled against the hospitality defendant if there are other intentional torts pled, e.g., assault, battery, false imprisonment, or defamation.

Negligent Infliction of Emotional Distress

Not all jurisdictions recognize **negligent infliction of emotional distress**. If they do, a negligent infliction of emotional distress (NIED) personal injury claim is based on the concept that all members of society have a duty to avoid causing another individual mental strain. Under this tort, an individual who

---

15. Restatement (2d) of Torts § 35–36.
16. www.findlaw.com.
17. Restatement (2d) of Torts § 46.

does not use due care in his or her actions, and, as a result, creates another individual's emotional distress may be responsible for damages. It is unlike intentional infliction of emotional distress since NIED goes to a duty of due care *not* intent.[18]

NIED will be pled if there is a negligence case brought against the hospitality business; this is an issue of taking reasonable care, not intent. Pleading NIED adds to the injury portion in a negligence case, since the plaintiff is seeking compensation for emotional damages.

Trespass

A **trespass** is an unlawful intrusion that interferes with one's person or property.

Every unlawful entry onto another's property is trespass, even if there is no harm done to the property. A person who has a right to come onto the land may become a trespasser by committing wrongful acts after entry. For example, a customer at a restaurant has the privilege of entering the restaurant and ordering a meal. However, if that same diner walks out without paying for the meal, they have become a trespasser since they have committed a wrongful act.

Permission to enter someone else's property, e.g., a hotel or restaurant, can be given either by **consent** or by **license**. Consent means giving permission or allowing another onto the land. For example, a hotel gives consent to people to walk through the lobby. Consent may be implied from all the circumstances. It is not necessary for the person walking through the lobby to get verbal or written consent to do so. The hotel is open for business and the lobby usually is a public space within the hotel.

Sometimes consent to enter another's land is called a license, or legal permission. This license is not necessarily a certificate and may or may not be in the form of a written agreement. For example, an electric company might have a license to enter the hotel property to maintain electrical lines or to read the electric meter. Even though the electric company has consent to enter the hospitality business's premises, electric company employees cannot act unreasonably when they make repairs, and they and the company are liable for any damage they cause to the property.[19]

At **common law**, a trespass is not *criminal* unless it is accomplished by violence or breaches the peace. Some modern statutes make *any* unlawful entry onto another's property a crime.

---

18. Restatement (2d) of Torts §436A.
19. Restatement (2d) of Torts §158.

When the trespass involves violence or injury to a person or property, it is always considered criminal, and penalties may be increased for more serious or malicious acts. Criminal intent may have to be proved to convict under some **statutory laws,** but in some states trespass is a criminal offense regardless of the defendant's intent.[20]

> Common law is also known as case law and is of two types — one where judgments passed become new laws if there are no statutes in place regarding this legal issue, and the other type of common law is when judges interpret the existing law and determine new boundaries and distinctions for the law.
> Statutory laws can be passed by various governmental agencies of a country. Thus, there are laws passed by federal and state governments and ordinances passed by towns and cities; all have the power of law. New laws are issued to meet the needs of the citizens, deal with the resolution of outstanding issues, and formalization of an existing law.

Conversion

Conversion is any unauthorized act that deprives an owner of personal property without his or her consent. The wrongdoer converts the goods to his or her own use and excludes the owner from the use and enjoyment of them — a fancy way to say "steals." Conversion is the tort side of the crime of **theft**.[21]

Theft is the generic term for all crimes in which a person intentionally and fraudulently takes the personal property of another without permission or consent and with the intent to convert it to the taker's use. In many states, if the value of the property taken is low (for example, less than $500) the crime is "**petty theft,**" but it is "**grand theft**" for larger amounts. Although **robbery** (taking by force), **burglary** (taking by entering unlawfully), and **embezzlement** (stealing from an employer) are all commonly thought of as theft, they are distinguished by the means and methods used.[22]

In the hospitality industry, a hospitality manager faces a high probability of suffering from the crimes of petty theft of services or products, grand theft of services or products, and potential embezzlement committed by one of the employees.

The tort of conversion will be used if one decides to sue the criminal perpetrator of a theft civilly.

20. www.realestate.findlaw.com.
21. Restatement (2d) of Torts §222A.
22. www.criminal.findlaw.com.

Intentional Interference with Contract Relations/ Interference with Prospective Contract

Both the tort of **interference with contract relations** and the tort of **interference with prospective contract** involve basically the same conduct by the defendant. In one tort, the interference takes place when a contract is already in existence, the other tort is when a contract would, with certainty, have been consummated but for the conduct of the individual interfering in the contract. For either of these torts to be actionable, the plaintiff must show the party inducing the breach intended it to happen.

If the actor had no knowledge of the existence of the contract or his or her actions were not intended to induce a breach, he or she cannot be held liable, even though an actual breach results from his or her acts. It is not enough that the actor intended to perform the acts that caused the result. He or she must have intended to cause the breach of an existing contract or the interference with the formation of the contract itself.

The claim of interference of contract can only be asserted against a stranger to the contractual relationship. If the person complained of was a party to the contract, then the claim should be brought as a breach of contract; since an individual cannot interfere with their own contract; they can only breach it.[23]

If some form of fraud is found in the interference with a contract, this could be a criminal matter as well.

Unfair Competition

Unfair competition is when one endeavors to substitute one's own goods or products in the market for those of another. This is accomplished by imitating the other product's name, title, size, shape, packaging, or other distinctive peculiarities.

The law of unfair competition serves five purposes:

- It seeks to protect the economic, intellectual, and creative investments made by businesses in distinguishing themselves and their products.
- It seeks to preserve the goodwill that businesses have established with consumers.
- It seeks to deter businesses from appropriating the goodwill of their competitors.

---

23. Restatement (2d) of Torts §766.

- It seeks to promote clarity and stability by encouraging consumers to rely on a merchant's goodwill and reputation when evaluating the quality of rival products.
- It seeks to increase competition by providing businesses with incentives to offer better goods and services than others in the same field.

Although the law of unfair competition helps protect consumers from injuries caused by deceptive trade practices, the remedies provided to redress such injuries are available only to business entities and proprietors. In general, businesses and proprietors injured by unfair competition have two remedies — **injunctive relief** (a court order restraining a competitor from engaging in a particular fraudulent or deceptive practice) and money damages (compensation for any losses suffered by an injured business).[24]

In the hospitality industry, it may be tempting to try to confuse a guest by mimicking a more successful competitor's product, service, or distinguishing marks or characteristics. Be aware this is actionable under the tort of unfair competition.

Interference with Business Relations

The law of unfair competition also prohibits businesses from intentionally inflicting injury upon a competitor's informal business relations through improper means or for an improper purpose.

Improper means include the use of violence and coercion to threaten competitors or intimidate customers. For example, it is unlawful for a business to blockade the entryway to a competitor's hotel, or impede the delivery of supplies to a competitor with a show of force. One pizza parlor cannot have someone standing in front of their competitor's restaurant threatening the customers entering.

The mere refusal to do business with a competitor, however, is not considered an improper means of competition, even if the refusal is motivated by spite.[25]

Misrepresentation

Misrepresentation is an assertion or manifestation by words or conduct that is not in accord with the facts.

---

24. Restatement (3d) of Torts § 1, 38–45.
25. Restatement (3d) of Torts § 16–17.

To create liability for the maker of the statement, a misrepresentation must:

- Be relied on by the listener or reader
- The speaker must know that the listener is relying on the factual correctness of the statement
- The listener's reliance on the statement must have been reasonable and justified
- The misrepresentation must have resulted in a pecuniary loss to the listener

A misrepresentation need not be *intentionally false* to create liability. A statement made with conscious ignorance or a reckless disregard for the truth can create liability. If the speaker is engaged in the business of selling products or services, any statement, no matter how innocent, may create liability if the statement concerns the character or quality of a product and the statement is not true. In such a case, the statement must be one of fact. This does not include so-called *puffing*, or the glowing opinions of a seller in the course of a sales pitch (such statements as "you'll love this hotel," or "it's the best meal you will ever have" will not create liability — they are opinions).

In the hospitality industry, we often suffer from extreme hyperbole of our products or services. This is not misrepresentation unless it is factually based. For example, it would not be misrepresentation to say our rooms are "beautiful." But if a picture of a room is posted in an advertisement and that is not in any way typical of a room at the hotel, the guest then has been intentionally misled into believing this is the type of room they are reserving.[26]

Fraud is the criminal side of misrepresentation.

Negligence

Negligence is conduct that falls below the standards of behavior established by law for the protection of others against unreasonable risk of harm. A person has acted negligently if he or she has departed from the conduct expected of a reasonably prudent person acting under similar circumstances.

Negligence is a tort in and of itself.

To prove negligence, a plaintiff must prove that:

- The defendant had a *duty* to the plaintiff
- The defendant *breached* that duty by failing to conform to the required standard of conduct

---

26. Restatement (2d) of Torts § 551–552.

- The plaintiff suffered *injury* (this could be a financial injury)
- The defendant's negligent conduct was the cause of the harm to the plaintiff (*causation*)[27]

An easy way to remember the elements of the tort of negligence is by the mnemonic D (duty) B (breach) I (injury) C (causation).

The Reasonable Person

The hypothetical **reasonable person** provides an objective by which the conduct of others is judged. In law, a reasonable person is not an average person or a typical person but a composite of the community's judgment as to how the typical community member should behave in situations that might pose a threat of harm to the public.

The concept of the reasonable person distinguishes negligence from intentional torts such as assault and battery. To prove an intentional tort, the plaintiff seeks to establish that the defendant *deliberately* acted to injure the plaintiff. In a negligence suit, however, the plaintiff seeks to establish that the failure of the defendant to act as a reasonable person caused the plaintiff's injury. The defendant had a duty to the plaintiff and, by acting unreasonably, that duty was breached.[28]

For example, it would not be intended to leave the floor of a hotel lobby wet and slippery, but a reasonable person would not have left such a potentially dangerous condition. By leaving the floor in this condition, it created an unreasonable risk of harm to those walking over it. Thus, if a guest is injured when they slip and fall on this wet floor, and this results in injury to the guest, the hotel may be held liable for negligence since the hotel did not act reasonably.

Actual Causation

Usually the major issue in the tort of negligence is not duty, breach, or injury; it is causation. There is **actual causation** and **proximate causation**.

Actual causation refers to a cause or factor without which the event could not have occurred. It is also termed as the "**but-for**" cause, or **cause in fact**, or **factual cause**. The "but-for" test is often used to determine actual causation. The test simply asks, "But for the existence of A, would B have occurred?" If the answer is yes, then factor A is an actual cause of the result B (the injury).[29]

---

27. Restatement (3d) of Torts §3,§6.
28. Restatement (2d) of Torts §463.
29. Restatement (2d) of Torts §431.

Proximate Causation

The concept of proximate causation limits a defendant's liability. Liability for negligence, based on proximate causation, is confined to the results or consequences that are *reasonably* related to the defendant's negligent conduct.

For example, a hotel's maid knocks over a plant on the balcony; this plant then falls on a chaise lounge sitting below the balcony; the chaise lounge then collapses due to the impact. Standing with their foot under the collapsing chaise lounge is the hotel lifeguard. When the chaise lounge collapses, it crushes the lifeguard's foot. Under the concept of proximate causation, would the negligence of the maid in knocking down the plant causing the collapse of the chaise lounge be the proximate cause of the broken foot?

In determining whether a defendant's negligence is the proximate cause of a plaintiff's injury, most courts focus on the foreseeability of the harm that resulted from the defendant's negligence. When applying this approach, the courts frequently instruct juries to consider whether the harm or injury was the "natural or probable" consequence of the defendant's negligence.

A minority of courts hold the view the defendant's negligence is the proximate cause of the plaintiff's injury if the injury is the "direct result" of the negligence. Usually, a plaintiff's injury is considered to be the direct result of the defendant's negligence if the injury follows an unbroken, natural sequence from the defendant's act and no intervening, external force acts to cause the injury.[30]

In the plant incident discussed above, proximate causation could be argued either way. Was the broken foot a foreseeable consequence of the maid's negligence? Was the lifeguard's injury a direct result of the maid's actions?

Defenses to Negligence

Contributory Negligence

Contributory negligence is one defense a defendant can use against a plaintiff in a negligence suit. Under the common-law rule of contributory negligence, a plaintiff whose own negligence was a contributing cause of his or her injury is barred from recovering from a negligent defendant.

For example, in our plant case discussed above, let us say the lifeguard was taunting the maid to see if he or she could hit the chaise lounge with the plant. In this case, the lifeguard's negligence—encouraging the maid to displace the plant—was a contributing factor to the lifeguard's injury. Under the doctrine

---

30. Restatement (3d) of Torts §29.

of contributory negligence, the lifeguard would potentially not be able to recover from the maid or hotel, due to his or her own negligence in encouraging the incident.

The doctrine of contributory negligence seeks to keep a plaintiff from recovering from the defendant when the plaintiff is also at fault. However, this doctrine often leads to unfair results.

For example, even if a defendant's negligence is the overwhelming cause of the plaintiff's injury, even slight negligence on the part of the plaintiff has the potential to completely bar his or her recovery. As a result, the courts and statutes have considerably weakened the doctrine of contributory negligence. In the U.S. only Alabama, The District of Columbia, Maryland, North Carolina, and Virginia now have pure contributory negligence as a defense to negligence.[31]

Comparative Negligence

The states that do not follow contributory negligence have now, either by court decision or statute, adopted some form of **comparative negligence** in place of pure, contributory negligence. Under comparative negligence or comparative fault, as it is sometimes known, a plaintiff's negligence is not a complete bar to his or her recovery. Instead, the plaintiff's damages are potentially reduced by whatever percentage his or her own fault contributed to the injury. This requires the jury to determine, by a percentage, the fault of the plaintiff and defendant in causing the plaintiff's injury.

For example, in the lifeguard scenario discussed above, suppose it is determined the lifeguard is 25 percent responsible for his or her injuries and the maid is 75 percent responsible. The lifeguard will then be allowed to recover 75 percent of the damages, since he or she was 25 percent responsible for their crushed foot.

Most states have adopted the "**50 percent rule**" of comparative negligence. Under this rule, the plaintiff cannot recover any damages if his or her negligence was as great as, or greater than, the negligence of the defendant. This rule partially retains the doctrine of contributory negligence, reflecting the view that a plaintiff who is largely responsible for his or her own injury is unworthy of compensation.

A minority of states have adopted "**pure comparative fault**." Under this rule, even a plaintiff who is 80 percent at fault in causing their injury may still recover 20 percent of damages, this reflecting the defendant's percentage of fault.[32]

---

31. www.negligence.uslegal.com.
32. Restatement (3d) §7, *Li v. Yellow Cab Co.*, 532P.2d 1226 (Cal. 1975).

Negligence and Criminal Acts

Regarding negligence and crimes, **criminal negligence** refers to a mental state of disregard as to known or obvious risks to human life and safety. An example would be leaving a loaded firearm within reach of a small child.

To be guilty of any crime, a person must act with a "*mens rea*" or "**criminal intent**." But criminal negligence may substitute for criminal intent under very specific circumstances. When it does, it can subject a negligent individual to serious charges such as child endangerment or manslaughter even when the defendant's actions were unintentional.

It is required to show a greater deal of culpability on the part of the defendant to prove *criminal* negligence than it would be to prove liability under *civil* negligence, since criminal cases require proof **beyond a reasonable doubt** for a conviction. But, if that degree of culpability is found, the individual can be found guilty of a crime.

Remember, to be found liable for a tort in civil cases, the plaintiff needs only to show, by a **preponderance of the evidence** that the defendant failed to follow the standard of conduct a reasonable person would have followed in the same situation. This is a significantly lower standard of proof than proof beyond a reasonable doubt.

Strict Liability

Strict liability is the absolute legal responsibility for an injury. It can be imposed on the wrongdoer *without* proof of carelessness, or fault, or negligence. For reasons of public policy, certain activities may be conducted only if the person conducting them is willing to insure others against the harm that results from the risks the activities create.

For example, the law distinguishes between domesticated and wild animals. The keeper of domesticated animals, which include dogs, cats, cattle, sheep, and horses is strictly liable for the harm they cause *only* if the keeper had actual knowledge that the animal had the particular trait or propensity that caused the harm, e.g., biting people. This particular trait must be a potentially harmful one, and the harm must correspond to the knowledge of the animal's owner. In the case of dogs, however, some jurisdictions have enacted statutes that impose absolute liability for dog bites without requiring knowledge of the dog's viciousness.

Keepers of species that are normally considered "wild" are always strictly liable for the harm these pets cause, whether or not the animal in question is known to be dangerous. Because such animals are known to revert to their natural tendencies, they are considered to be wild no matter how well trained or domesticated they are.

Strict liability will also be imposed if harm results from the miscarriage of an activity that, although lawful, is unusual, extraordinary, exceptional, or inappropriate in light of the place and manner in which the activity is conducted. Common hazardous activities that could result in strict liability include storing explosives, flammable liquids, or blasting caps; accumulating sewage; and emitting toxic fumes. Although these activities may be appropriate or normal in one location, they may not be appropriate in another.

For example, storing explosives in quantity in a hotel storage facility will create an unusual and unacceptable risk and thus strict liability. However, if these explosives were stored in the middle of a large, uninhabited forest, strict liability will be imposed only if the explosives were stored in an unusual or abnormal way.

Once it is established the activity is abnormally dangerous and strict liability attaches, no matter how careful one is, there still will be liability if there are any injuries associated with that activity.[33]

Damages in Tort Cases

Damages in tort are awarded generally to place the claimant in the position in which he or she would have been had the tort not taken place.[34]

Compensatory damages, called **actual damages**, are paid to compensate the claimant for loss, injury, or harm suffered as a result of another's breach of duty.[35]

General damages compensate the claimant for the non-monetary aspects of the specific harm suffered. This is usually termed "**pain and suffering.**" Examples of this include physical or emotional pain and suffering, disfigurement, loss of reputation, loss or impairment of mental or physical capacity, loss of enjoyment of life, and in some jurisdictions **loss of consortium** (loss of the comfort of a significant other).[36]

Special damages compensate the plaintiff for quantifiable monetary losses suffered. For example, extra costs, repair or replacement of damaged property, lost earnings (both historically and in the future), loss of irreplaceable items,

---

33. *Rylands v. Fletcher*, L.R. 1 Ex. 265 (1866).
34. Restatement (2d) of Torts § 902.
35. Restatement (2d) of Torts § 903.
36. Restatement (2d) of Torts § 924.

additional domestic costs, and so on. These damages can include direct losses (such as amounts the plaintiff had to spend to try to **mitigate** problems) and **consequential** or economic losses resulting from lost profits in a business. Injured victims have a responsibility to act reasonably to limit or "mitigate" losses incurred. If a plaintiff fails to act reasonably to mitigate injuries, the defendant will not be held liable for incremental losses that otherwise could have been avoided.[37]

Nominal damages are very small damages awarded to show that the loss or harm suffered was technical rather than actual.[38] Nominal damages are *not* pursued in tort law; they are only pursued in contract law. No injury, no tort, no **contingency** basis (a personal injury attorney will not handle the case unless there is significant injury and thus potentially significant damages).

Punitive damages, also called **exemplary damages**, may properly be imposed under tort law to further a state's legitimate interests in punishing unlawful conduct and deterring its repetition. The most important indices of the reasonableness of a punitive damage award are the degrees of reprehensibility of the defendant's conduct. The U.S. Supreme Court has held punitive damages must bear some relationship to the potential harm.[39]

Punitive damages are *only* available in tort law—not contract law. An individual cannot be subjected to punitive (punishing) damages for breaching a contract.

Crimes against a Hospitality Business

The three most common crimes against a hospitality business are:

- Consumer theft of services—a guest leaves without paying a bill or a guest refuses to pay
- Fraudulent payment of a bill, e.g., the use of an unauthorized credit card, bad check, or counterfeit money
- Internal theft of assets—embezzlement of money by employees

Consumer Theft of Services

As a hospitality manager, it is part of one's job to calm a legitimately unhappy guest or customer and fashion a solution that is fair to the guest and the

---

37. Restatement (2d) of Torts §918.
38. Restatement (2d) of Torts §907.
39. *BMW of North Dakota, Inc. v. Gore*, 517 U.S. 559 (1996).

business. However, many times the consumer has no intention of paying for the services they have used — whether it is a hotel room or a restaurant meal.

In the foodservice industry, a customer that leaves without paying their restaurant bill is said to have "**skipped**." This means they have evaded paying the cashier or wait staff. In the lodging industry, it is said the guest has "**walked**."

In lodging, the best way to limit the possibility of a guest "walking" is to verify the guests' payment information on check-in. If paying by credit card, the card should be authorized for an appropriate amount for the stay intended. If cash is to be used, payment for the room should be taken, in its entirety, on check-in. If a hospitality business accepts personal checks, then they need to be authorized using the business's established protocol. At minimum, identification needs to be seen and copied for future reference.

Fraudulent Payment

Credit Cards

Hospitality managers should use the services of a **credit card verification service**. Although there is a fee involved for each transaction, these services guarantee the business will receive their money for legitimate credit card charges.[40]

In some cases, the issue of "**chargebacks**" can be of concern to a hospitality business. This is when a guest pays the bill using their credit card, but then expresses concerns as to the service or meal they have received, and then they protest all or part of the bill to their credit card company.

Unless the guest can be appeased, the business may face the loss of all or part of that guest's revenue. Since the credit card company wants to appease their customer, the credit card company will delete the charge, thus the amount that was deposited into the hospitality business's bank account for that meal or service is now "charged-back" in favor of the credit card customer.

Each credit card company has its own procedures for customer complaints, and it is important to become familiar with the policies associated with each credit card the hospitality business accepts. It is important to remember the credit card company must be fair to both its credit customers and to the hospitality business.[41]

The federal government has passed laws prohibiting the fraudulent use of credit cards — whether the business patron does not have the right to use the

---

40. www.experian.com.
41. Truth in Lending Act, 1968.

questioned credit card or if the patron is using the credit card to defraud the business. Individuals who fraudulently use credit cards in interstate commerce to obtain goods or services of $1,000.00 or more in any given year could be subject to a fine and prison terms of up to ten years.[42]

Additionally, every state has passed laws prohibiting individuals from taking advantage of hospitality services without paying for them. These laws are strict and often carry fines or prison terms for those found guilty. As in many areas of the law, the specific provisions of these state statutes vary widely. Interestingly, many of these laws favor the hospitality operation by requiring an accused defendant to prove that he or she did not intentionally try to avoid payment of a bill.

Cash

When guests attempt to defraud a business by using cash, they are either:

- A **quick-change** artist — one who intentionally tries to confuse or distract a cashier when paying the bill, or
- An individual using **counterfeit money**

To foil a quick-change artist, it is important to train cashiers to take their time making change, and keep the bill given for payment outside the register, in plain view, until change has been made. Then there is no confusion as to what denomination the payment amount was.

As for counterfeiting, it would be best for a manager to enroll cashiers in a counterfeit-detection training program. These are usually offered by local law enforcement agencies.

Personal Checks

The acceptance of **personal checks** by a hospitality business raises the risks of non-payment for services to that business. Guests may inadvertently or deliberately write checks for amounts they do not have sufficient funds in the bank for, or even write checks against closed or nonexistent accounts or banks.

There are services the hospitality business can use that will help with this issue. These services convert a paper check into an electronic item at the point of sale.

How this conversion works:

---

42. U.S. Code Title 18 Part 1 Chapter 47 § 1029.

- The check is authorized, capturing banking information and the amount of the check.
- Once the check is approved, there will be a receipt issued that the guest will sign.
- The guest will even get their check back.
- When the guest signs the receipt it allows the presentation of the check with the bank, electronically, and then the funds will be deposited into the hospitality business's bank account.[43]

Internal Theft of Assets

Employees steal from a company usually in two ways:

- Embezzlement
- Theft of company property

Embezzlement

Embezzlement is when money or property legally entrusted to one person is fraudulently converted to that person's own use.[44]

A hospitality business can guard against embezzlement by implementing financial controls that will verify:

- Product sales receipts
- Service sales receipts
- Deposits
- Accounts receivable
- Accounts payable

Another way to protect the business against embezzlement is to take out a **fidelity bond**. A fidelity bond is a guarantee against dishonesty losses from employees whose tasks include the handling of financial assets.

It also must be considered that employees are given many opportunities to defraud guests. This could come in the form of:

- Charging guests for items not purchased
- Imprinting additional credit card charges and then pocketing the cash difference
- Overcharging with the intent of keeping the overage

---

43. www.telecheck.com.
44. www.merriam-webster.com/dictionary.

- Purposely short-changing guests when making change
- Charging higher prices for products or services, recording the proper price, and then keeping the overcharge

Theft of Company Property

It is tempting for employees in the hospitality industry to take company property. Most everything can be used in their homes—towels, food, trash bags, even furniture.

Some ways to prevent this theft:

- Adequately screen employees at hiring
- Create a friendly work environment that discourages theft
- Limit theft opportunities

Even guests many times cannot pass up taking the stray bathrobe or fluffy towel.

Although it is impossible to prevent all theft in the hospitality industry, it is imperative employees are treated with respect to discourage theft on their part. It is crucial to train employees to be alert to guest pilferage.

If it is found there has been theft by an employee, human resources or the hospitality manager can take appropriate actions.

If a guest has found the bathrobe irresistible, and it is hotel policy, it can be charged to the guest's account. To save goodwill, the hotel should contact the guest and delicately inquire if the guest inadvertently placed the robe in their luggage. Most people are honest and once "caught" will admit their "mistake."

It is important for the hospitality business to place in the room, discreetly and as a courtesy, a price list of items that are available for purchase. Then there is less likelihood of a dispute when that $80.00 charge for the missing bathrobe appears on the guest's bill.

Chapter Summary

The hospitality manager dreads the thought of an intentional tort or crime being committed on property, but these sometimes do occur.

More likely to happen is the failure of an employee or guest to conform to a required standard of conduct. In the hospitality industry, it is imperative to always be alert to conditions that could trigger liability for the tort of negligence. Unreasonable conduct can be anything from leaving a set of stairs wet and slippery, to not monitoring conduct at the swimming pool, to not fixing that broken shower. Remember, it is only in tort when those staggering punitive damages can be imposed.

Avoid creating strict liability conditions—conditions so dangerous liability cannot be avoided, no matter how carefully the task was performed. Do not store or use unusually explosive materials; shun allowing wild animals on property.

Hire carefully, and train staff well to avoid consumer theft of services, fraudulent payments, and theft of company property. The hospitality staff must be chosen for their honesty, loyalty, and attentiveness.

Key Terms

Crime
Public duty
Tort
Private duty
Negligence
Assault
Battery
Intent
Defamation
Libel
Slander
Invasion of privacy
Intrusion
Public disclosure of private facts
False light
Appropriation
Disparagement
Fraud
False advertising
Unfair competition
Lanham Trademark Act
Uniform Deceptive Trade Practices
    Act
Puffing
False imprisonment
Kidnapping

Intentional infliction of emotional
    distress
Negligent infliction of emotional
    distress
Trespass
Consent
License
Common law
Statutory law
Conversion
Theft
Petty theft
Grand theft
Robbery
Burglary
Embezzlement
Interference with contract relations
Interference with prospective con-
    tract
Unfair competition
Injunctive relief
Interference with business relations
Misrepresentation
Negligence
Reasonable person
Actual causation

Proximate causation
But-for
Cause in fact
Factual cause
Contributory negligence
Comparative negligence
50 percent rule
Pure comparative fault
Criminal negligence
Mens rea
Criminal intent
Beyond a reasonable doubt
Preponderance of the evidence
Strict liability
Damages
Compensatory damages
Actual damages
General damages

Pain and suffering
Loss of consortium
Special damages
Mitigate
Consequential damages
Nominal damages
Contingency
Punitive damages
Exemplary damages
Skipped
Walked
Credit cards
Credit card verification service
Chargebacks
Quick-change
Counterfeit money
Personal checks
Fidelity bond

Chapter Six

Property

Chapter Objectives

What is the nature of real property?

What does a deed do?

Which types of deeds are there?

What is personal property?

What is the difference between shipment and destination contracts?

Who is a *bona fide* purchaser?

How does personal property become a fixture?

What are trade fixtures?

What are the considerations in leasing real property?

Who is a transient guest?

Who is a tenant?

What rights and responsibilities do transient guests and tenants have?

What duties does the hospitality business have toward a transient guest or tenant?

What is a condo hotel?

What is a timeshare?

Nature of Real Property

Although the terms **real property** and **real estate** are often used inter-changeably, technically the term real property *encompasses much more than the term real estate.*

The generic definition of real property consists of *land, real estate, and the rights that are part of ownership of real estate.* When one owns land, one owns not only the surface of the land, but also according to common law from the "Depths of Hell to the Heights of Heaven," and the owner may have rights to the use of any abutting or underground water source. This is subject to modern day commercial flights, rights reserved by others to mine minerals under the land, and water regulations.

> Real estate is the land and all the improvements to it, such as houses, trees, fences, and other *permanently* attached items.

Along with ownership of the land and real estate come rights of real property ownership such as the right to:

- *Dispose of the land*—sell, mortgage, or give it away
- *Use the land* in any way one sees fit as long as the use complies with local laws—zoning
- *Possess the properties*—occupy and receive any income generated from the land such as rents or sale of crops
- *Quiet enjoyment* of the real estate. The owner of real property decides who can access the property. Anyone coming onto the land without the owner's permission is a trespasser.[1]

Commercial Property

Commercial property is land that has been zoned for business use. These business ventures can range from shopping malls, to car dealerships, to physicians' offices. Commercial properties are meant to conduct entrepreneurial activities. Some jurisdictions such as Florida allow multi-use condominiums where individuals can live and work.[2]

---

1. Towers-Romero, S., *Essentials of Florida Real Estate Law* (2007): 4–5.
2. Florida Statutes § 718.404.

Commercial properties will have features such as parking lots, and customer and delivery entrances. These properties must abide by the **Americans with Disabilities Act** — dictating access for those that are handicapped — the **Occupational Safety and Health Administration Act**, and other federal and state regulations that apply directly to businesses.

Essential Elements of a Deed

A deed is a *written instrument* that conveys title to real property. *Only* a deed transfers title. With every deed there are two parties — a **grantor** (the one conveying the land) and the **grantee** (the one receiving title). The actual ownership of the land transfers when the grantee voluntarily accepts the deed from the grantor. A deed is not only a document recording the conveyance of land, it is also a contract setting forth the contractual agreement between the parties.

As a contract, the deed must have all the requirements of such, including offer, acceptance, consideration, and capacity of the grantor to transfer the property. The grantor must be of sound mind and legal age (see Contract chapter as to legal capacity). An individual that is under 18, has impaired mental capabilities; or is adjudged mentally incompetent cannot sign a deed. The *grantee* of the property does *not* have to have the legal capacity to take the real estate; they only need the capacity to accept it.

The essential elements of a deed are:

1. Under the **Statute of Frauds**, deeds must be in writing.
2. They must meet contractual elements discussed above.
3. The grantor and grantee must be clearly identifiable. The *grantor* must be identified by name, and they must sign the deed. If there is no signature on the deed, then the land cannot be conveyed. Under the **USA Patriot Act** there is now a requirement that all financial institutions, including "persons involved in real estate closings and settlements," establish anti-money laundering programs. Under the Patriot Act *grantees* of real estate will have to provide proof of their identity to establish they are not involved in any money laundering schemes.

"Persons involved in Real Estate Closings and Settlements must comply with OFAC [Office of Foreign Assets Control] regulations relative to verifying the identity of their parties, maintaining records for at least five years, consulting the OFAC list of known or suspected terrorists, reporting suspicious transactions and reporting cash transfers in excess of $10,000."[3]

4. The property conveyed must be adequately described.
5. The *grantor* must sign the deed.
6. There must be language of conveyance. The deed must contain language that shows the grantor intends to convey. For example, "the grantor does hereby grant, bargain, sell, or transfer" to the grantee.
7. The deed must be properly executed.
8. The grantor must deliver the deed and the grantee must accept the deed. Until the deed is delivered and accepted, the grantor is still liable for any damages occurring to the property. Once the deed is delivered and accepted by the grantee, then the grantee becomes liable for any damages to the real estate.[4]

Clauses Required in a Deed

Certain clauses must be contained in a deed:

1. Date of the deed — the date of execution by the *grantor*.
2. The names of the parties to the deed.
3. The **granting clause** — words of conveyance such as "grants, bargains, sells."
4. **Consideration** given — this can be a small amount — $10.00 or such. The entire amount paid for the property need not be stated. If the clause "for love and affection" is used, the implication is this is a **gift deed**.
5. The *habendum* **clause**. The "have and to hold" clause. If the word forever is used it is a **fee simple** transfer — unqualified ownership in the real property. If the words for the life of the grantee are used, it is a **life estate** — the estate is limited to the length of a specific lifetime.
6. The fact the grantor is **seized of the land** — they own the land so conveyed.
7. The land is free of **encumbrances** — the grantor has not encumbered the land. For example, there are no easements or liens against the property except as stipulated in the deed itself.[5]

---

3. USA Patriot Act §352.
4. Towers-Romero, S. 126–127.
5. Towers-Romero, S. 127.

Types of Deeds

General Warranty Deed

The highest and best deed for the *grantee* is the **general warranty deed**. This form of deed contains full warranties to the grantee of present and future title protection by the grantor. The warranties given allow the grantee to pursue legal action against the grantor, now and in the future, if any of the warranties are not true. These warranties include:

1. **Covenant of seisin**. This is an assurance by the grantor they have legitimate possession of the property and have the ability to transfer their interest to the grantee.
2. **Covenant of quiet enjoyment**. This is the grantor's promise there are no present outstanding claims or unresolved issues as to the property that may interfere with the grantee's enjoyment of it.
3. **Covenant against encumbrances**. The grantor assures there are no outstanding liens, judgments, or other legal actions that will affect the grantee's ownership.
4. **Covenant of further assurances.** In case a claim does arise against the property, the grantor will supply evidence or testimony to prove the transfer of the land was legitimate, and the grantee has full ownership.
5. **Covenant to warrant forever**. The grantor promises they will not take any action to undermine the ownership rights of the grantee once conveyance of the property has been made.

To assure the grantee, all such covenants are, and will be honored by the grantor, it is imperative that a **title examination** is completed prior to the transfer of any ownership.[6]

Title examinations determine whether the title to a property is marketable. They inform the grantee if the property being conveyed is free and clear of any liens, encumbrances or judgments that may have arisen during prior ownership.[7]

---

6. Towers-Romero, S. 128.
7. www.uslegal.com.

Special Warranty Deed

In a **special warranty deed**, the grantor only warrants that the grantor, or their representative has done nothing to encumber or put a **cloud on the title** (a title defect). This is much less protection for a grantee than a general warranty deed, wherein the grantor warrants to the grantee every possible title protection now and in the future.

Special warranty deeds are usually executed when there is a potential title defect. If a grantor is only willing to convey such a deed, this should alert the grantee of potential title issues.[8]

Quitclaim Deed

In a **quitclaim deed** the grantor makes *no* warranties as to the quality of the title being conveyed to the grantee. The grantor does not warrant they will defend the title interest conveyed, nor does the grantor warrant any interest in the property that is being transferred.

Quitclaim deeds are very helpful in clearing clouds on a title. For example, if a lien has been placed against the property, or a recorded mortgage has been paid in full, but a mortgage satisfaction has not been recorded prior to the conveyance of the land to the grantee, these clouds need to be removed. The most efficient method of accomplishing this is to have the holder of the lien or mortgage (the grantors in this situation) execute a quitclaim deed releasing any interest they may have in the property being conveyed. The grantor signs a quitclaim deed and thus transfers all interests they may have in the real property, yet they make no claims to ownership. Quitclaim deeds are also used extensively in divorce settlements where one party needs to release their real estate interest to the other party.

If the holder of the lien, mortgage, or other interest in the property being conveyed cannot be found, or they will not execute a quitclaim deed, there will need to be a suit to quiet title prior to the conveyance of the real estate to the grantee.[9]

Personal Property

The opposite of real property is **personal property**. This is property that is *not* real property. It is movable and not permanently attached to the land. Per-

---

8. Towers-Romero, S. 131.
9. Towers-Romero, S. 131–132.

sonal property can be *tangible*—property that has its own value, such as tables, chairs, and microwaves, or it can be *intangible*—property that represents value such as stocks and bonds. Other terms for personal property are *chattel* or *personalty* (real property is referred to as *realty*).

Real property can become personal property by the act of *severance* of the property from the land. For example, if there is an apple tree on the land, the apple *on the tree* is still real property, but once the apple falls off the tree, it is now moveable and thus is personal property. However, if there is a crop planted on the land, and it is cultivated *annually*—it is planted every year, this is considered personal property because of its impermanent nature.[10]

Bill of Sale to Transfer Personal Property

The **bill of sale** is a legal document used to transfer the ownership of personal property to any named recipient.

Most bill of sale forms require the following information:

- Amount of consideration paid for the transfer of title and date of purchase
- Name and address of the seller
- Name and address of the buyer
- Specific information about the asset being transferred from the seller to the buyer
- Guarantee from the seller that the item is free from all claims
- Any representations or warranties
- Signature of the seller(s)
- Signature of a notary public (A bill of sale can also be witnessed by someone not a party to the transaction, but notarization is best.)

Does a bill of sale have to be recorded? Generally, a bill of sale does not have to be recorded, but recordation may be required as proof of ownership.

Who must sign a bill of sale? The owners of the property being sold must sign. If the property is owned jointly, both owners must generally sign it. This is to protect the buyer from having the other joint owner saying they did not intend to sell the item.[11]

---

10. Towers-Romero, S. 5–6.
11. www.uslegal.com.

Shipment versus Destination Contracts

In the hospitality industry, there are many times an item of personal property will need to be shipped. So when does ownership and responsibility over that piece of personal property pass to the buyer of that item? This is where the differentiation between shipment and destination contracts comes into play.

When two parties enter into a contract to buy and sell merchandise, it is best to specify who carries the liability and risk during shipment of the product. If there are no specific provisions stated by the parties, the Uniform Commercial Code will come into play.

Shipment Contracts

If the contract does not require the seller to deliver the merchandise to a specified destination, then the risk of loss passes to the buyer when the seller delivers the merchandise to the shipping carrier. This type of contract is called a **shipment contract**.

The following is a list of common terms that designate shipment contracts:

- **FOB (free on board)**: Also known as **point of origin**. This places the risk of loss plus shipping and loading costs at the FOB point (usually the seller's factory or warehouse) onto the buyer.
- **FAS (free alongside ship)**: This requires the seller to bear the risk of loss and costs for transferring the merchandise to a specified ship or port. The risk passes to the buyer once the merchandise reaches the dock alongside the ship.
- **CIF (cost, insurance, and freight)**: This indicates that the price for the merchandise includes the cost for shipping and insuring the merchandise to the buyer's delivery point.
- **C & F (cost and freight)**: This indicates that the price for the merchandise includes the cost of shipping, but not the cost of insuring the merchandise. The buyer bears the risk of not having his or her shipment insured.[12]

---

12. UCC Article 2 §§ 2-319–321.

Destination Contracts

If the contract does require the seller to deliver the merchandise to a specified destination, then the risk of loss does not pass until the seller has delivered it to that destination. This type of contract is called a **destination contract**.

The following is a list of common terms that designate destination contracts:

- **FOB Destination**: This is similar to FOB, but now the risk of loss does not get transferred until the merchandise reaches the destination point.
- **Ex-ship**: The seller will bear the risk of loss until the merchandise has been unloaded from the ship.
- **No arrival, no sale**: This means that there is no contract unless the merchandise arrives to the buyer. The seller may have to compensate the buyer if the merchandise arrives damaged.[13]

What Happens If It Can't Be Determined If It Is a Shipment or Destination Contract?

In the case where the terms of the contract are so ambiguous that it is extremely difficult or impossible to determine whether the contract is a shipment or a destination contract, the UCC provides additional guidelines.

In *Windows, Inc. v. Jordan Panel Systems Corp.*, 177 F.3d 114 (2nd Cir. 1999), the Second Circuit Court of Appeals ruled:

Where the terms of an agreement are ambiguous, there is a strong presumption under the UCC favoring shipment contracts. "Unless the parties 'expressly specify' that the contract requires the seller to deliver to a particular destination, the contract is generally construed as one for shipment."[14]

Bona Fide Purchaser

A *bona fide* **purchaser** (BFP) — referred to more completely as a *bona fide* **purchaser for value without notice** — is a term used in the law of property. It refers to an innocent party who purchases personal or real property without notice of another party's claim to the title of the property.

---

13. UCC Article 2 §§ 2-322 & 324.
14. UCC Article 2 §§ 2-503:24, 503:26.

To be a BFP:

- The property must be purchased for value — the BFP must pay for the property, it cannot be a gift.
- The BFP must take without notice — either **actual** or **constructive notice** of the claim against the property. The BFP must be innocent. Actual notice is when there is an express delivery of information to an individual. Constructive notice occurs if one had exercised ordinary care and diligence they would have possessed notice of another's interest in the property.
  For example, if someone is buying real estate and sees someone living there, they would be on constructive notice to investigate further to see who actually holds good title to the property.

If recordation is required, once the BFP records they will take valid (good) title to the property despite the competing claims of the other party. Any parties with claim to ownership in the property will then have to bring a cause of action (a suit) against the party that made the fraudulent conveyance.[15]

Personal Property in a Real Property Sale

In any real property transaction, it is extremely important to distinguish what is and what is not personal property. Personal property is *not* a basis for assessment of real estate taxes; it will *not* usually be used to collateralize a loan; it will *not* be automatically transferred with the real estate deed; the transfer of personal property will *not* usually come under the purview of the Statute of Frauds.

If any personal property is to be included in a real estate transaction, it must be listed in the contract so it will be transferred with the sale of the property. If it is not so listed, the seller is entitled to remove such personal property upon completion of the sale.

Possible examples of personal property in a real estate transaction would be computers, televisions, bookcases, and so on. One shouldn't jump to the conclusion that everything inside a structure is personal property; it may actually be a **fixture**. A fixture is an item of personal property that is transformed into an item of real property based on several requirements.

---

15. U.C.C Article 8 §8-302.

How Does Personal Property Become a Fixture?

To become a fixture, the piece of personal property must become part of the real property. An example of this would be a bookcase that is specifically made for a particular house; it is permanently affixed to a wall, and removing it would cause major damage to the house.

It is very important to determine what is and what is not a fixture. As a fixture, and thus real property, a bank issuing a mortgage will use the item for collateral, and if an item is deemed a fixture, it will automatically be transferred with the real estate.

So how do the courts decide if something is or is not a fixture? There is a mnemonic device to easily remember the elements of a fixture—M-A-R-I-A.

M—*Method of attachment*—if removing the item is going to damage the property the item is usually deemed a fixture.

A—*Adaptability*—is the item specifically made for the real estate? If so it is probably a fixture.

R—*Relationship of the parties*—in a residential situation, if an item is attached to the real estate, it usually will be considered a fixture, for example, a carpet. But if a rug is part of a commercial venture, and that rug has the business logo on it, it will usually be deemed a **trade fixture** (see below) and thus be removable by the former owner.

I—*Intent of the parties*—what did the parties intend of the item? If the buyer just loves the chandelier and keeps mentioning it prior to the signing of the contract, and the seller says, "The chandelier is all yours," the chandelier becomes a fixture.

A—*Agreement*—this step seems superfluous, but if more parties to a real property contract would put what goes with the real estate, many court cases would be avoided.[16]

Trade Fixtures

A **trade fixture** is a piece of equipment on or attached to real estate which is used in a trade or business. They are items that are used as identification for that business, e.g., special art work, unique counters, and distinctive decorations.

---

16. Towers-Romero, S. 6–7.

Trade fixtures differ from other fixtures in that they may be removed from the real estate (even if attached) at the end of the tenancy of the business, while ordinary fixtures attached to the real estate become part of the real property. Trade fixtures should be removable by the **tenant** *without* causing serious damage to the property, and they must be removed within the time specified in the lease or deed or else they become part of the real estate.

To determine if an item is a trade fixture, one must look at:

- What the parties to the contract intended? Is that a specially made rug for that restaurant—a rug with the logo of the restaurant or special pattern? If the answer is yes, the item, most likely, will be considered a trade fixture and will be taken by the lessee or owner when they leave.
- What is the agreement between the parties? To avoid conflicts, if an item is intended to be removed as a trade fixture, this should be listed in the contract. Not doing so leads to lawsuits.

Leasing of Property — Real and Personal

Leasing is a contractual agreement by which one party conveys an estate in property, either real or personal, to another party for a limited period, subject to various conditions, in exchange for something of value.

A lease contract can involve any property that is not illegal to own. Common lease contracts include agreements for leasing real estate; manufacturing, business, and farming equipment; and consumer goods such as automobiles, televisions, stereos, and appliances.

Leases are governed by Article 2A of the UCC for leases of goods; the Statute of Frauds (a writing is required) for real estate; state and federal statutes; and common law.

A lease is created when:

- A property owner (the offeror or **lessor**) makes an offer to another party (the offeree or **lessee**).
- The offeree accepts the offer.
- The offer must authorize the offeree to possess and use property owned by the offeror for a certain period of time *without gaining ownership.*
- A lease must also contain consideration, which means that the offeree must give something of value to the offeror. Consideration usually consists of money, but other items of value may be given.

- The offeror must deliver the property to the offeree, or make the property available to the offeree.

When the lease is signed, the property owner (offeror) then is called the lessor, and the user of the property is then called the lessee (offeree).

Leases of Goods

Generally, a lease for *goods* may be written or oral. Most states recognize oral lease contracts that are for a year or less. However, oral agreements are not favored legally since they often lead to ambiguity about the obligations of each party since memories fade over time. Under the UCC, an oral lease contract is not enforceable by way of action or defense unless:

- The total payments to be made under the lease contract, excluding payments for options to renew or buy, are less than $1,000.
- There is some writing signed by the party against whom enforcement is sought, or by that party's authorized agent, sufficient to indicate that a lease contract has been agreed to between the parties and describes the goods leased and the lease term.[17]

A court may void an **unconscionable lease**. A lease is unconscionable if it unduly favors one party over the other. For example, assume that a small-business owner leases kitchen equipment for 30 years in order to operate a restaurant. The lease contains a clause stating that the lessor may revoke the agreement without cause and without notice. If the lessee performs his or her obligations under the lease, but the lessor revokes the lease without notice, the clause allowing termination without notice may be found to be unconscionable. A determination of unconscionable must be made by a judge or jury based on the facts of the case. The fact finder may consider factors such as the relative bargaining power of the parties, other terms in the lease, the purpose of the lease, and the potential loss to either party as a result of the terms of the lease.

> Some courts are holding in commercial leases of goods, there is the **implied warranty of suitability** — the leased property be fit for *general purposes*. The warranty of **fitness for a particular purpose** may be applicable if the lessor knew how the lessee planned to use the goods,

---

17. UCC Article 2A §2A-201 Statute of Frauds.

and the lessee relied on the expertise of the lessor in choosing the goods leased for that particular purpose.[18]

If a lessor defaults on his or her obligations under the lease, the lessee may sue the lessor for damages. The measure of damages can vary. If a lessor breaches the lease by sending nonconforming goods or goods that were not ordered by the lessee, the lessee may reject the goods, cancel the lease, and sue the lessor to recover any monies already paid and for damages caused by the shipment of the nonconforming goods.

If the lessee defaults on obligations under the lease, the lessor may cancel the lease, withhold or cancel delivery of the goods, or lease the goods to another party and recover from the original lessee any difference between the amount the lessor would have earned under the original lease and the amount the lessor earns on the new lease.[19]

Essential Elements of a Real Estate Lease

In a real estate lease there needs to be the following information:

- Length of the lease
- Start date and end dates of the lease
- Lease rent amount
- Is it a net, net-net, or triple net lease?

A **Net lease** is a type of commercial real estate lease in which the lessee (tenant) pays for their space, as well as for part or all of certain "usual costs" (expenses associated with operating, maintenance and use of the property). These costs would be ones that the **landlord** would usually have to pay.

Expenses incorporated into net leases may include taxes, utilities, janitorial services, property insurance, property management fees, sewer, water, and trash collection. Net leases almost always favor the lessor (landlord) and should be negotiated to include caps on the maximum amount a landlord can increase fees charged to the tenant each year.

---

18. www.legalmatch.com.
19. UCC Article 2A §§2A-101 & 102.

A **double net lease** is a type of net lease in which the lessee (tenant) pays all or part of taxes and insurance associated with use of the property. These fees are paid in addition to the monthly rent.

A **triple net lease** is also known as **Net Net Net Lease** or **NNN Lease**. This is a type of net lease in which the tenant pays *all* the taxes, insurance, and maintenance associated with use of the property. These fees are paid in addition to the tenant's regular monthly rent. These leases almost always favor the landlord and should be carefully negotiated to limit how much the landlord can increase NNN fees charged to the tenant.

Can the Real Property Be Assigned or Subleased?

A lessee usually may **assign** a lease to a third party, or **assignee**. An assignment conveys all rights under the lease to the assignee for the remainder of the lease term, and the assignee then assumes a contractual relationship with the original lessor.

However, unless the lessor agrees otherwise, the original lessee will still retain their original duties under the lease agreement until the lease expires. Thus, if the original lessee was not released from the original lease by the lessor and if the assignee defaults, the original lessee will still have to fulfill all their duties under the original lease, including paying rent. Generally, an assignment is valid unless it is prohibited by the original agreement with the lessor.

An assignment differs from a **sublease**. In a sublease, the original lessee gives temporary rights under the lease to a third party (a **sublessee**), but the third party does *not* assume a contractual relationship with the lessor.

In a sublease, the original lessee retains the same rights and obligations under the original lease, but forms a second contractual relationship with the sublessee. In return, the sublessee gets temporary use of the property. Like assignments, subleases are generally valid unless they are prohibited by the lessor in the original lease.

The problem with a sublease is if the original lessee defaults on the lease, and there is no provision in the sublease giving the sublessee the right to take over the original lease made with the lessor, then the sublessee is "out in the street." The original contract was between the lessor and the lessee only. That is why it is so important, as a sublessee, to protect one's right to continue the original lease even if the original lessee defaults.[20]

---

20. Towers-Romero, S. 214.

Insurance for the Tenant

A landlord will require a tenant to take out **insurance** to protect not only the tenant's property but to protect the landlord from monetary recovery from potential legal suits initiated by third parties. For example, if a customer comes onto the property and slips and falls, the lessor wants to be protected from any suits initiated by that customer that slipped and fell.

The lessee's insurance carrier must be approved by the lessor. Copies of the insurance contract will need to be delivered to the lessor. It is required that the lessor be notified if there are any changes or cancellations to the lessee's insurance policy.

When and How the Parties Can Terminate the Lease

This is an example of a termination clause in a real estate lease:

NOW, WHEREFORE, in consideration of mutual promises contained herein and for other good and valuable consideration, the receipt and sufficiency of which is hereby acknowledged, it is agreed as follows:

1. *Termination.* The parties agree that in lieu of the original expiration date of October 31, 2024, the lease shall terminate on March 1, 2024 (termination date). Prior to the termination date, the tenant shall quit the premises and surrender and return the premises to the landlord, "as is" in broom clean condition.
2. *Lease Termination Fee.* In consideration for the tenant being relieved of further obligations under the lease after the termination date, the tenant and landlord agree that the tenant shall pay a lease termination fee of seventy thousand dollars ($70,000.00). This payment shall be made to landlord by March 1, 2024.
3. *Mutual Release.* Upon the tenant satisfying the obligations set forth in this agreement, the landlord releases, discharges and waives any claims known or unknown, against tenant, its successor, assigns, officers or directors, arising out of or in any way connected with the lease through the date hereof, and tenant releases, discharges and waives any claims, known or unknown, against the landlord, its successors, assigns, officers or directors, arising out of or in any way connected with the lease through the date hereof.
4. *Binding upon Successors and Assigns.* This agreement shall be for the benefit of and be binding upon the parties hereto and their respective successors and assigns.

5. *Final Agreement.* This agreement shall constitute the final agreement and understanding of the parties on the subject matter hereof. This agreement may be modified only by a further writing signed by the parties.
6. *Attorney Fees.* If any legal action is commenced to enforce or interpret the terms of this lease termination agreement, the prevailing party shall be entitled to reasonable attorney's fees and costs in addition to any other relief to which the prevailing party may be entitled.

Common Area Maintenance

Common area maintenance (CAM) refers to costs required for a tenant's *pro rata* (proportional) share of the upkeep of common areas and amenities such as the parking lot, external lighting, trash removal, and street cleaning. When obtaining quotes for retail space or office space, one should always ask about tenant CAM expenses. A lower per-square-foot rental rate may be negated by high CAM expenses.

Because CAM fees can be complicated and expensive, it is highly advisable to have an attorney review any lease that has CAM (or other special fee) requirements before a hospitality business owner signs the lease. It is especially important to consider the amount CAM can be increased in any particular time period and how often CAM expenses can be raised. If CAM appears to be an onerous aspect of leasing that particular property, perhaps another property should be considered.

When Are Landlord and Tenant Relationships Established?

Generally, a landlord and tenant relationship exists if:

- The property owner consents to occupancy of the premises
- The tenant acknowledges that the owner has title to the property and a future interest in the property
- The owner actually has title to the property
- The tenant receives a limited right to use the premises
- The owner transfers possession and control of the premises to the tenant
- A contract to lease/rent exists between the parties[21]

21. Towers-Romero, S. 188.

Transient Guests versus Tenants

In the hotel business, it is important to take the concept of tenancy one step further, whether a guest is **transient** (a temporary stay) or a tenant (a form of lessee). The determination of this status will seriously affect what a hospitality manager can and cannot do with regard to the tenant versus the transient guest.

Courts have considered several factors in determining the guest's status, such factors include:

1. Length of stay—shorter means transient.
2. Existence of a lease or other "special contract for the room." This would point to the guest being a tenant.
3. Receipt of mail by the guest—usually means they are a tenant.
4. Access to cooking facilities—with the new "extended stay" hotels the guest can be deemed either tenant or transient.
5. Degree of control over the space (such as whether the person has his or her own key to their own lock, not the hotel's key)—this usually means they are a tenant.
6. Whether the person has another residence—if they do, they usually would be considered transient.
7. The extent to which the person has made the dwelling his or her home for the time being—for example, if they start decorating the room. If this is the case, this would make them more of a tenant.

These factors allow the court to determine whether the person has possession and control over the space in the manner that an official tenant would. A unilateral intention on the part of the occupant to remain indefinitely is not enough to create a tenant; all the circumstances of the transaction must be considered.[22]

> For example, in *Bourque v. Morris* (cited in the footnote), the court held a person was a transient guest at a hotel even though he had stayed there for more than three months and had no other home. While those factors were significant, the court also noted that "the operation of the premises as a licensed hotel, the rudimentary nature of the accommodations furnished, without cooking, bathing or toilet facilities in the room [were] some indication that only a temporary living arrangement was intended."

---

22. *Bourque v. Morris*, 190 Conn. 364, 369 (1983), *State v. Anonymous*, 34 Conn. Sup. 603, 605 (1977).

But, in *State v. Anonymous* (cited in the footnote), the court held the state had not proven that a person was a transient guest when he had rented an efficiency apartment for four weeks on a week-to-week basis.

So, now the criteria for determining a tenant from a transient guest have been discussed, that determination will differentiate the duties of the hotel to that guest.

Duties to a Transient Guest

The very first and most important "public duty" of the hotel is the duty to receive guests. But, this duty is not absolute and is subject to lawful excuses. Hotels may generally deny accommodations to a prospective guest for the following reasons:

- If the person is unwilling or unable to pay for a room or other establishment privileges
- If the person is visibly under the influence of alcohol, other drugs, or creating a public nuisance
- If the person's use of a room or accommodation would violate the facility's maximum capacity
- If the innkeeper reasonably believes the person will use the room or facility for an unlawful purpose
- If the innkeeper reasonably believes the person will bring in something that would create an unreasonable danger or risk to others

Generally speaking, to avoid liability for *refusal to receive* a prospective *transient guest*, hotels must reasonably believe a person is unable or unwilling to pay, plans to use the room or premises for an unlawful purpose, or plans to bring a potentially dangerous object onto the premises.

Right to Evict People Admitted as Guests

Hotels may generally **evict** a transient guest and keep the room rental payment for the following reasons:

- Disorderly conduct
- Nonpayment of charges
- Using the premises for an unlawful purpose or act
- Bringing property onto the premises that may be dangerous to others
- Failing to register as a guest
- Using false pretenses (e.g., a fake ID) to obtain accommodations

- Being a minor unaccompanied by an adult registered guest
- Violating federal, state, or local hotel laws or regulations
- Violating a conspicuously posted hotel or motel rule
- Failing to vacate a room at the agreed checkout time

The general rule, to avoid liability for *evicting a transient guest*, the guest must have refused to pay, or the innkeeper must reasonably have believed the person used the room or premises for an unlawful purpose, or brought a potentially dangerous object onto the premises.

Some State Innkeepers Laws

Alabama Code: See Section 34-15-17: Managers of hotels may remove, cause to be removed or eject from such hotel, in the manner provided in this section, any guest of said hotel or visitor thereto, both hereinafter referred to in this section as "guest," who, while in said hotel or on the hotel premises, is intoxicated, profane, lewd, brawling or who shall indulge in any language or conduct or otherwise conducts himself in such fashion as to disturb the peace and comfort of other guests, proprietor or employees of such hotel. Hotels must give oral notice to leave the premises and return the unused portion of any advance payment.

Alaska: See Title 8 of the Alaska Statutes, Chapter 56, "Hotels and Boardinghouses" which discusses such issues as registration, refusal to register, liability for valuables, and baggage liability.

Arizona: See Title § 33-301 of the Arizona Revised Statutes. Arizona has special provisions for the posting of minimum and maximum innkeeper rates.

California: See California Civil Code, Sections 1861–1865. With proper written notice, signed by the guest, hotels may evict guests who refuse to depart at checkout time and there is a need to accommodate another arriving guest. Moreover, if a guest refuses to leave, the hotel owner may enter the room and take possession of the guest's personal property, rekey the door, and make the room available to the new guests.

Colorado: See Title 12 of the Colorado Revised Statutes Annotated, 12-44-302 codifies common law with respect to refusing accommodations to certain persons.

Florida: See Florida Statutes Annotated, FSA 509.141. In addition to the usual reasons for evicting guests, Florida hotels may evict a person for injuring the facility's reputation, dignity, or standing.

Georgia: See Chapter 43 of the Georgia Code, 43-21-2, et seq.; 48-13-50, et seq. Georgia has a very comprehensive statute that expressly outlines the rights and duties of hotels; much of it is carried over from common law.

Idaho: See Titles 39 of the Idaho Code, Sections 39-1805 and 1809. The statute follows the common law general reasons for denying accommodations to or evicting guests. The statute expressly permits hotel owners to enter the rooms of guests who fail to pay and leave. The innkeeper may then remove the guest's personal property and hold this towards an innkeepers' lien.

Iowa: See Iowa Code Annotated 137C.25C and 137C.25. Iowa follows the general rules for denying accommodations and for evictions.

Kansas: See Kansas Statutes Annotated, 36-604 and 602. Kansas adds a few more categories to the general rights to evict guests: failing to register as a guest, using false pretenses to obtain accommodations, exceeding the guest room occupancy limits, or being a minor unaccompanied by a parent or guardian.

Louisiana: See Louisiana Statutes Annotated 21:75 and 76. Louisiana expressly requires that a hotel owner notify a guest at least one hour before the time to leave, before he or she may legally evict the guest. After this, the hotel may have law enforcement personnel remove the guest and their personal belongings.

Minnesota: See Minnesota Statutes Annotated 327.73. Minnesota follows the general rules for denying accommodations and for evictions.

Missouri: See Missouri Revised Statutes, 315.075 and 315.067. Missouri follows the general rules for denying accommodations and for evictions.

Montana: See Montana Code Annotated 70-6-511 and 70-6-512. Montana follows the general rules for denying accommodations and for evictions and expressly adds the right to evict guests for refusing to abide by reasonable hotel standards or policies.

North Carolina: See Chapters 72 of the North Carolina General Statutes, Article 1. North Carolina has express provisions that address liability for lost baggage, losses by fire, safeguarding of valuables, and hotel rights for negligence of the guest. North Carolina also has an express provision for the admittance of pets to hotel rooms.

Oregon: See Chapters 699 of the Oregon Revised Statutes, "Innkeepers and Hotelkeepers." Oregon's thorough statutory provisions cover liability for valuables, baggage, and other property. Special provisions address personal property left at a hotel for more than 60 days. Guests who refuse to leave or pay are deemed "trespassers" under Oregon law and may be removed by force without the hotel incurring liability.

Rhode Island: See RIGL 5-14-4 and 5-14-5. Rhode Island follows the general rules for denying accommodations and for evictions.

South Carolina: See South Carolina Statutes Annotated, SCSA 45-2-60 and 45-2-30. South Carolina follows the general rules for denying accommodations and for evictions.

Tennessee: See Tennessee Code Annotated 68-14-605 and 68-14-602. Tennessee follows the general rules for denying accommodations and for evictions.

Utah: See the Utah Code Annotated, UCA 29-2-103. Utah follows the general rules for denying accommodations and for evictions.

Duties to a Tenant

If it is deemed the guest is a tenant, as opposed to a transient guest, then the rules of leasehold must be followed. These vary in each state, but the basics are:

- The tenant has the right of peaceful possession. This means that even though the landlord keeps legal title to the property, the tenant has the use of the property. The rented room or apartment is considered home. With this goes the right of privacy. No one may invade a "home" without legal authority.
- The dwelling place must be safe and sanitary.
- There must be notice given to evict a tenant — the form and time period for notice depends on each state and the length of time the tenant occupies the unit.[23]

Duties of a Tenant

As a tenant, the guest must:

- Use the property only as a dwelling
- Pay the rent
- Keep the property reasonably clean
- At the end of the rental term, return the property to the landlord in the same condition in which it was received, except for reasonable wear and tear[24]

Condo Hotel Owners

A **condo hotel** is a building used both as a condominium and a hotel.

Condo hotels are typically high-rise buildings developed and operated as luxury hotels, usually in major cities and resorts. These hotels have condominium units which allow an individual to own a full-service vacation home. When the owner is not using the property, the hotel chain will rent and manage

---

23. Towers-Romero, S. 189–190.
24. Towers-Romero, S. 194.

the condo unit as it would any other hotel room. Any rental revenue obtained for the owner is shared with the hotel management company.

Homeowner's association fees (HOAs) are levied on the owner of the individual condo units, just as there would be association fees levied on any other type of condominium ownership. HOAs cover such items as maintenance and insurance on the condo property.

Condo hotels are very attractive to individuals who want the convenience of a hotel, the ease of rental when they are not using the unit, and the brand name associated with the condo hotel.[25]

Timeshares

Unlike a condo hotel, where the owner owns all the time in the particular unit, a **timeshare** only creates ownership for a particular portion of the year. Timeshares are created when ownership of a unit, in a multi-unit building, is divided into time segments, usually fifty-two — one for each week of the year.

A timeshare is considered real property and the purchaser receives a deed or some other evidence of property ownership. What one is buying is an undivided interest in a living unit. The percentage of ownership is based on how many weeks the individual has purchased. For example, if one buys one week they own an 1/52nd interest in the unit.

The timeshare owner, like any other owner in real estate, will have to pay real estate taxes. As a partial owner of the timeshare units, they will be required to pay their share of maintenance costs as well. Maintenance costs would include such services as housekeeping, repair, utilities, landscaping, insurance, and pool maintenance costs, if a pool is included in the timeshare property.[26]

Chapter Summary

Property is divided into two main categories — real and personal. Real property is land and anything attached to it. It also includes what are called fixtures. Fixtures originally could be considered personal property, but with the way they are attached to the real property; their customization for the property; and the intent to make them part of the property; they lose their personal property nature and become real property. Trade fixtures are slightly

25. www.condohotelcenter.com.
26. Towers-Romero, S. 8.

different from regular fixtures in the fact that a business will actually take these with them when they move. Why? They are representative of the business itself, e.g., a special patterned rug or specific decorations indicative of that hospitality enterprise.

Personal property can be divided into tangible and intangible. Tangible personal property is anything that has value in and of itself, e.g., a couch, a necklace, a table. Intangible personal property does not have a value itself; it represents value, e.g., a copyright, a bankbook. The value is not in the item the value is in what the item represents.

Real and personal property can be bought and sold, or it can be leased. Leases are legal agreements that allow an individual or business to use land or personal property for a specified period of time. The lessee must pay the lease rent and comply with all the requirements of the lease to allow them continued use of the property. Land leases must be in writing under the Statute of Frauds, and personal property leases are influenced by the UCC.

It is important that guests of a hospitality property be categorized either as a tenant or as a transient guest. This determination will establish the hospitality business's obligations to the guest, and the guest's obligations to the hospitality business.

Key Terms

Real property
Real estate
Commercial property
Americans with Disabilities Act
Occupational Safety and Health
    Administration Act
Grantor
Grantee
Statute of Frauds
USA Patriot Act
Granting clause
Consideration
Gift deed
Habendum clause
Fee simple
Life estate

Seized of the land
Encumbrances
General warranty deed
Covenant of seisin
Covenant of quiet enjoyment
Covenant against encumbrances
Covenant of further assurances
Covenant to warrant forever
Title examination
Special warranty deed
Cloud on the title
Quitclaim deed
Personal property
Bill of sale
Shipment contract
FOB (free on board)

Point of origin

FAS (free alongside ship)

CIF (cost, insurance, and freight)

C & F (cost and freight)

Destination contract

FOB destination

Ex-ship

No arrival, no sale

Bona fide purchaser for value without notice

Actual notice

Constructive notice

Fixture

Trade fixture

Tenant

Leasing

Lessor

Lessee

Unconscionable lease

Implied warranty of suitability

Fitness for a particular purpose

Net lease

Landlord

Double net lease

Triple net lease

Net Net Net lease

NNN Lease

Assign

Assignee

Sublease

Sublessee

Insurance

Common area maintenance

Pro rata

Transient

Evict

Condo hotel

Homeowner's association fees

Timeshare

Chapter Seven

How to Select Employees

Chapter Objectives

What are the legal requirements when hiring an employee?

What does the EEOC do?

What does the ADA do?

What does the ADEA do?

When is an employee eligible to work in the U.S.?

What does the Fair Labor Standards Act do?

What is sexual harassment and what needs to be done to prevent it?

What is the FMLA?

What is a W-2?

When is a 1099 used?

What is FUTA?

How can an employee be legally terminated?

What is WARN?

When can an employer monitor what the employee is doing?

Job Descriptions

When writing a job description, it is imperative that only the requirements necessary for the job be listed. These must only specify the list of skills required for that position. To list any additional requirements can lead to legal liability. Some permissible requirements would be educational level, certifications, licensing, language skills, and knowledge of equipment, and age if related to serving alcohol or working late hours.

Job qualifications cannot violate the law, e.g., age, gender, race, and marital status cannot be put into a job description unless it is a **bona fide occupational qualification**, a BFOQ.

BFOQs are employment qualifications that employers are allowed to consider while making decisions about hiring and retention of employees. The qualification must relate to an essential job duty and the BFOQ must be considered necessary for the operation of the particular business.

BFOQs allow the hiring of individuals based on race, sex, age, and national origin if these characteristics are critical for the duties of the job. This is an exception and complete defense to **Title VII of the Civil Rights Act of 1964**. The Civil Rights Act protects employees from discrimination based on religion, sex, age, national origin and race in the workplace. To prove a BFOQ, the employer must show the specific class of employee sought is reasonably necessary for the operation of the business.[1]

An example of this is the notorious "Hooters® case." In this case, Nikolai Grushevski filed a complaint against a Hooters® franchisee in Corpus Christi, Texas when his application to become a waiter was allegedly rejected because he was a male.

Hooters'® defense was BFOQ. Hooters® stated, "Being female is reasonably necessary to the performance of the Hooters Girls® job duties."[2] This case was settled out of court. At this time there are no male waiters at Hooters®.

---

1. www.findlaw.com. In *Bostock v. Clayton County, Georgia*, discussed and cited previously, the Supreme Court held that firing individuals because of their sexual orientation or transgender status violates Title VII's prohibition on discrimination because of sex.

2. *Grushevski v. Texas Wings Inc., et al.*, C.A. NO. 09-cv-00002, April 13, 2009.

Applications

When doing the company's application, it is imperative the application does not require the applicant to disclose such things as their marital status, whether they have children or not, whether they own a home, or other information that does not focus on the qualifications needed specifically for the job.

Employment applications must be identical for all applicants and all job positions. What will differentiate the applicants will be their educational and experiential backgrounds. If in doubt about what can be asked on job applications, consult with an attorney.[3]

Job Interviews

The **Equal Employment Opportunity Commission** limits what can be asked during a job interview:

- Questions cannot screen out minorities or females.
- Consider why each question needs to be answered. If it is necessary to judge an applicant's competence — only then is the question permissible.
- Are there any less discriminatory questions that can be asked to judge an applicant's qualifications?

Do not just pick questions "from the air." Questions asked need to be written; answers and notes taken in reference to the questions asked need to be written down as well. It is important to be prepared in case a discrimination trial is filed against the interviewer and the company.

Questions that can and cannot be asked:

- Age, unless it is for a job involving alcohol, dangerous materials, or late night work — then it is important a *minimum* age is established
- No race, religion, national origin questions
- No physical trait qualification questions unless a BFOQ — such as the need to lift a certain weight, e.g., the requirement to lift 50 pounds for a delivery company
- If specific educational requirements are required, then it is OK to ask

---

3. www.dol.gov; www.eeoc.gov.

- No questions as to home ownership
- It is OK to ask about present and former employers and job related references[4]

Pre-Employment Testing

The areas that a potential employee can be tested in are:

- To see if the person has the required job skills, e.g., computer skills or food preparation ability
- Psychological testing to see if the person can handle stress and how they will fit into the job and organization

Any test given must be documented as a valid indicator of the ability needed for the job or organization.[5]

Background Checks

Background checks can be run when hiring employees. To do so, the employer will need the person's name and social security number.

Appropriate information that can be sought during a background check would be information that the applicant puts on their job application — such as:

- Training
- Education
- Criminal record
- Credit report
- Use of online social media

This information cannot be shared with parties outside the organization, or this would be a violation of privacy.

If employment is denied based on a background check, this needs to be documented. An explanation of why the applicant was not hired must be given

---

4. www.eeoc.gov.
5. www.dol.gov.

to the prospective employee. In that way, the applicant can explain the reason for the situation in question or can correct a possible mistake on the part of the collector of information.[6]

References

Can an employer ask for references from a potential employee? Yes. The problem is these references may not be helpful.

Most former employers will only give very limited information regarding their former employee, the former employer being fearful of potential lawsuits against them for **defamation**. Although the truth is a complete defense to the tort of defamation, many employers will not want to risk a legal suit.

Safe information a former employer can provide would be:

- The former employee's name
- Dates of employment of the former employee
- Job title
- The name and title of the individual giving the reference

Classified Ads

Up through the 1960s help wanted ads were classified into "**Help Wanted-Male**" and "**Help Wanted-Female**." Then, in 1969, the EEOC ruled only if there was a specific BFOQ could an employer discriminate on the basis of gender.

Today, thanks to Title VII of the Civil Rights Act of 1964, ads cannot discriminate as to race, color, religion, sex, and national origin.

Who Must Comply with This Law?

Any employer that is engaged in an industry that affects interstate commerce and who has fifteen or more employees for each working day in each of the twenty or more calendar weeks in the current or preceding calendar year.[7]

---

6. www.eeoc.gov.
7. ibid.

Affirmative Action

Affirmative Action is a good faith effort to redress past or present discrimination. Yet, affirmative action has come under U.S. Supreme Court scrutiny.

> In the 2003 case of *Gratz v. Bollinger*[8] six justices decided the Michigan University undergraduate policy of awarding "racial bonus points" to minority applicants was not "**narrowly tailored**" enough to pass constitutional muster. This undergraduate policy assigned extra points to any minority applicant without any individual review of their background, experiences, or qualities.

What *Gratz* accomplished was to allow the continuation of the doctrine of affirmative action, but requires **strict scrutiny** of when and how it could be used.

In *Fisher v. University of Texas at Austin I*, 570 U.S. 297 (2013), the USSC stated the 5th Circuit Court of Appeals should apply strict scrutiny to determine the constitutionality of the University's race sensitive admission's policy, and in *Fisher II*, 579 U.S. ___, 136 S. Ct. 2198, 195 L, Ed, 2d 511, (2016) the USSC held the Court of Appeals for the 5th Circuit correctly found that the University of Texas at Austin's undergraduate admission policy survived strict scrutiny. Strict scrutiny is a method of judicial review that courts use to determine the constitutionality of a particular law. To pass the strict scrutiny test, the legislature must have passed the law to further a "compelling governmental interest," and must have narrowly tailored the law to achieve that interest.

Americans with Disabilities Act

The 1990 **Americans with Disabilities Act** (ADA) states there can be no discrimination against those with disabilities in public accommodations, transportation, telecommunications, and in employment. No business under the ADA shall discriminate against a qualified individual on the basis of disability with regard to job application procedures; hiring, advancement, or discharge of employees; employee compensation; job training; and other terms, conditions, and privileges of employment. Title I of the ADA applies to employers (including state or local governments) with fifteen or more employees; to em-

---

8. 539 U.S. 506.

ployment agencies; and to labor organizations and joint labor-management committees with any number of employees.[9]

The ADA requires that any individual who, with or without **reasonable accommodation**, can perform the essential functions of an employment position that such an individual holds or desires cannot be denied employment for that position if they are qualified. Consideration shall be given to the employer's judgment as to what functions of a job are essential. To protect him or herself, the employer should prepare a written description before advertising or interviewing applicants for the position. This description shall be considered to be evidence of the essential functions of the job.

What Is Reasonable Accommodation?

The term "reasonable accommodation" may include:

- Making existing facilities used by employees readily accessible to and usable by individuals with disabilities.
- Job restructuring, part-time or modified work schedules, reassignment to a vacant position, acquisition or modification of equipment or devices, appropriate adjustment or modifications of examinations, training materials or policies, the provision of qualified readers or interpreters, and other similar accommodations for individuals with disabilities.

In making these reasonable accommodations, the employer should be able to do so without incurring **undue hardship**, or put the health or safety of their hospitality guests in jeopardy.

For example, hiring someone with a communicable disease, such as a carrier of typhoid would put the health of guests at a hotel or restaurant at risk. Thus, this individual could not be reasonably accommodated under the ADA.

The term "undue hardship" means an action requiring significant difficulty or expense.

In determining whether accommodation under the ADA would impose an undue hardship on a business, factors to be considered include:

- The nature and cost of the accommodation needed
- The overall financial resources of the facility or facilities involved in the provision of reasonable accommodation

---

9. www.ada.gov.

- The effect on expenses and resources, or the impact of such accommodation upon the operation of the business
- The overall size of the business — with respect to the number of its employees
- The number, type, and location of its facilities
- The type of operation or operations of the business, including the composition, structure, and functions of the workforce of such a business entity; the geographic separateness, administrative or fiscal relationship of the facility or facilities in question in regard to the business entity[10]

Thus, the larger the business, the more needed changes could be considered reasonable, since the larger business has the finances, space, and staff to allow for the assimilation of a disabled individual.

If an employer has any questions as to whom must be considered for a position under the ADA, they can always consult with the EEOC for clarification.

Age Discrimination

Under the **Age Discrimination in Employment Act 1967** (ADEA), workers cannot be discriminated against if they are over 40 years of age. This includes the area of hiring, firing, promotions, layoffs, compensation, benefits, job assignments, and training.

ADEA applies to all employers who:

- Are engaged in an industry affecting interstate commerce (most every industry will affect interstate commerce within the meaning of the ADEA)
- Has twenty or more employees for each working day in each of twenty or more calendar weeks in the current or preceding calendar year[11]

It is a good policy to hire based on experience and qualifications, not age.

---

10. ibid.
11. www.eeoc.gov; www.dol.gov.

Verification of Eligibility to Work

Knowing if a potential hire is eligible to work in the U.S. will be a major area of concern in the hospitality industry. The labor intensive work required in the industry, attracts potential employees who may not have the proper papers to work in the U.S.

Under the **1986 Immigration Reform and Control Act** (IRCA) an employer cannot knowingly hire people who do not have the right to work in the U.S. It is the duty of the employer to verify that all employees are legally authorized to work. IRCA applies to all businesses regardless of size. Thus if a business has only one employee, they still must comply with this Act.

To comply with IRCA, the employer must have the new hire fill out an **I-9** form. I-9 forms are available at www.uscis.gov.

To prove they are eligible to work, employees must present original documents, not photocopies. The only exception to this is that an employee may present a certified copy of a birth certificate.

Acceptable I-9 Documents

Employees are required to present either one of the documents from List A or one of the following documents from List B *and* one of the documents from List C.

List A (Documents that establish both identity and employment eligibility)

- United States Passport
- Permanent Resident Card or Alien Registration Receipt Card (I-551)
- Employment Authorization Document (I-766)
- For aliens authorized to work only for a specific employer, foreign passport with Form I-94 authorizing employment with this employer
- A foreign passport containing a Form I-551 stamp or Form I-551 printed notation

List B (Documents that establish identity only)

- A driver's license issued by a state or outlying possession
- An ID card issued by a state or outlying possession
- A Native American tribal document
- A Canadian driver's license or ID card with a photograph (for Canadian aliens authorized to work only for a specific employer)
- A school ID card with a photograph

- Voter's registration card
- U.S. military card or draft record
- Military dependent's ID Card

List C (Documents that establish employment eligibility only)

- Social Security account number card without employment restrictions
- Original or certified copy of a birth certificate with an official seal issued by a state or local government agency
- Certification of Birth Abroad
- U.S. Citizen ID Card (I-197)
- A Native American tribal document
- Employment authorization document issued by the Department of Homeland Security (DHS)
- Identification Card for Use of Resident Citizen in the United States (I-179)

Employers *cannot* specify which documentation they will accept from the employee to prove the ability to work.

The employer has three business days to fill in the I-9 form. The identity and employment eligibility documents must be examined within three business days of the date paid employment begins.

If the employee is unable to present the actual documents to satisfy the I-9 regulations within those three days, the employee must present a receipt for application of replacement document(s) and the actual document(s) within (90) ninety days.

Retaining Form I-9

To calculate how long to keep an employee's Form I-9, enter the following:

1. Date the employee began work for pay　1. _____
   A. Add three years to the date on line 1.　A. _____

2. The date employment was terminated　2. _____
   B. Add one year to the date on line 2.　B. _____

3. Which date is later; A or B?　3. _____
   C. Enter the later date.　C. _____

Employers must retain Form I-9 until the date on Line C.[12]

---

12. www.uscis.gov.

Fair Labor Standards Act of 1938

The **Fair Labor Standards Act (FLSA)** protects the health and education of young workers. It prescribes standards for the basic minimum wage and overtime pay, and it affects most private and public employment.

The federal **minimum wage** as of July 24, 2009, is $7.25 per hour (still the same as of this writing in 2021). Unless the employee is exempt from receiving overtime, such as if the employee is in a supervisory position; any work after 40 hours per week must be compensated at one and one-half times an employee's regular rate of pay. An employee is exempt from receiving overtime pay if they are employed as a bona fide executive, administrative, professional, or outside sales employee, or employees of certain seasonal amusement or recreational establishments.

To qualify for the *administrative* employee exemption, all the following tests must be met:

- The employee must be compensated on a salary or fee basis at a rate not less than $684 per week.
- The employee's primary duty must be the performance of office or non-manual work directly related to the management or general business operations of the employer or the employer's customers.
- The employee's primary duty includes the exercise of discretion and independent judgment with respect to matters of significance.

To qualify for the *learned professional* employee exemption, all the following tests must be met:

- The employee's primary duty must be the performance of work requiring advanced knowledge, defined as work which is predominantly intellectual in character and which includes work requiring the consistent exercise of discretion and judgment.
- The advanced knowledge must be in a field of science or learning.
- The advanced knowledge must be customarily acquired by a prolonged course of specialized intellectual instruction.

To qualify for the *creative professional* employee exemption, the following tests must be met:

- The employee's primary duty must be the performance of work requiring invention, imagination, originality or talent in a recognized field of artistic or creative endeavor.

To qualify for the *computer* employee exemption, the following tests must be met:

- The employee must be compensated either on a salary or fee basis at a rate not less than $684 per week.
- The employee must be employed as a computer systems analyst, computer programmer, software engineer, or other similarly skilled worker in the computer field performing the duties described below.

The employee's primary duties must consist of:

- ○ The application of systems analysis techniques and procedures, including consulting with users, to determine hardware, software or system functional specifications
- ○ The design, development, documentation, analysis, creation, testing or modification of computer systems or programs, including prototypes, based on and related to user or system design specifications
- ○ The design, documentation, testing, creation, or modification of computer programs related to machine operating systems
- ○ A combination of the aforementioned duties, the performance of which requires the same level of skills

To qualify for the *outside sales* employee exemption, all the following tests must be met:

- The employee's primary duty must be making sales (as defined in the FLSA), or obtaining orders, or contracts for services, or selling the use of facilities for which consideration will be paid for by the client or customer.
- The employee must be customarily and regularly engaged away from the employer's place or places of business.

Highly compensated employees: Beginning on January 1, 2020, an employee with total annual compensation of at least $107,432 is deemed exempt from overtime, under section 13(a)(1) of the FLSA, if the employee customarily and regularly performs any one or more of the exempt duties or responsibilities of an executive, administrative or professional employee.

The exemptions provided by the FLSA Section 13(a)(1) apply only to "white collar" employees who meet the salary and duties tests set forth in Part 541 regulations. The exemptions do not apply to manual laborers or other "blue collar" workers who perform work involving repetitive operations with their hands, physical skill, and energy. FLSA-covered, non-management employees in production, maintenance, construction, and similar occupations such as carpenters, electricians, mechanics, plumbers, iron workers, craftsmen, operating engineers, longshoremen, construction workers, and laborers are entitled to a minimum wage and overtime premium pay under the FLSA, and are not exempt under Part 541 regulations no matter how highly paid they might be.[13]

Many states have their own minimum wage laws. In cases where an employee is subject to both the state and federal minimum wage laws, the employee is entitled to the higher of the two minimum wages.

Youth Employment

An employee must be at least sixteen years old to work in most non-farm jobs and at least eighteen to work in non-farm jobs that have been declared to be hazardous by the Secretary of Labor. Youths fourteen and fifteen years old may work outside school hours in various non-manufacturing, non mining, non-hazardous jobs under the following conditions:

- No more than 3 hours on a school day or eighteen hours in a school week
- Eight hours on a non-school day or 40 hours in a non-school week
- Work may not begin before 7 a.m. or end after 7 p.m., except from June 1 through Labor Day, when evening hours are extended to 9 p.m. Different rules apply in agricultural employment.

Tip Credit

Employers of "tipped employees," such as wait staff and bartenders, must pay a cash wage of at least $2.13 per hour to these employees if the employer is claiming a **tip credit** against their minimum wage obligation. If an em-

---

13. www.dol.gov.

ployee's tips combined with the employer's cash wage of at least $2.13 per hour do not equal the minimum hourly wage, the employer must make up the difference.[14]

Requirements for the Use of Tip Credits

The employer must provide the following information to a tipped employee before the employer may use the tip credit:

- The amount of cash wage the employer is paying a tipped employee, which must be at least $2.13 per hour.
- The additional amount claimed by the employer as a tip credit.
- The tip credit claimed by the employer cannot exceed the amount of the tips actually received by the tipped employee.
- All tips received by the tipped employee are to be retained by the employee except for a valid **tip pooling** arrangement (see below).
- The tip credit will not apply to any tipped employee unless the employee has been informed of these tip credit provisions.

The employer may provide oral or written notice to its tipped employees informing them of the above listed items. An employer who fails to provide the required information *cannot* use the tip credit provisions.

A hospitality owner or manager who intends to use the tip credit provisions should have a written agreement that the tipped employee must sign upon hire. Although the law allows for verbal notice of the use of tip credit, this will not protect the employer if the employee decides to sue for back wages months or years later.

---

14. ibid.

Table of Minimum Hourly Wages for Tipped Employees, by State

Jurisdiction	Basic Combined Cash & Tip Minimum Wage	Maximum Tip Credit against Minimum Wage Rate	Minimum Cash Wage[1]	Minimum Monthly Tips
FEDERAL: Fair Labor Standards Act (FLSA)	$7.25	$5.12	$2.13	More than $30
STATE LAW DOES NOT ALLOW TIP CREDIT				
Minimum rate same for tipped and non-tipped employees				
Alaska			$10.19	
California			$12.00 if have 25 or fewer employees $13.00 with 26 or more employees	
Guam			$8.25	
Minnesota Large employer[2] Small employer[2]			$10.00 $8.15	
Montana Large business Small business			$8.65 sales over $110,000 $4.00 sales under $110,000 and not subject to FLSA	
Nevada			$8.25 if no health insurance provided $7.25 if health insurance provided	See note 10.
Oregon			$11.25	
Washington			$13.50	
STATE LAW ALLOWS TIP CREDIT				
Arizona	$12.00	$3.00	$9.00	Not specified
Arkansas	$10.00	$7.37	$2.63	More than $20

Jurisdiction	Basic Combined Cash & Tip Minimum Wage	Maximum Tip Credit against Minimum Wage Rate	Minimum Cash Wage[1]	Minimum Monthly Tips
Colorado	$12.00	$3.02	$8.98	More than $30
Connecticut	$11.00			
Hotel, restaurant		$4.62	$6.38	
Bartenders		$2.37	$8.23	
Delaware	$9.25	$7.02	$2.23	More than $30
District of Columbia	$15.00	$10.00	$5.00	Not specified
Florida	$8.56	$3.02	$5.54	
Hawaii	$10.10	$0.75	$9.35	More than $20
Hawaii: Tip Credit in Hawaii is permissible if the combined amount the employee receives from the employer and in tips is at least $7.00 more than the applicable minimum wage.				
Idaho	$7.25	$3.90	$3.35	More than $30
Illinois	$10.00	40%	$6.00	$20
Indiana	$7.25	$5.12	$2.13	Not specified
Iowa	$7.25	$2.90	$4.35	More than $30
Kansas	$7.25	$5.12	$2.13	More than $20
Kentucky	$7.25	$5.12	$2.13	More than $20
Maine	$12.00	$6.00	$6.00	More than $30
Maryland	$11.00	$7.37	$3.63	More than $30
Massachusetts	$12.75	$7.80	$4.95	More than $20
Michigan	$9.65	$5.98	$3.67	Not specified
Missouri	$9.45	$4.72	$4.73	Not specified
Nebraska	$9.00	$6.87	$2.13	Not specified
New Hampshire	$7.25	55%	45%	More than $30
New Jersey[3]	$11.00	$7.87	$3.13	Not specified
New Mexico	$9.00	$6.65	$2.35	More than $30
New York	$11.80			
Food service workers		$3.95	$7.85	Not specified.
Service Employees in All Establishments		$1.95	$9.85	

Jurisdiction	Basic Combined Cash & Tip Minimum Wage	Maximum Tip Credit against Minimum Wage Rate	Minimum Cash Wage[1]	Minimum Monthly Tips
North Carolina[4]	$7.25	$5.12	$2.13	More than $20
North Dakota	$7.25	33%	$4.86	More than $30
Ohio[5]	$8.70	$4.35	$4.35	More than $30
Oklahoma[6]	$7.25	$5.12	$2.13	Not specified
Pennsylvania	$7.25	$4.42	$2.83	More than $30
Rhode Island	$10.50	$6.61	$3.89	Not specified
South Dakota	$9.30	$4.65	$4.65	More than $35
Texas	$7.25	$5.12	$2.13	More than $20
Utah	$7.25	$5.12	$2.13	More than $30
Vermont Hospitality employees	$10.96	$5.46	$5.46	More than $120
Virginia	$7.25	$5.12	$2.13	Not specified
Virgin Islands[11]	$10.50	$6.30	$4.20	Not specified
West Virginia[7]	$8.75	$6.13	$2.62	Not specified
Wisconsin[8]	$7.25	$4.92	$2.33	Not specified
Wyoming	$7.25	$5.12	$2.13	More than $30

The above figures are from *July 1, 2020.*

Footnotes

1. Other additional deductions are permitted, for example for meals and lodging.

2. Minnesota. Effective August 1, 2014, a large employer means an enterprise whose gross revenue is not less than $500,000. A small employer means an enterprise whose gross revenue is less than $500,000.

3. In New Jersey, in specific situations where the employer can prove to the satisfaction of the Department of Labor and Workforce Development that if the tips actually received exceed the creditable amount, a higher tip credit may be taken.

4. North Carolina. Tip credit is not permitted unless the employer obtains from each employee, either monthly or each pay period, a signed certification of the amount of tips received.

5. Ohio. For employees of employers with gross annual sales of less than $305,000, the state minimum wage is $7.25 per hour. For these employees, the state wage is tied to the federal minimum wage of $7.25 per hour, which requires an act of Congress and the President's signature to change.

6. Oklahoma. For employers with fewer than 10 full-time employees at any one location who have gross annual sales of $100,000 or less, the basic minimum rate is $2.00 per hour.

7. West Virginia. The state minimum wage law applies only to employers with six or more employees and to state agencies.

8. Wisconsin. $2.13 per hour may be paid to employees who are not yet 20 years old and who have been in employment status with a particular employer for 90 or fewer consecutive calendar days from the date of initial employment.

9. The following states do not have state minimum wage laws: Alabama, Louisiana, Mississippi, South Carolina, and Tennessee. Georgia has a state minimum wage law, but it does not apply to tipped employees.

10. Nevada. The state's minimum wage rates may be increased annually based upon changes in the cost of living index, which would in turn increase the minimum cash wage for tipped employees.

11. U.S. Virgin Islands. After December 31, 2018, and each year thereafter, the Virgin Islands Wage Board may increase the territory's minimum wage to a rate equal to not more than 50 percent of the average private, nonsupervisory, nonagricultural hourly wage; after 2020, the Wage Board may increase the minimum cash wage for tipped tourist service and restaurant employees to 45% of the minimum wage.[15]

Tip Pooling

If you are an employer who does not take a tip credit (discussed above) — that is, you pay the full minimum wage, whether because of state law or personal choice — then you can include back of the house employees, such as cooks and dishwashers, in your tip pool. This is an update to the U.S. DOL FLSA, as of March 2018.

If you do take a tip credit out of employees' wages, then your tip pool can only include the customer-facing employees who would ordinarily receive more than $30 in tips per month. If you take a tip credit for bartenders or wait staff, these individuals should not have to tip share with non-tipped employees (those who you aren't taking a tip credit for).

It's important to note that tip pooling laws prohibit employers, managers, and supervisors from participating in the tip pool. The position of "supervisor" or "manager" is determined based on the DOL duties test. Under the duties test, a person qualifies for supervisor or manager status if they are exempt under the overtime rule, supervise at least two other employees, and have the authority to make hiring and firing decisions.

---

15. Division of Communications, Wage and Hour Division, U.S. Department of Labor.

Additionally, another stipulation to the rule is that owners must inform employees of the pool's existence and the format by which the pool will be distributed, such as hours worked. Finally, make sure to check any new state laws that might include tip pooling laws specific to your area.

Retention of Tips

The FLSA prohibits any arrangement between the employer and the tipped employee whereby any part of the tip received becomes the property of the employer. For example, even when a tipped employee receives at least $7.25 per hour in wages directly from the employer, the employee may not be required to turn over his or her tips to the employer.

Penalties for FLSA Violations

Employers may be assessed civil monetary penalties of up to $2,074 for each willful or repeated violation of the minimum wage or overtime pay provisions of the law, and up to $13,227 for each employee who is the subject of a violation of the Act's child labor provisions. In addition, a civil monetary penalty of up to $60,115 may be assessed for each child labor violation that causes death or serious injury to any minor employee, and such assessments may be doubled, up to $120,230, when the violations are determined to be willful or repeated (effective date of penalty amounts, January 14, 2021).

The law also prohibits discriminating against or discharging workers who file a complaint or participate in any proceeding under the Act.[16]

Employment at Will

It has been a well-settled principle of common law in the U.S. that an employee who is hired for an indefinite period of time, without an employment contract, is terminable at will by the employer without restriction. This means an employer may dismiss their employees for good cause, for no cause, or even for a reason that is morally wrong, without being liable for a legal wrong. Under this rule, employees are correspondingly free to quit at any time, and for any reason.

In contrast to **employment at will**, a contract of employment for a specified period ordinarily may be terminated only for "good cause" or "just cause."

---

16. www.dol.gov.

Even where there is a written contract for a definite time period, however, other contractual provisions might render the employment relationship terminable at will. For example, employers can terminate employment contracts at will where they provide for a definite term, but also provide that either party could terminate the contract by giving notice to the other party.

There are also **union workers**. These groups of employees are covered by collective bargaining agreements and usually can only be terminated for cause.

The 1935 **National Labor Relations Act** (NLRA) guarantees workers the right to organize and form a union. The employer cannot:

- Threaten employees if they try to unionize
- Threaten to shut down if the employees unionize
- Interfere with the formation of a union
- Try to coerce non-unionization
- Discriminate against union members
- Terminate union members who participate in a strike

The **National Labor Relations Board** (NLRB) requires employers to post notices in the workplace, or online, informing workers of their rights to unionize, under the National Labor Relations Act.[17]

The notice, required to be posted, is similar to Department of Labor notices already posted in workplaces across the country. Furthermore, the poster will be provided free of charge by the federal government. Some business groups and their allies say this new rule is too onerous, and that it benefits labor unions.

Sexual Harassment

It is unlawful to harass a person (an applicant or employee) because of that person's sex. Harassment can include **sexual harassment**, such as unwelcome sexual advances, requests for sexual favors, and other verbal or physical harassment of a sexual nature.

Sexual harassment can include offensive remarks about a person's sex. For example, it is illegal to harass a woman by making offensive comments about women in general, e.g., making crude jokes about the private parts of a woman during work hours.

Both the victim and the harasser can be either a woman or a man, and the victim and harasser can be the same sex.

---

17. www.nlrb.gov.

Although the law doesn't prohibit simple teasing, offhand comments, or isolated incidents that are not very serious, harassment is illegal when it is so frequent or severe that it creates a **hostile or offensive work environment**, or when it results in adverse employment decisions (such as the victim being fired or demoted).

The harasser could be the victim's supervisor, a supervisor in another area, a co-worker, or someone who is not an employee of the employer, such as a client or customer.[18]

In the hospitality industry, since there is so much interaction between employees, customers, guests, and others employed in the industry, it is extremely important to be aware when sexual harassment is creating a hostile work environment. In the case of sexual harassment, the policy of "the customer is always right" does *not* apply.

As an employer, there must be reasonable care taken to prevent and correct sexual harassment in the workplace. If the company is large enough, it is advantageous having a company **ombudsman**—a neutral third party that the "harassed" individual feels comfortable and safe in making their complaint. Supervisors must be trained in how to recognize sexual harassment.

All complaints must be documented in writing and investigated. The resolution of the complaint must also be documented and kept in all the parties' files for the period of the **statute of limitations** for that particular jurisdiction. Have the employee[s] involved sign the form stating how the matter was resolved.

To avoid liability for sexual harassment, it is important to show:

- The complaint was investigated substantially.
- Immediate corrective actions were taken against the harasser.
- If a remedy is needed to put the harassed individual back to where they were prior to the harassment, e.g., restoring their job or wages — this must be done promptly.
- Prove preventative measures have been taken to avoid future occurrences of harassment.

It is important to have a policy in place in the employee manual that shows how serious sexual harassment is considered by the company, and that action will be taken against the harasser.

There must be **zero tolerance** in all cases of reported sexual harassment.

---

18. www.eeoc.gov.

Here is an example from the State of South Dakota's Department of Labor and Regulation of what can be put in an employee manual in reference to the company's handling of sexual harassment.

> *Division of Human Rights*
> *Harassment, including Sexual Harassment*
> [Company Name] is committed to providing a work environment that is free of discrimination and unlawful harassment. Actions, words, jokes, or comments based on an individual's sex, race, ethnicity, age, religion, or any other legally protected characteristic will not be tolerated.
>
> If you believe you have been the victim of harassment, or know of another employee who has, report it immediately. Employees can raise concerns and make reports without fear of reprisal.
>
> Any supervisor who becomes aware of possible harassment should promptly advise their supervisor [or the Human Resources Representative] who will handle the matter in a timely and confidential manner.[19]

Family and Medical Leave Act

The **Family and Medical Leave Act** (FMLA) provides an entitlement of up to 12 weeks of job-protected, unpaid leave during any 12-month period to eligible, covered employees for the following reasons:

- Birth and care of an eligible employee's child, within one year of birth, or placement for adoption or foster care of a child with the employee, within one year of placement
- Care of an immediate family member (spouse, child, or parent) who has a serious health condition.
- Care of the employee's own serious health condition that does not allow the employee to perform the essential functions of their job. (*Author's Note — To the reader, please also refer to Chapter Three for a discussion of the new state mandates for paid family leave, and, the offering of temporary federal paid family leave due to the COVID pandemic.*)

---

19. www.dlr.sd.gov.

FMLA requires that the employee's group health benefits be maintained during the leave. FMLA is administered by the **Employment Standards Administration Wage and Hour Division** within the **U.S. Department of Labor.**

The FMLA applies to all:

- Public agencies, including local, state, and federal employers, and local education agencies (schools); and
- Private sector employers who employ 50 or more employees at least 20 workweeks in the current or preceding calendar year—including joint employers and successors of covered employers.

(Author's note: On July 16, 2020, the Wage and Hour Division announced a Request for Information (RFI) to be published in the Federal Register seeking the public's feedback on the administration and use of the law—FMLA.)

The Family and Medical Leave Act and National Defense Authorization Act

The **National Defense Authorization Act** (NDAA) amends FMLA to permit a "spouse, son, daughter, parent, or next of kin" to take up to 26 workweeks of leave to care for a "member of the Armed Forces, including a member of the National Guard or Reserves, who is undergoing medical treatment, recuperation, or therapy, is otherwise in outpatient status, or is otherwise on the temporary disability retired list, for a serious injury or illness."

The NDAA also permits an employee to take FMLA leave for "any qualifying exigency (as the Secretary of Labor shall, by regulation, determine) arising out of the fact that the spouse, or a son, daughter, or parent of the employee is on active duty (or has been notified of an impending call or order to active duty) in the Armed Forces in support of a contingency operation."[20]

FMLA Rights and Responsibilities Notice

Each time the eligibility notice of FMLA is provided, the employer is also required to provide a written notice detailing the specific expectations and obligations of the employee under FMLA and explain any consequences of a failure to meet these obligations. If leave has already begun, the employer should mail the notice to the employee's address of record. The employer must translate this notice in any situation where it is obligated to translate the general

20. www.dol.gov.

notice into a language in which employees are literate. The written notice must include information on:

- Leave designated and counted against the employee's annual FMLA leave entitlement if it qualifies as FMLA leave
- The applicable twelve-month period for the FMLA entitlement
- Requirements for the employee to furnish certification of a serious health condition, serious injury or illness, or qualifying exigency arising out of active duty or call to active duty status, and the consequences of failing to do so
- Employee's right to substitute paid leave, whether the employer will require the substitution of paid leave, the conditions related to any substitution, and the employee's entitlement to take unpaid FMLA leave if the employee does not meet the conditions for paid leave
- Requirement for the employee to make any premium payments the employer requires to maintain health benefits, the arrangements for making such payments, and the possible consequences of the failure to make such payments on a timely basis
- Employee's status as a "key employee" and the potential consequence that restoration may be denied following FMLA leave, explaining the conditions required for such denial
- Employee's rights to maintenance of benefits during FMLA leave and to restoration to the same or an equivalent job upon return from leave (as long as they are not deemed a key employee)
- Employee's potential liability for payment of health insurance premiums paid by the employer during the employee's unpaid FMLA leave if the employee fails to return to work after taking FMLA leave

The specific notice may include other information such as whether the employer will require periodic reports of the employee's status and intent to return to work.

If the specific information provided to the employee under FMLA changes, the employer must provide a written notice that refers to the prior notice given and sets forth any changes in such information. This notice of changes should be provided within five business days of any change.

FMLA Designation Notice

When the employer has enough information to determine whether the leave is being taken for a FMLA qualifying reason, the employer must notify the employee in writing whether the leave is designated and will count as FMLA leave within five business days. The employer must also notify the employee, in writing, if it determines that the leave is not FMLA qualifying and will not be designated as FMLA leave.

The employer must notify the employee of the number of hours, days, or weeks that will be counted against the employee's FMLA entitlement.[21]

Recordkeeping under FMLA

Under the Fair Labor Standards Act, employers are required to make, keep, and preserve records pertaining to their obligations under FMLA. Employers must keep the records for no less than three years and make them available for inspection, copying, and transcription by Department of Labor representatives upon request. Records kept in computer form must be made available for transcription and copying.

Covered employers who have eligible employees must maintain records that must disclose the following:

- Basic payroll and identifying information (including name, address, and occupation)
- Rate or basis of pay
- Terms of compensation
- Daily and weekly hours worked per pay period
- Additions to or deductions from wages
- Total compensation paid
- Dates of FMLA leave taken by FMLA eligible employees
- Copies of all written notices given to employees as required under FMLA
- Documents describing employee benefits or employer paid and unpaid leave policies and practices
- Premium payments for employee benefits
- Records of disputes between the employer and the employee regarding FMLA

Records and documents relating to medical certifications, recertifications or medical histories of employees or employees' family members, created for the purposes of FMLA, are required to be maintained as confidential medical records in separate files/records from the usual personnel files.[22]

---

21. ibid.
22. 29 C.F.R. §825.500.

Federal Income Tax and
Social Security and Medicare Taxes

As an employer, federal income taxes must be withheld from employees' wages. At the end of the year, the employer must complete a **W-2 Wage and Tax Statement** to report wages, tips and other compensation paid to an employee. A copy of this form must be provided to the employee by January 31st of the following year. A copy of the W-2 must also be sent to the Social Security Administration (SSA). Employers can prepare and file up to twenty W-2s at a time at the Social Security Administration's website.[23]

1099s

There are over a dozen different types of Form 1099, each for reporting different kinds of income. These are forms used by the **Internal Revenue Service (IRS)** to track individual income that isn't reported on a W-2.

Contract workers, business investors, and independent contractors will have more income reported on 1099s than reported on a W-2. Businesses and entities that make payments to contract workers, business investors, and independent contractors have the obligation to prepare and file the appropriate Form 1099.

Social Security and Medicare

As an employer and an employee in the United States, **Social Security and Medicare** taxes must be paid. These tax payments contribute to the employee's coverage under the U.S. Social Security system. Social Security and Medicare taxes are partly paid by the employer and partly paid by the employee. The employer must withhold the employee's portion of both programs from the employee's paycheck. These taxes must be deducted even if the employee does not expect to qualify for Social Security or Medicare benefits.

> Social Security coverage provides retirement benefits and medical insurance (Medicare) benefits to individuals who meet certain eligibility requirements.

In general, U.S. Social Security and Medicare taxes apply to payments on wages for services performed as an employee in the United States, regardless of the citizenship or residence of either the employee or the employer. In limited sit-

---

23. www.irs.gov.

uations, these taxes will be collected from an employee's wages for services performed outside the United States.

International Social Security Agreements

The U.S. government has entered into social security agreements with foreign countries to coordinate social security coverage and taxation of workers employed for part or all of their working careers in these foreign countries. These agreements are referred to as **Totalization Agreements**. Under these agreements, dual coverage and dual contributions (taxes) for the same work are eliminated. The agreements generally make sure that social security taxes are paid only to one country.[24]

Federal Unemployment Tax

Federal Unemployment Tax (FUTA) is reported separately from federal income tax and Social Security and Medicare taxes (on IRS Form 940), and the employer pays for FUTA, and any state unemployment taxes, out of their own funds. Employees do not pay these taxes, nor do they have them withheld from their pay.[25]

Unemployment Claims

Under unemployment law, each state sets its own criteria for an employee filing for unemployment.

An employee cannot get unemployment if there is:

- Insubordination on the job
- Habitual lateness or excessive absences
- Drug abuse on the job
- Disobedience of legitimate company policies
- Gross negligence or neglect of duty
- Dishonesty

Employers are given the chance to dispute a claim. They also have the right to appeal if they do not agree with the state's decision as to the employee's claim.[26]

---

24. www.ssa.gov.
25. www.irs.gov.
26. www.dol.gov.

Earned Income Tax Credit

The **Earned Income Tax Credit** (EITC) is a refundable federal income tax credit for low to moderate income working individuals and families. Congress originally approved this tax credit legislation in 1975, in part to offset the burden of Social Security taxes and to provide an incentive to work. When EITC exceeds the amount of taxes owed by the employee, it results in a tax refund to the employee.

To qualify for EITC, the employee must have earned income from employment, self-employment or another source and meet all the following rules:

1. Have a valid Social Security number
2. Have earned income from employment, self-employment or another source
3. Cannot use the married, filing separate filing status
4. Must be a U.S. citizen or resident alien all year, or a nonresident alien married to a U.S. citizen or to a resident alien and choose to file a joint return and be treated as a resident alien
5. Cannot be the qualifying child of another person
6. Cannot file Form 2555 or 2555-EZ (related to foreign earned income)
7. Adjusted gross income and earned income must meet the allowable limits
8. Investment income must meet or be less than the amount listed on the Income Limits, Maximum Credit Amounts and Tax Law Updates Page
9. If the employee is married and filing jointly, the spouse must also meet the EITC rules[27]

Workers' Compensation

Workers' compensation is a form of insurance that provides wage replacement and medical benefits for employees who are injured in the course and scope of employment. Workers' compensation is used to allow for a mandatory relinquishment of the employee's right to sue his or her employer for the tort of negligence. The trade off between assured, limited coverage and the lack of

---

27. www.irs.gov.

recourse, outside the workers' compensation system, is known as "the compensation bargain."

While plans differ between jurisdictions, provisions can be made for weekly payments to the injured employee in place of wages (functioning in this case as a form of disability compensation for economic loss, past and future); reimbursement or payment of medical and like expenses (functioning in this case as a form of health insurance); and benefits payable to the dependents of workers killed during employment (functioning in this case as a form of life insurance). State statutes establish the framework for workers' compensation insurance requirements.

Federal statutes, as to workers' compensation, are limited to federal employees or those workers employed in some significant aspect of interstate commerce.[28]

Termination of Employees

To avoid liability for **wrongful termination**, it is imperative to do regular employee evaluations. In that way, if an employee is not performing as required, there is a record of that non-performance. Also, by performing regular evaluations, the employee has been given reasonable notice of their dereliction and thus, knows they must correct their actions or face the consequences.

It is important that any company rules or regulations be properly and evenly applied to all employees. These rules and regulations need to be put in writing in an employee manual.

If disciplinary action against an employee is required, keep a written record of this discipline — when, how, and against whom the action was taken, and keep this record in the employee's files. If the employee comes to work drunk or presents a danger to others or themselves, they must be terminated immediately. This action must be fully documented — preferably by several individuals.

When firing an employee, an employer cannot:

- Violate the employee manual
- Deny accrued benefits
- Fire due to legitimate illness or absence
- Fire for attempts at unionization

---

28. www.dol.gov.

- Fire for reporting violations of the law — e.g., reporting safety concerns to OSHA
- Fire for belonging to a protected class of workers, e.g., those over 40
- Fire without notice under The Worker Adjustment and Retraining Notification Act (see below)
- Fire if the employee was verbally promised that employment would continue
- Fire in violation of a written employment contract

The Worker Adjustment and Retraining Notification Act

The **Worker Adjustment and Retraining Notification Act** (WARN) was enacted on August 4, 1988, and became effective on February 4, 1989. WARN is a provision that protects workers, their families, and communities by requiring most employers with 100 or more full-time employees to give notice if there will be a plant closing or mass layoff. Private, for-profit employers and private, nonprofit employers are covered, as are public and quasi-public entities which operate in a commercial context and are separately organized from the regular government. Regular federal, state, and local government entities which provide public services are *not* covered under WARN.

WARN provides notification 60 calendar days in advance. Employees entitled to notice under WARN include managers and supervisors, as well as hourly and salaried workers.

WARN requires that notice also be given to employees' representatives, the local chief elected official, and the state's dislocated workers' unit. Advance notice gives workers and their families some transition time to adjust to the prospective loss of employment, to seek and obtain other jobs, and, if necessary, to enter skill training or retraining that will allow these workers to compete successfully in the job market.

What Triggers Notice?

Plant Closing: A covered employer must give notice if an employment site (or one or more facilities or operating units within an employment site) will be shut down, and the shutdown will result in an employment loss (as defined later) for 50 or more employees during any 30-day period.

Mass Layoff: A covered employer must give notice if there is to be a mass layoff which does not result from a plant closing, but which will result in an employment loss at the employment site during any 30-day period for 500 or more employees, or for 50–499 employees if they make up at least 33% of the employer's active workforce.

Sale of Businesses

In a situation involving the sale of part or all of a business, the following requirements apply:

(1) In each situation, there is always an employer (seller or buyer of the business) responsible for giving notice.

(2) If the sale, by a covered employer, results in a covered plant closing or mass layoffs, the required parties (employees and supervisors) must receive at least 60 days' notice.

(3) The seller of the business is responsible for providing notice of any covered plant closing or mass layoffs which occur up to and including the date/time of the sale.

(4) The buyer of the business is responsible for providing notice of any covered plant closing or mass layoffs which occur after the date/time of the sale.

(5) No notice is required if the sale does not result in a covered plant closing or mass layoff.

Employment Loss

The term "employment loss" means:

(1) An employment termination, other than a discharge for cause, voluntary departure, or retirement

(2) A layoff exceeding six months; or

(3) A reduction in an employee's hours of work of more than 50% in each month of any six-month period. Thus, a plant closing or mass layoff need not be permanent to trigger WARN.

Exceptions: An employee who refuses a transfer to a different employment site within a reasonable commuting distance does *not* experience employment loss. An employee who accepts a transfer outside this distance within 30 days after it is offered or within 30 days after the plant closing or mass layoff, whichever is later, does not experience an employment loss. In both cases, the transfer offer must be made before the closing or layoff, and there must be no more than a six-month break in employment, and the new job must not be deemed a constructive discharge. These transfer exceptions from the "employment loss" definition apply only if the closing or layoff results from the relocation or consolidation of part or all of the employer's business.[29]

---

29. www.dol.gov; www.doleta.gov.

Trade Adjustment Assistance

Trade Adjustment Assistance (TAA) is a federal program established under the **Trade Adjustment Assistance Reauthorization Act 2015.** It was designed to help trade-affected workers who have lost their jobs as a result of increased imports, or shifts in production to facilities outside the United States.

The TAA program offers a variety of benefits and reemployment services to help unemployed workers prepare for and obtain suitable employment. Workers may be eligible for training, job search and relocation allowances, income support, and other reemployment services.

The Department of Labor published a Final Rule implementing the Trade Adjustment Assistance Reauthorization Act of 2015 on August 21, 2020 (85 FR 51896). The Final Rule is codified at 20 CFR Part 618. Section 236 of the Trade Act of 1974, as amended, it establishes six criteria that trade-affected workers must meet prior to the approval of training under the TAA Program. These criteria are found in regulations at 20 CFR 618.610.

If the new criteria are met, to obtain TAA services and benefits, a group of three or more workers, their union, or other duly authorized representatives must file a petition. Petition forms may be obtained from the local State Employment Security Agency or from any agency designated by the state's governor to provide reemployment services under the TAA program. If certified, each worker in the group may then apply separately for individual services and benefits through their local One-Stop Career Center.[30]

Workplace Surveillance

If an employee is using a company computer, phone, etc., they should *not* expect privacy, they should expect monitoring. To ascertain if there is the tort of invasion of privacy against the employer for such monitoring, these questions must be addressed:

- Did the employee have a legitimate expectation of privacy? If the answer is yes, there may be an invasion of privacy.
- Did the employer give advanced notice of surveillance? If the answer is no, there may be an invasion of privacy.
- Was the monitoring work related? If the answer is no, there is a strong presumption of the tort of invasion of privacy.

---

30. www.doleta.gov.

- Was the monitoring done in a reasonable manner? If the answer is no, there is a likelihood of an invasion of privacy. There may even be the torts of intentional or negligent infliction of emotional distress.

As an employer, a printed form should be handed to each employee according to company policy in regard to monitoring and privacy. This form needs to be signed by the employee and kept in their personnel file.[31]

Chapter Summary

The hiring and firing of employees is complex and well regulated under various laws. It is important, when hiring, not to violate Title VII of the Civil Rights Act. Yet, if an employer can prove that there is a BFOQ that allows for violation of the Civil Rights Act, then the employee can be chosen under this altered employment job description.

A key agency in the pre-employment process is the EEOC. The EEOC limits what can and cannot be asked or done to a prospective employee. The ADA is another law that puts limitations on an employer discriminating against an employee that has one of the disabilities recognized under this Act. ADEA prohibits discrimination against workers who are aged 40 or over.

It is imperative that an employer know if an employee is eligible to work in the U.S. The completion of the I-9 and the secure keeping of these forms for the prescriptive time is required.

Minimum wages must be paid to employees under the Fair Labor Standards Act, even if the bulk of the employees' wages come from tips.

Sexual harassment is a major area of concern for employers. There must be zero tolerance of any type of harassment, including the creation of a hostile work environment.

The Family and Medical Leave Act protects employees' positions if they are required to take time to care for an ill family member, for birth or adoption of a child, or to care for their own serious health issues.

Employers must withhold and report all wages of the employee on a W-2. If the worker is an independent contractor, then a 1099 must be completed.

The Federal Unemployment Tax is designed to assist employees that have lost their jobs and Workers' Compensation is to assist employees that have been injured while on the job.

---

31. www.gao.gov.

To legally terminate an employee, the employee manual must be followed, and regular employee evaluations must be given.

WARN provides 60 days' notice to employees in the case of mass layoffs or plant closings.

Workplace surveillance is governed by the concept of the expectation of privacy on the part of the employee. If the employee is using company equipment, they usually can expect surveillance of its use.

Key Terms

Bona Fide Occupational Qualification
Title VII of the Civil Rights Act of 1964
Equal Employment Opportunity Commission
Defamation
Help Wanted-Male
Help Wanted-Female
Affirmative action
Narrowly tailored
Strict scrutiny
Americans with Disabilities Act
Reasonable accommodation
Undue hardship
Age Discrimination in Employment Act 1967
1986 Immigration Reform and Control Act
I-9
Fair Labor Standards Act
Minimum wage
Tip credit
Tip pooling
Employment at will
Union workers
National Labor Relations Act

National Labor Relations Board
Sexual harassment
Hostile or offensive work environment
Ombudsman
Statute of limitations
Zero tolerance
Family and Medical Leave Act
Employment Standards Administration Wage and Hour Division
U.S. Department of Labor
National Defense Authorization Act
W-2 Wage and Tax Statement
Internal Revenue Service
Social Security and Medicare
Totalization Agreements
Federal Unemployment Tax
Earned Income Tax Credit
Workers' compensation
Wrongful termination
Worker Adjustment and Retraining Notification Act
Trade Adjustment Assistance
Trade Adjustment Assistance Reauthorization Act 2015
Workplace surveillance

Chapter Eight

Trade Name, Trademark, Service Mark, and Trade Dress

Chapter Objectives

What is a trade name?

What is a trademark?

How does a business obtain a trademark?

What are the benefits of registering a trademark?

How can a business lose a trademark?

What are service marks?

What is trade dress?

What does the concept of trade dress do for a business?

What are trade secrets?

How are copyrights different from patents?

What is fair use?

Does anyone have to be paid if a hospitality business plays copyrighted music or movies?

Before a business establishes commercial relations with its customers, it needs to create an image for itself. Consumers must be able to distinguish between products that are offered in the marketplace. Without any distinguishing characteristics, customers will feel the nondescript business is interchangeable with any other business supplying the same type of goods or services. Part of a business's identity is the goodwill it establishes with customers, which includes its reputation for quality and value.

The four main devices used by businesses to establish a unique image and identity are **trade names**, **trademarks**, **service marks**, and **trade dress**.

Trade Names

A trade name is used by companies to distinguish a business from others in the same field. A trade name may be the actual name of a business owner or an assumed name, also known as a **DBA — Doing Business As**.

To establish trade name infringement by another business, the plaintiff business must establish it owned the right to operate the business under that particular trade name, and the defendant business violated this right by using a similar name in an attempt to pass their business off as the plaintiff's. The use of the "infringing" trade name must cause confusion in the mind of the consumer as to which business they are patronizing.

For example, it would *not* be confusing if a hospitality business selling sandwiches used the name Best Western and the hotel chain Best Western® used the same name. One business sells sandwiches and the other rents rooms.

The right to use a trade name is established by the first use of the name. Some states will require its registration as well. Thus, the first business that uses the name and files that particular trade name will acquire the right to use it against all other businesses in that particular state.

Some states do not allow registration of the trade name, and without the registration requirement, it is more difficult to prove ownership of the name. In this case, to establish infringement, the enterprise must show the business and trade name are inseparable in the mind of the public. The trade name will only be acquired in a non-registration state through public use.

Under federal law, a business may only acquire the rights to a trade name if it is used by a business to identify products or services and it is distinctive enough. Only then would the trade name be protected under the **Lanham Trademark Act**.[1] Under state laws, trade names are regulated by state statute and common-law doctrines.

---

1. 15 U.S.C. § 1051 et seq.

Trademarks

A trademark is a word, symbol, or phrase used to identify a particular manufacturer or seller's products; it distinguishes those items from the products of another.[2] For example, the ® following the name of a product shows it has been registered with the federal government as that company's trademark, e.g., Hilton Hotels®. Trademarks make it easier for consumers to quickly identify the source of a given good.

Trademarks are governed by state and federal law. Originally, state common law was the main source of protection for trademarks. However, in the late 1800s, the U.S. Congress enacted the first federal trademark law. Since then, federal trademark law has consistently expanded, taking over much of the ground initially covered by state common law. The main federal statute is the Lanham Act, which was enacted in 1946 and was most recently updated on December 27, 2020, under the Trademark Modernization Act of 2020 (TMA). The TMA becomes effective one year after its signature into law—December 2021. The TMA introduces significant amendments to the Lanham Act designed to modernize trademark examination procedures and combat the increasing numbers of trademark registrations covering marks not used in commerce.[3]

In order to serve as a trademark, a mark must be *distinctive*—that is, it must be capable of identifying the source of a particular good. In determining distinctiveness, the courts group trademarks into four categories based on the relationship between the mark and the underlying product:

(1) Arbitrary or fanciful
(2) Suggestive
(3) Descriptive
(4) Generic

Arbitrary Marks

An arbitrary or fanciful mark is a mark that bears no logical relationship to the underlying product. For example, Applebee's® and TGIF® bear no inherent relationship to the underlying product of being a restaurant. Arbitrary or fanciful marks are inherently distinctive—i.e., capable of identifying an underlying product—and are given a high degree of protection.

---

2. 15 U.S.C. §1127.
3. 15 U.S.C. §1051 et seq.

Suggestive Marks

A suggestive mark is a mark that evokes or suggests a characteristic of the underlying good. For example, Panera Bread® is suggestive of a restaurant, but does not specifically describe the underlying product. Some exercise of imagination is needed to associate the word with the underlying product. At the same time, however, the word is not totally unrelated to the underlying product. Like arbitrary or fanciful marks, suggestive marks are inherently distinctive and are given a high degree of protection.

Descriptive Marks

A descriptive mark acquires secondary meaning when the consuming public primarily associates that mark with a particular producer, rather than the underlying product. Thus, for example, the term Holiday Inn® has acquired a secondary meaning because the consuming public associates that term with a particular provider of hotel services, and not with hotel services in general. The public need not be able to identify the specific producer, only that a product or service comes from a single producer. When trying to determine whether a given term has acquired a secondary meaning, courts will often look to the following factors:

- The amount and manner of advertising using the mark
- The volume of sales associated with the mark
- The length and manner of the mark's use
- How consumers understand the mark's usage[4]

Generic Marks

Generic marks are marks that describe the general category in which the underlying product belongs. For example, the words "Hotel" and "Restaurant" are generic terms, and they receive no protection under trademark law. Under some circumstances, terms that are not originally generic can become generic over time. For example, aspirin, thermos, and dry ice were originally trademarks. The owner of these trademarks allowed these marks to be used in a generic sense; in other words, all acetylsalicylic acid was called aspirin, all vacuum flask bottles were called thermos, and all frozen

---

4. www.uspto.gov.

carbon dioxide became dry ice. Once this happened, these marks lost their trademark protection.

How to Acquire a Trademark

In the U.S., trademark protection is granted only to marks that are used to identify and distinguish goods or services in commerce. This typically occurs when a mark is used in conjunction with the actual sale of goods or services. So, by being the first to use the mark in commerce, this protects the mark. Is it beneficial to register a trademark with the **U.S. Patent and Trademark Office** (PTO)? Yes, this further establishes the trademark holder's legal claim to it, and establishes a date of registration.[5]

Descriptive marks only qualify for registration and protection after they have acquired a secondary meaning. Until they do, they do not qualify for trademark protection.

Applications for trademark registration are subject to approval by the Patent and Trademark Office. A registration may be rejected if the mark is generic, or if it is a descriptive mark that has not acquired a secondary meaning. The mark cannot be immoral or scandalous. Certain geographic marks may not be able to be trademarked, e.g., San Francisco, or marks that are likely to cause confusion with an existing mark.[6]

Some states have their own registration systems under state trademark law. If a trademark is only registered in the state where one is doing business, then only state protection is given to the mark.

Benefits of Trademark Registration

Federal registration gives the party holding the trademark the right to use the mark nationwide. It is constructive notice that the mark is owned by the person that registered it. This enables the trademark holder to bring an infringement suit in federal court.[7]

A company or a person has the right to use a trademark prior to filing registration with the USPTO. Then the "TM" (trademark) or "SM" (service mark—see below) designations are used to alert the public to a claim of ownership.

However, the federal registration symbol "®" may *only* be used after the USPTO actually registers a mark—not while an application is pending.

---

5. 15 U.S.C. § 1127(a).
6. 15 U.S.C. § 1052.
7. 15 U.S.C. § 1121.

Service Marks

A service mark is the same as a trademark except that it identifies and distinguishes the source of a service rather than a product. The terms "trademark" and "mark" are commonly used to refer to both trademarks and service marks.

For example, a theme park may be called Texas Cowboy® which would be a service mark since a theme park is a service, not a product; while the Texas Cowboy Burger®, the hamburger they sell, would hold a trademark.[8]

Trade Dress

Trade dress is a product or business physical appearance, such as size, shape, color, design, and texture. This may refer to the product or business itself or its packaging, wrapping, labeling, presentation, or advertisement method.

There is potential trade dress infringement if the trade dress of two businesses is sufficiently similar to *likely* cause confusion among the consuming public. Restaurants many times either accidentally or purposely copy each other's décor, wait staff uniforms, or architectural style. If this emulation becomes too similar, then one business usually sues the other. The victor in this suit will be the restaurant with the more established and recognized trade dress. The remedies for trade dress infringement include **injunctive relief** — thus the restaurant held infringing would be restrained from using the offending trade dress, or there may be **monetary damages** awarded — the winning restaurant would be given compensation for any losses suffered from the infringement.

At the federal level, trade dress infringement is governed primarily by the Lanham Trademark Act (15 U.S.C.A. § 1051 et seq.); at the state level, it is governed by intellectual property statutes and common-law doctrines. Both state and federal laws prohibit businesses from duplicating, imitating, or appropriating a competitor's trade dress in order to pass off their merchandise to unwary consumers.

To establish a claim for trade dress infringement, a company must demonstrate the distinctiveness of its product's appearance. Trade dress will not receive protection from infringement unless it is unique, unusual, or widely

---

8. www.uspto.gov.

recognized by the public. Courts have found a variety of trade dress to be distinctive, including waitress uniform stitching, linen patterns, and the interior and exterior features of commercial establishments. In certain contexts, courts may find that distinctive color combinations are protected from infringement, as when a federal court found the silver, blue, and white foiled wrapping in which Klondike® ice cream bars are packaged to be part of an identifiable trade dress.[9]

Goods that are packaged or promoted in an ordinary, unremarkable, or generic fashion normally receive no legal protection under the law of trade dress. Many times in a casual dining restaurant, one will see the wait staff in black pants, white shirts, and ordinary ties. This is a rather ordinary uniform that would be difficult to protect as trade dress.

The law of trade dress serves four purposes:

- First, the law seeks to protect the economic, intellectual, and creative investments made by businesses in distinguishing their products.
- Second, the law seeks to preserve the good will and reputation that are often associated with the trade dress of a particular business and its merchandise.
- Third, the law seeks to promote clarity and stability in the marketplace by encouraging consumers to rely on a business's trade dress when evaluating the quality of a product.
- Fourth, the law seeks to increase competition by requiring businesses to associate their own trade dress with the value and quality of the goods they sell.

Under state and federal law, it is advantageous for businesses to register their trademarks, service marks, and trade names with the government. Conversely, trade dress has no formal registration requirements and receives legal protection simply by being distinctive and recognizable. Like unregistered trademarks, an unregistered trade dress is entitled to protection if it is distinctive, either inherently or through an acquired distinctiveness (or secondary meaning). If an unregistered trade dress is inherently distinctive, there is no need to prove that the trade dress has a secondary meaning; if the trade dress is descriptive, it is protectable upon a showing of secondary meaning; and if it is generic, it is not entitled to protection.

---

9. *AmBrit v. Kraft*, 812 F.2d 1531 (11th Cir. 1986).

Trade Secrets

The intangible assets of a business include not only its trade name and other identifying devices but also its inventions, creative works, and artistic efforts. These are broadly defined as **trade secrets**. This body of commercial information may consist of any formula (McDonald's® secret sauce), pattern, process, program, tool, technique, mechanism or compound that provides a business with the opportunity to gain advantage over competitors. Although a trade secret is not patented or copyrighted, it is entrusted only to a select group of people. The law of **unfair competition** awards individuals and businesses property rights in any valuable trade information they discover and attempt to keep secret through reasonable steps.

A trade secret:

- Is information that has either actual or potential independent economic value by virtue of not being generally known,
- Has value to others who cannot legitimately obtain the information, and
- Is subject to reasonable efforts to maintain its secrecy.

All three elements are required; if any element ceases to exist, then the trade secret will also cease to exist. Otherwise, there is no limit on the amount of time a trade secret is protected.

The owner of a trade secret is entitled to its exclusive use and enjoyment. A trade secret is valuable not only because it enables a company to gain advantage over a competitor, but also because it may be sold or licensed like any other property right. In contrast, commercial information that is revealed to the public, or at least to a competitor, retains limited commercial value. Consequently, courts vigilantly protect trade secrets from disclosure, appropriation, and theft. Businesses or opportunistic members of the public may be held liable for any economic injuries that result from their theft of a trade secret. Employees may be held liable for disclosing their employer's trade secrets, even if the disclosure occurs after the employment relationship has ended.[10]

The **Defend Trade Secrets Act of 2016 (DTSA)** amended the Economic Espionage Act to establish a private civil cause of action for the misappropriation of a trade secret. This cause of action provides trade secret owners with a uni-

---

10. *Kewanee Oil Company v. Bicron Corp.*, 416 U.S. 470 (1990).

form, reliable, and predictable way to protect their valuable trade secrets anywhere in the country. The DTSA does not preempt existing state trade secret law, thus giving trade secret owners the option of state or federal venues.

U.S. courts can protect a trade secret by (a) ordering that the misappropriation stop, (b) that the secret be protected from pubic exposure, and (c) in extraordinary circumstances, ordering the seizure of the misappropriated trade secret. At the conclusion of a trade secret case, courts can award damages, court costs, reasonable attorneys' fees and a permanent injunction, if warranted.

Copyrights versus Patents

Copyright law gives individuals and businesses the exclusive rights to any original works they create, including movies, books, musical scores, sound recordings, dramatic creations, and pantomimes. **Patent law** gives individuals and businesses the right to exclude all others from making, using, and selling specific types of inventions, such as mechanical devices, manufacturing processes, chemical formulas, and electrical equipment.

Federal law grants these exclusive property rights in exchange for full public disclosure of an original work or invention. The inventor or author receives complete legal protection for their intellectual efforts, while the public obtains valuable information that can be used to make life easier, healthier, or more pleasant.

Like the law of trade secrets, patent and copyright law offer protection to individuals and businesses that have invested considerable resources in creating something useful or valuable and wish to exploit that investment commercially. Unlike trade secrets, which may be protected indefinitely, patents and copyrights are protected only for a finite period of time. Applications for copyrights are governed by the Copyrights Act (17 U.S.C.A. §401), and patent applications are governed by the Patent Act (35 U.S.C.A. §1).

Copyrights

Copyrights are a group of exclusive rights granted by the federal government. The Congress of the United States has the power, "To promote the progress of science and useful arts, by securing for limited times to authors and inventors the exclusive right to their respective writings and discoveries." This is known as the Intellectual Property Clause.[11]

---

11. U.S. Constitution Article I, section 8, Clause 8.

The issuance of a copyright gives the owner of the copyright the right to reproduce the copyrighted work. It means only the owner of the copyright can produce *derivative* works — those works that are based on the original copyrighted material.

Copyright protection is automatic. Once the work is completed and fixed, in a **tangible medium of expression**, the creator of the work obtains a common law copyright whether or not they actually register the work with the federal government.

There is no longer any need to attach the copyright symbol to establish a copyright, although it is suggested to do so.[12] The usual notice is "Copyright © 2022 by the name of the creator of the work, or other holder of the copyright such as a publishing house or news organization." If no copyright notice were included on the work, a person using the work may be unaware the work is copyrighted. The person may think the work is in the **public domain** — it is available for anyone to use. Of course, once an individual is notified, there is a copyright on the material, they are no longer an innocent party to infringement. To prove copyright infringement, the copyright holder must show the new work is substantially similar to the original work, the copyright is still in force, and the person infringing on the work had violated the copyright.[13]

Following the Copyright Act of 1976, copyrights would last for the life of the author plus fifty (50) years. In 1998, the **Sonny Bono Copyright Term Extension Act (CTEA)** extended copyright protection to the duration of the author's life plus *seventy* (70) years, or ninety-five years for works made for hire, dated from the year of its first publication or a term of 120 years from the year of its creation, whichever expires first. The CTEA applies to existing as well as future copyrights. The practical result of this was to prevent a number of works, beginning with those published in 1923, from entering the public domain in 1998, and beyond.[14] This law is sometimes cited as the "**Mickey Mouse® Act.**" Why? The copyright on Mickey® was about to expire under the former copyright law. The CTEA allowed Disney® to maintain control over this very valuable property. Under the CTEA, works made in 1923 or afterwards that were still protected by copyright in 1998, would not enter the public domain until January 1, 2019, or later. Mickey Mouse® specifically, having first appeared in 1928, will be a public domain work in 2024, or afterward, depending on the date of the product's creation. Will Mickey® be saved again? Only time will tell.

---

12. Berne Convention Implementation Act of 1988, signed by the United States March 1, 1989.

13. www.copyright.gov.

14. Public Law 105-298, 112 Stat. 2827.

Once a work has been copyrighted, anyone that copies it, uses it for a derivative work, displays the work to the public as their own, or performs the work without the copyright holder's permission, has potentially committed copyright infringement. The only exception to this would be what is called the **fair use** of the material.

Fair Use

Federal courts have been using the common law form of fair use since the mid-1800s, but the 1976 Copyright Act, section 107, codified this defense to copyright infringement. Fair use is a legal doctrine that recognizes that scholarly quoting of brief passages or use of a work for teaching purposes would not dilute the economic returns of the copyright holder, and thus should be a defense of copyright infringement. What fair use allows is the use of a copyrighted work for criticism, teaching, scholarship, research, or the reporting of the news.[15]

How Does Copyright Law Affect the Hospitality Industry?

Every time a restaurant or hotel plays music, they need to pay to do so. This is not just paying the subscription to SiriusXM® for streaming music but paying for the right to use it with the **music licensing societies**.

Music Licensing Societies

A difficult issue regarding royalties and the use of copyrighted music is how does a composer, lyricist, and music publisher get a licensing fee from everyone performing a copyrighted song? **ASCAP—The American Society of Composers, Authors, and Publishers, BMI—Broadcast Music Incorporated**, and **SESAC—Society of European Stage Authors and Composers**, were created to solve this problem. These organizations keep track of whose music is being played. They then collect royalties from restaurants, nightclubs, hotels, and other businesses that play copyrighted music. Even churches, schools, and non-profits may have to pay licensing fees unless they are exempted under section 110 of the Copyright Act.[16]

---

15. www.copyright.gov.
16. 17 U.S.C § 110.

Music licensing societies sell a **blanket license**, which allows a music user, such as a hotel or restaurant, to perform any of the groups' copyrighted works, as much or as little as they wish. Licensees pay an annual fee — from $500 up. The license saves the hospitality business from having to keep track of all the music used, and avoids having to negotiate licenses with all the copyright holders. It also prevents inadvertent copyright infringement on ASCAP's, SESAC's, and BMI's members.

There are also "per program" licenses. These authorize a hospitality business to use all the works under the groups' copyright, but the hospitality business will have to keep track of all the music used. A complication to this form of license is that a music user must get rights to any music used in programs *not* covered under the "per program" license. The main advantage of the "per program" license is, it is less expensive than the blanket license. When fees have been collected under either the blanket or per program license, BMI, SESAC, and ASCAP then distribute these amounts to the copyright holders they represent.[17]

Motion Picture Licensing Societies

Another area of copyright concern, especially with hotels, is the showing of motion pictures and other audiovisual works. If these are not being used for personal, private, or home use, a separate license that authorizes the public performance of that work must be obtained.[18]

Even if a motion picture is shown in a "semi-public" place such as a lodge, golf clubhouse, or summer camp, this is considered a public performance and subject to copyright control.[19]

Enter the **Motion Picture Licensing Corporation (MPLC)**. This organization licenses the public performance of motion pictures. The MPLC represents 1,000 producers and distributors from major Hollywood studios to independent and foreign producers, and licenses in over 40 countries worldwide.[20]

There are also **Criterion Pictures USA** and **Swank Motion Pictures**; both are suppliers of rental non-theatrical (not in theaters) feature entertainment movies that are licensed for public performance in the United States.[21]

Large hotel chains may circumvent these motion picture societies by licensing directly with the studio for a motion picture's public use.

---

17. www.bmi.com; www.sesac.com; www.ascap.com.
18. 17 U.S.C § 202.
19. Senate Report No. 94-473, page 60; House Report No. 94-1476, page 64.
20. www.mplc.org.
21. www.swank.com; www.criterionpicusa.com.

Non-Compliance with Copyright Law

What if the hospitality business violates copyright law? Non-compliance with the Copyright Act is considered infringement and carries steep and significant penalties for both the exhibitor and anyone that contributes to the infringing conduct. Unlicensed public performances are federal violations and can be subject to a $150,000 penalty per exhibition.[22]

Chapter Summary

There are four main ways a business can create a public image of itself. These are trade names, trademarks, service marks, and trade dress.

A trade name identifies the company and distinguishes it from other companies in the same type of business. If another company infringes on the use of a trade name, and because its use of this trade name confuses the public into thinking it is another business, then the business that first used the trade name could sue the imposter company.

Trademarks are words, symbols, or phrases that identify a particular manufacturer or seller's products and distinguish them from the products of another. The mark must be distinctive to be protected. They are acquired when a business is the first to use the mark in commerce. By registering a trademark, it allows the holder to bring an infringement suit in federal court.

Service marks are the same as trademarks except these are used for services — not products.

Trade dress is a product's or business's physical appearance, e.g., its size, shape, color, design, and texture. In the hospitality industry, this could include the architectural design of a building or the uniforms of the wait staff.

Intangible assets of a business are its trade secrets. These include its inventions, creative works, and ingredients in a recipe. Although they cannot be patented or copyrighted, if the owner of the trade secret wants to keep them secret, the owner is still entitled to their exclusive use and enjoyment.

Copyrights give a business the exclusive right to use and profit from creative works they produce, including movies, books, music, dramatic works, brochures, or any other product that is copyrightable. If another business or person wishes to use a copyrighted work, and this use does not come under the fair use doctrine, then the user of the copyrighted material will have to pay the holder of the copyright, royalties.

---

22. www.copyright.gov.

Patents give a patent holding business the right to exclude all others from using, making, or selling a product that infringes on the business's patented invention. For a business to use another's patent, they will have to pay the patent holder an agreed upon license fee.

Key Terms

Trade names
Lanham Trademark Act
Trademarks
Service marks
Trade dress
DBA — Doing Business As
U.S. Patent and Trademark Office
Injunctive relief
Monetary damages
Trade secrets
Unfair competition
Defend Trade Secrets Act of 2016
   (DTSA)
Copyright law
Patent law
Tangible medium of expression
Public domain

Sonny Bono Copyright Term Extension Act
Mickey Mouse® Act
Fair use
Music licensing societies
ASCAP — The American Society of Composers, Authors, and Publishers
BMI — Broadcast Music Incorporated
SESAC — Society of European Stage Authors and Composers
Blanket license
Motion Picture Licensing Corporation
Criterion Pictures USA
Swank Motion Pictures

Chapter Nine

Safety and Security of Guests and Their Property

Chapter Objectives

What are the key points for guest safety and security?

What control does the federal government have over hotels?

What is an innkeeper's duty to receive guests?

How should guest information be kept?

How can guests' privacy be assured in their rooms?

How should the guest reservation policy be set?

When can a guest be evicted?

What are innkeepers' liens?

What is an innkeeper's duty to a non-guest?

Is there a duty to provide safe premises?

What responsibility does an innkeeper have for guests' personal property?

What is a bailment?

What is mislaid, lost, and abandoned property?

There have been special concerns regarding the safety and security of guests since hospitality businesses first opened their properties to the public at large.

Hotels have a long history as "**innkeepers**." As innkeepers, under **common law**, places of accommodation were held to a very high standard. Weary travelers that reached wayside inns as night approached could not be arbitrarily turned away to face potential robbers on the roads. There were laws put in place that regulated prices and the adequacy of the quarters furnished. Most modern innkeeper's laws are based on these historic considerations.

Key Points as to Safety and Security of Guests

- Hotels are not liable for every accident or loss that occurs on the premises, nor do they insure the absolute safety of every guest.
- Hotels have a general duty to exercise "**reasonable care**" for the safety and security of their guests.
- Hotels have a general duty to reasonably protect guests from harm caused by other guests or non-guests.
- Hotels have an affirmative duty to make the premises reasonably safe for their guests. This obligation includes a twofold duty either to correct a hazard or warn of its existence. The hotel must not only address visible hazards but must also make apparent hidden dangers or hazards.
- Hotels are not liable for harm to person or property unless "fault" can be established against the hotel.
- Hotels may be "vicariously liable" for the **negligence** of their employees.
- Hotels are generally liable for damages if they cannot honor a confirmed reservation because of "overbooking."
- Hotels may generally sue for damages or retain deposits if confirmed reservations are not honored by prospective guests.
- Hotels may generally evict registered guests for a variety of well-established reasons (see below).
- Hotels may retain personal possessions of evicted guests as security for room charges.
- Hotels are generally not required to have lifeguards on duty at the hotel's swimming pools, except by state statute. However, conspicuous "No Lifeguard" warning signs are minimally required, and most states statutes require lifesaving equipment in the pool area, such as

poles to reach a swimmer in trouble and some sort of flotation device that is readily available.

- Hotels are generally not liable for valuables that are not secured in the hotel safe if a conspicuous notice is posted of the availability of a safe or safe deposit box. If there is liability for valuables under state statute, there is generally a limitation on the amount unless some sort of gross negligence on the part of the hotel can be proven by the guest.
- Hotels are generally not liable for harm to guests caused by criminal acts of others unless fault on the part of the hotel is established.

Federal Government Authority over Hotels

The federal government has limited involvement in the private relationships between hotels and guests, although there are three areas where the federal government can step in.

- Under Title 42 of the U.S. Code, Chapter 21, Sub-chapter II (Public Accommodations) prohibits discrimination under the **Civil Rights Act of 1964** applicable to "any inn, hotel, motel, or other establishment which provides lodging for transient guests."
- Under a phase-in provision, hotels must meet the requirements of the **Americans with Disabilities Act (ADA)**; any new or renovated hotel facility must comply with the Act's mandates for public access and/or removal of physical barriers.
- The **Hotel and Motel Fire Safety Act of 1990** (as amended in 1996) imposes additional safety requirements upon hotel facilities above and beyond those found in local building codes.[1]

The Federal Civil Rights Act guarantees all people the right to "full and equal enjoyment of the goods, services, facilities, privileges, advantages, and accommodations of any place of public accommodation, without discrimination or segregation on the ground of race, color, religion, or national origin."[2]

---

1. www.usfa.fema.gov.
2. www.archives.gov.

States are free to enact their own statutes regarding innkeepers' rights and duties, so long as they do not abridge federal rights; and most states have done so.

Americans with Disabilities Act (ADA)

The right to public accommodation is guaranteed to disabled citizens under the Americans with Disabilities Act, which precludes discrimination by businesses on the basis of disability.

The 1991 ADA standards apply to all hotels that began construction before March 15, 2012, provided that no alterations to guest rooms have taken place since that date. For all hotels built or which have undergone alterations to accessible guest rooms on or after March 15, 2012, the 2010 ADA standards apply.

To meet these requirements, lodging facilities must comply with certain regulations published by the **Justice Department**. The regulations contain detailed architectural requirements called the **ADA Standards for Accessible Design** (Standards), 28 C.F.R. pt. 36, Appendix A.

The Standards are designed to ensure accessibility for individuals with a wide variety of different disabilities, such as people who are blind or have low vision, people who are deaf or hard of hearing, people with limited use of hands or arms, individuals with mobility impairments who use canes, crutches, braces or walkers, people who use wheelchairs, and people who have a combination of disabilities. Thus, the Standards include architectural requirements that address the different needs of people with each of these types of disabilities.

For example, the Standards include requirements for **Braille** and raised letter signs and cane-detectable warnings of safety hazards for people who are blind or have low vision. The Standards require lodging facilities to install visual fire alarms and to have rooms that are equipped for people who are deaf or hard of hearing. The Standards require door hardware, heating and air conditioning controls, and faucet controls that do *not* require tight pinching, twisting, or grasping for people with limited use of hands or arms. For people who use mobility aids because they cannot walk or have problems walking or climbing stairs, the Standards require there be ways of traveling throughout the facility that do not use steps, stairs, or other abrupt level changes. The Standards also require doors with 32 inches of clear passage width and ramps and curb cuts for people who use wheelchairs, crutches, and other mobility aids.

Lodging facilities must comply with all the requirements in the Standards that are applicable. A difference in inches or, in some cases, a difference of a fraction of an inch can pose a serious safety hazard or result in the denial of access for persons with disabilities, full compliance with the Standards is essential.[3]

Duty to Receive Guests

The very first and most important "public duty" of the hotel is the duty to receive guests. This duty is not absolute and is subject to lawful excuses. Hotels may generally deny accommodations to a prospective guest for the following reasons:

- If the person is unwilling or unable to pay for a room or other establishment privileges
- If the person is visibly under the influence of alcohol or other drugs, or creating a public nuisance
- If the person's use of a room or accommodation would violate the facility's maximum capacity
- If the innkeeper reasonably believes the person will use the room or facility for an unlawful purpose, e.g., prostitution or drug sales
- If the innkeeper reasonably believes the person will bring in something that would create an unreasonable danger or risk to others, e.g., explosives or wild animals

Privacy of Guest Information

In November 2009, the Washington Supreme Court ruled that people do not give up their right to privacy when they check into a hotel.

In the case of *State v. Jorden* No 76800-5, the court overturned the conviction of a man arrested following a police sweep of motel guest registries in Lakewood, Washington. The court's opinion agreed with a (***amicus curiae***) friend-of-the-court brief filed by the **ACLU** of Washington, which argued that searching hotel registries without suspicion of a crime violates privacy guarantees of the Washington Constitution.

"This is a great victory for privacy rights in Washington State," said Doug Klunder, director of the ACLU-WA's Privacy Project, and author of the amicus brief in the case. "This decision ensures that people can stay in a hotel without

---

3. www.ada.gov.

worrying that their government is collecting information about their personal lives, their travel patterns, or the company they keep."

Under the "Lakewood Crime-Free Hotel Motel Program," the Pierce County Sheriff's Department routinely viewed the guest registries at local hotels, checking names for outstanding warrants. On March 15, 2003, deputies examined the registry at the Golden Lion Motel. After finding outstanding warrants for Timothy Jorden, they entered his room, found drugs, and arrested him. A trial court convicted Jorden, and his conviction was upheld by the state court of appeals.

The ACLU brief said police violated Jorden's right to privacy under the Washington Constitution. The ACLU asserted that hotel registration records are private, and police may not access them without reasonable suspicion of a crime. Giving police blanket access to hotel records could allow the government to learn about all guests' personal information, not just outstanding warrants.

"Guest registrations at a hotel adjacent to a convention center will have a high correlation with attendees of that convention, revealing the guest's profession, hobbies or political leanings," wrote Klunder in the ACLU brief. "Even details of intimate association can be determined from guest registers by examining which people are registered in the same or adjacent rooms."

Agreeing, the court's majority opinion said, "The information contained in a motel registry — including one's whereabouts at the motel — is a private affair under our state constitution, and a government trespass into such information is a search ... A random, suspicionless search is a fishing expedition, and we have indicated displeasure with such practices on many occasions."[4]

Guest Privacy within Their Rooms

When Can a Hotel Employee Enter a Guest's Room without Permission from the Guest?

Generally, if a guest is using their hotel room in an ordinary manner, then there is a limited right of privacy in the room. However, if there is suspicion on the part of the hotel that the room is being used for illegal acts, then the hotel management may enter. Under no circumstances can the hotel authorize

---

4. www.aclu-wa.org/cases/state-v-jorden.

the *police* to conduct a search of the guest's room without the guest's consent or without a proper search warrant.

Other Legitimate Reasons Why a Hotel Employee May Enter a Room

- To stop a guest from disturbing other guests or from destroying the hotel property
- To carry out housekeeping duties
- To perform necessary maintenance

Can the Hotel Disclose Which Room a Guest Is Staying In?

No. It is a violation of the right of privacy if the hotel discloses to another person which room a guest is staying in.

Guest Reservations

Most hotels have well-established policies for making, confirming, and holding reservations placed by prospective guests. A confirmed reservation generally constitutes a binding agreement (in essence, a "reservation contract") between the hotel and prospective guest. If the guest fails to use the reservation, the hotel is generally entitled to damages. On the other hand, if the hotel breaches a reservation contract, the guest can sue the hotel for damages. If the hotel actually has accommodations available but fails to supply them as agreed, it may be liable for breach of its duties as an innkeeper.

Hotel overbooking often presents problems, and many hotels, especially large hotel chains have adopted a pledge that requires their assistance in securing comparable accommodations if, for any reason, a room should not be available for a patron who holds a valid, confirmed reservation. A few states have enacted legislation that addresses hotel overbooking.

Florida, for example, makes the hotel responsible for "every effort" to find alternate accommodations and up to a $500 fine for each guest turned away because of over-booking.[5]

---

5. Florida Statutes Annotated, §509 et seq.

Right to Evict Persons
Admitted as Guests

Hotels may generally evict a transient guest and keep the room rental payment, despite the **eviction**, for the following reasons:

- Disorderly conduct
- Nonpayment
- Using the premises for an unlawful purpose or act
- Bringing property onto the premises that may be dangerous for others
- Failing to register as a guest
- Using false pretenses to obtain accommodations
- Being a minor unaccompanied by an adult registered guest
- Violating federal, state, or local hotel laws or regulations
- Violating a conspicuously posted hotel or motel rule
- Failing to vacate a room at the agreed checkout time
- (See Chapter Six for transient versus tenant guest duties.)

Innkeeper's Liens

Many states have retained the common law right of an "**innkeeper's lien**." If a hotel has properly evicted a guest, or if a guest refuses to leave or pay, the hotel may take into its possession the personal property of the guest and hold it as security for hotel charges. Innkeeper's liens differ from other liens in that the hotel need not take physical possession of the guest's personal property, but may simply prevent its removal from the hotel until the debt is satisfied. Hotels cannot sell the goods or personal property until there has been a final judgment in an action to recover charges.

Duty to Persons Who
Are Not Guests

A person who is not a guest (or intends immediately to become a guest) generally has no right to enter or remain on the premises over the objection of the hotel. Nor can a non-guest use a public area of the premises, such as lobbies or hallways, without the consent of the hotel. Despite the fact that the hotel has held itself out to the public with an invitation to enter and seek out accommodations, any person who enters without the intention of accepting an invitation for accommodation remains on the premises only with consent of the hotel.

A widely acknowledged exception to this general rule is that a non-guest or stranger coming to the hotel at the request or invitation of an existing guest has a right to enter the premises for that purpose; otherwise, the guest would be unfairly deprived of a privilege necessary for his or her comfort while at the hotel. However, the hotel may revoke such permission if the non-guest engages in conduct which would justify his or her eviction.

There is no duty to permit non-guests into the hotel public areas for the purpose of soliciting business from hotel guests. On the contrary, there is a duty to protect guests from bothersome or troublesome non-guests. Accordingly, most hotels have posted notices that prohibit solicitation of any kind on the premises.

Invitees versus Licensees versus Trespassers

The legal theory of "premises liability" holds owners and occupiers of property legally responsible for accidents and injuries that occur on that property. The kinds of incidents that give rise to premises liability claims can range from a **slip and fall** on a sidewalk to an injury suffered on an amusement park ride.

The liability of owners and occupiers of property will vary depending on the legal rules and principles in place in the state where the premises liability injury occurred. In some states, the court will focus on the status of the injured visitor in determining the liability of the owner or occupier. In other states, the focus will be on the condition of the property and the activities of both the owner and visitor.

In states that focus only on the status of the visitor to the property, there are generally four different labels that may apply: **invitee, social guest, licensee, or trespasser**.

An *invitee* is someone who is invited onto the property of another, such as a customer in a store. This invitation usually implies the property owner/possessor has taken reasonable steps to assure the safety of the premises.

A *licensee* enters a property for his or her own purpose, or as a social guest, and is present at the consent of the owner.

Finally, a *trespasser* enters without any right whatsoever to do so.

In many states that look to the legal status of the injured person, the trend is toward distinguishing only between those lawfully on the property (invitees, social guests, licensees) and those on the property unlawfully (trespassers). If the person is on the hotel property unlawfully then, except in a few states, there is no duty of care owed to that person. Remember a licensee or invitee becomes a trespasser if they show they have no intention of doing business with the hotel or other hospitality venue, or if the licensee or invitee commits a crime while on the premises.[6]

Condition of the Property and Nature of Activities

In states where consideration is given to the condition of the property and the activities of the owner and visitor, a uniform standard of care is applied to both invitees and licensees. This uniform standard requires the exercise of reasonable care for the safety of the visitor. In order to satisfy the reasonableness standard owed to invitees and/or licensees, an owner has a continuing duty to inspect the property in order to identify dangerous conditions and either repair them or post warnings as appropriate. An owner can be found liable if he or she has knowledge of a dangerous condition, fails to take reasonable steps to fix or warn of that condition, and a visitor (invitee and/or licensee) suffers an injury as a result.

Determining whether the standard of reasonableness required by an owner toward licensees (and in some states, both licensees and invitees) has been met requires an examination of numerous factors, including:

- Circumstances under which the visitor enters the property
- Use to which the property is put
- Foreseeability of the accident or injury that occurred
- Reasonableness of the owner/possessor's effort to repair or warn of a dangerous condition

Trespassers on Property

With respect to trespassers, if the owner knows that it is likely trespassers will enter the property; he or she may be charged with a duty to give reasonable warning to prevent injury. This requirement applies only with respect to artificial conditions that the owner has created or maintains and knows may be likely to cause serious injury or death, e.g., a pond or lake that is not fenced. However, even in cases where there is a dangerous artificial condition, a

---

6. Towers-Romero, S. *Essentials of Florida Real Estate Law,* 2007.

landowner does not necessarily need to give warning to potential trespassers if the condition is obvious.

Children on Property

A landowner's duty to warn is different with respect to children who are *not* authorized to be on property. A property owner/possessor must give warning if he or she knows (or should know) that children are likely to be on the premises, and that a dangerous condition on the premises is likely to cause serious bodily injury or death. In order to find liability, the owner/possessor's need to maintain the dangerous condition, and the burden to the owner/possessor, of eliminating it must be low when compared with the potential risk to children. Furthermore, the owner/possessor must have failed to exercise reasonable care to eliminate the danger of protecting children coming on to the property.

Comparative Fault

One of the most commonly used limitations on a property owner/possessor's liability is the argument that the injured person was partially at fault for what happened. A visitor has a duty, in most cases, to exercise reasonable care for his or her own safety. Where that care is not exercised appropriately, the plaintiff's recovery may be limited or reduced by his or her own negligence. Most states adhere to a "**comparative fault**" system in personal injury cases, meaning that an injured person's legal damages will be reduced by a percentage that is equivalent to his or her fault for the incident. So, if it is decided that an injured person was 25% liable for an accident, and the total damages were $10,000, he or she would receive only $7,500.

Duty to Provide Safe Premises

The duty of a hotel to provide safe premises is based on the common-law duty owed to business and social invitees of an establishment. Under common law, hotels must exercise reasonable care for the safety of their guests. Hotels may be found negligent if they knew or should have known upon reasonable inspection of the existence of a danger or hazard and failed to take action to correct it and/or warn guests about it. Accordingly, hotels have an affirmative duty to inspect and seek out hazards that may not be readily apparent, seen or appreciated by patrons and guests. If the risk of harm or damage was foreseeable, and the hotel failed to exercise reasonable care to either eliminate the risk or warn guests of its existence, the hotel may be liable for any resulting harm or damage caused by its negligence ("**proximate cause**").

However, the law does not protect hotel guests from their own negligence. An "open and obvious" hazard, such as a bathroom tile floor that becomes slippery when wet after reasonable use, is not a basis for liability. On the other hand, if a poorly maintained bathroom fixture results in standing water on the tile floor, and an unsuspecting guest enters the bathroom and slips on the tile, the hotel would most likely be liable for damages. Likewise, standing water on any floor in the hotel, if left standing beyond a *reasonable time* for management to have detected and eliminated it, may result in liability for the hotel.

Hotel swimming pools are a major topic for litigation. It is important that "**NO DIVING**" signs are posted in highly visible areas. There is no minimum requirement regarding the number or nature of posted warnings, but a hotel's diving-accident history is critical in establishing what would be considered "adequate," "sufficient," or "satisfactory" posted warnings in any legal matter. Statutes in most states do not require the presence of lifeguards at hotel pools. However, "**NO LIFEGUARD**" warnings should be posted and visible from all angles of the pool, and basic rescue equipment must be maintained and available poolside.

Harm or Damage Caused by Other Guests

Hotels have an affirmative duty to exercise reasonable care for the safety and security of their patrons. This obligation may include the duty to evict or otherwise restrain drunken or disorderly guests or patrons who may possibly cause harm to other guests or to their property. However, the hotel also has a duty not to cause foreseeable injury or harm to the drunken or disorderly guest as a result of the eviction. Under those circumstances, hotels must seek more reasonable alternatives, such as contacting police and arranging safe transport of the drunken or disorderly guest, or escorting the person back to his/her room (if this can be done safely without the risk of recurring problems).

If the hotel actually creates the risk of harm by serving alcohol to an already-intoxicated person, other laws come into play, most notably; the state **dram shop** acts (see Chapter Ten). These laws generally provide that third parties, injured by intoxicated persons, may sue the seller/provider of the alcohol (in this case, the hotel). Hotels can also lose their liquor licenses for serving minors.

Hotels may be liable for the personal injury of guests caused by the criminal act of another patron or guest if it can be established that the hotel was negligent or at fault. Criminal acts of other patrons do not always fall into the category of foreseeable risks hotels can protect against. Nonetheless, in assessing potential fault of the hotel, several factors will be considered. Was the injury or harm reasonably preventable? Who was in charge of security? Were the security personnel properly trained? Is there a past history of crime at the hotel? Were assessments of security risks ever established for the hotel? Were the security personnel uniformed? Were there an adequate number of security people on hand to handle routine matters as well as potential emergencies or crises?

For example, numerous court decisions nationwide have found hotels liable for failing to provide adequate locks on doors and windows. While the lodging industry does not recognize an official "standard of security," there are several minimum safety and security measures that indicate compliance with "standard practices," and have been used to establish legal precedent. These would include dead-bolt locks, viewing devices (peepholes) on room doors, chain locks, communication devices (telephones to enable emergency calls for assistance), and track (lock) bars for sliding glass doors. Closed circuit television has been found to be invaluable to assure reasonable security in facilities with several entrances, high-risk parking lots, or remote locations.

Natural Disasters, Acts of God, Public Enemies, Catastrophic Exposures

Common law and most state statutes excuse hotels from liability if guests are injured or harmed as the result of an act of God or natural disaster. Hotels are generally not liable for harm caused by public enemies. Most hotel insurance policies exclude coverage for catastrophic or widespread disasters which affect a great number of insureds or an unmanageable number of claimants. Acts of war, damages arising from nuclear energy, and certain exposures to pollutants are routinely eliminated from coverage. Notwithstanding, hotels are sensitive to enabling guests to vacate the premises in an orderly and speedy fashion in the event of a catastrophe.

Good Samaritan Acts

Laws regarding **Good Samaritan Acts** generally apply to hotel personnel in emergencies. Most states have Good Samaritan Acts that generally shield persons from liability if they try to save a life but fail. Florida was one of the first states to enact new legislation allowing hotel desk clerks, among others, to revive heart attack victims using automated defibrillators, without fear of exposure to unreasonable lawsuits.[7]

Responsibility for Personal Property of Guests

Keys

In the hotel industry, the standard for keys and locks has gone electronic — the cards that one swipes to get into the room. These "keys" offer much better security for the guest since they cannot be easily duplicated; the hotel has record of each time someone enters the room, how long they have stayed, and who entered, e.g., housekeeping, maintenance, or the guest. The traditional hotel keys were too easily lost and duplicated, especially if they were "accidentally" taken when the guest checked out.

Liability for Guest Personal Property

To limit liability for guests' **personal property, an in-room** safe or access to a safe deposit box must be available. Room safes are generally recommended only if they contain digital keypads, and the guest assumes all responsibility for getting into the safe and keeping the combination confidential.

The hotel needs to post notices announcing the availability of a safe or safe deposit box. Such notices should be posted so that a reasonable person would see them. It is best to post these notices in several places, e.g., at registration, on the room door with emergency exit information, and in the hotel informational book left in the room.

It is important to post notices that announce the limits on the hotel's liability for the loss of personal property (depending on state law). It needs to be made clear that certain items must be deposited in the safe or safe deposit box, e.g., money, jewels, bank notes, or other negotiable securities.

In Vermont, for example, the state puts a ceiling on liability for personal property of $300 unless the guest provides a statement of value to the hotel upon checking in and the hotel acknowledges that value.[8]

---

7. Florida Statutes Annotated, § 509 et seq.
8. www.vermont.gov.

When a hotel requests that a guest state a "declared value" for valuables, the hotel generally has the right, on behalf of its insurer, to inspect the valuables.

A hotel is generally not liable for a guest's loss of luggage or other personal items, which are lost in areas other than the guest's private room, unless the hotel or its employees are at fault.

Bailment

Many times, a hotel will be asked to hold something for a guest or a contractor. A hotel may also ask another business to loan the hotel something temporarily for a specific time period. This is called a **bailment**.

A bailment is the temporary placement of control over personal property by one person, the **bailor**, into the hands of another, the **bailee**. A bailment is made for a designated purpose upon which the parties have agreed.

These are either oral or written contractual relationships since the bailor and the bailee either expressly or impliedly have bound themselves to the terms of this agreement. The bailee receives only control or possession of the property, while the bailor retains the ownership interest in it. During the specific period a bailment exists, the bailee's interest in the property is superior to that of all others, including the bailor, unless the bailee violates some term of the agreement. Once the purpose for which the property has been delivered has been accomplished, the property will be returned to the bailor or otherwise disposed of pursuant to the bailor's directions.

For example, a contractor working to refurbish a portion of the hotel brings their tools onto the hotel property. They do not wish to remove them each evening after a day's work. The contractor asks the hotel if there is a locked room where they can store them; the hotel agrees to this. This is now a bailment; the contractor is the bailor (the titleholder of the tools); and the hotel is the bailee (they have possession of the tools on property).

Another example of a bailment would be if the hotel is hosting a large convention and needs extra kitchen equipment. They do not want to buy this equipment for one evening; so they go to a neighboring hotel and ask if they could borrow these items. The neighboring hotel agrees to loan the items for free. Now, the neighboring hotel is the bailor (the one owning the equipment) and the hotel asking to borrow the equipment is the bailee (they will have temporary possession of the kitchen items).

A guest bailment would occur if the guest sends an item of clothing to the hotel laundry. The guest would be the bailor (titleholder to the item) and the hotel laundry would be the bailee (in possession of the items for cleaning).

A bailment is not the same as a sale, which is an intentional transfer of ownership of personal property in exchange for something of value. A bailment involves only a transfer of possession or custody, not of ownership.

Categories of a Bailment

There are three types of bailment:

(1) For the benefit of the bailor and bailee
(2) For the sole benefit of the bailor
(3) For the sole benefit of the bailee

A bailment for the mutual benefit of the parties is created when there is an exchange of performances between the parties. A bailment for the cleaning of the item of clothing (discussed above) is a bailment for mutual benefit. The bailee receives a fee for the cleaning in exchange for his or her work, and the bailor receives cleaned garments.

A bailor receives the sole benefit from a bailment when a bailee acts gratuitously—for example, the contractor storing his or her tools as discussed above.

A bailment is created for the sole benefit of the bailee when both parties agree the property, temporarily in the bailee's custody, is to be used to his or her own advantage without giving anything to the bailor in return. The hotel borrowing kitchen equipment, for free, from the neighboring hotel would be an example of this bailment.

Elements of a Bailment

Three elements are generally necessary for the existence of a bailment: delivery, acceptance, and consideration.

Actual possession of, or control over property must be delivered to a bailee in order to create a bailment.

The delivery of actual possession of an item allows the bailee to accomplish his or her duties toward the property without the interference of others.

Control over property, although not necessarily the same as actual delivery of the property, suffices as constructive delivery of the item(s). By giving the bailee the access to control the property, the bailor gives the bailee the means to take custody of the property, without its actual delivery. The law construes such action as the equivalent of the physical transfer of the item(s). The delivery of the keys to a safe-deposit box is constructive delivery of its contents.

The second requisite to the creation of a bailment is the express or implied acceptance of possession or control of the property by the bailee. A person cannot unwittingly become a bailee. Because a bailment is a contract, knowledge and acceptance of its terms are essential to its enforcement.

Consideration, the exchange of something of value, must be present for a bailment to exist. Unlike the consideration required for most contracts, in a bailment as long as one party gives up something of value, such an action is regarded as good consideration. It is sufficient consideration that the bailor suffers the loss of the use of the property by relinquishing its control to the bailee; the bailor has given up — the immediate right to control the property.

Rights and Liabilities of a Bailment

The duty of care that must be exercised by a bailee varies, depending on the type of bailment.

In a bailment for *mutual benefit*, the bailee must take *reasonable care* of the bailed property. A bailee who fails to do so may be held liable for any damages incurred from his or her negligence. For example, in the cleaning example above, the hotel laundry must use reasonable care in the handling of the garment.

When a bailor receives the sole benefit from the bailment, the bailee has a *lesser duty* to care for the property and is financially responsible only if he or she has been *grossly negligent or has acted in bad faith* in taking care of the property. For example, in the case of the contractor storing his or her tools in the room on the hotel's property; the hotel will not be liable unless they are grossly negligent or act in bad faith in regard to the tools stored.

In contrast, a bailee for whose sole benefit property has been bailed must exercise *extraordinary care* for the property. The bailee can use the property only in the manner authorized by the terms of the bailment. The bailee is liable for all injuries to the property from failure to properly care for it. For example, in the borrowing of the kitchen items by the hotel from another hotel, the bailee hotel must use extraordinary care in their use and cleaning.

Once the purpose of the bailment has been completed, the bailee usually must return the property to the bailor or account for it, depending upon the terms of the contract. If, through no fault of his or her own, the return of the property is delayed or becomes impossible — for example, when it is lost during the course of the bailment, or when a hurricane blows the property into the ocean (take note Florida and other hurricane prone areas) — the bailee will not be held liable for non-delivery on demand. In all other situations, however, the bailee will be responsible for the *tort of conversion* (see Chapter Five) for unjustifiable failure to redeliver the property, as well as the property's unauthorized use.

The provisions of the bailment contract may restrict the liability of a bailee for negligent care or unauthorized use of the property. Such terms may not, however, absolve the bailee from all liability for the consequences of his or her own fraud or negligence. The bailor must be given notice of all such limitations on liability. Any such restrictions on liability cannot violate public policy. Similarly, a bailee may extend his or her liability to the bailor by contract provision.

Termination of a Bailment

A bailment is ended when its purpose has been achieved; when the parties agree that it is terminated, or when the bailed property is destroyed. A bailment created for an indefinite period is terminable at will by either party, as long as the other party receives due notice of the intended termination. Once a bailment ends, the bailee must return the property to the bailor or possibly be liable for the tort of conversion (see above).

Property with Unknown Owners

Mislaid Property versus Lost Property

Mislaid property refers to a property that has been left intentionally in a certain place and later forgotten. When a property is left in a certain place by the owner with the intention of taking it later, and if the owner finds it difficult to locate the property, then such a property is called mislaid.

For example, a wallet found in a restaurant lying on a counter near the cash register will be regarded as mislaid rather than lost. Under common law principles, the finder of a mislaid object has a duty to turn it over to the owner of the premises. This is based on the theory that the true owner is likely to return to that location to search for his or her mislaid item.

However, if the true owner does not return within a reasonable time, the property becomes that of the owner of the premises, for example the restaurant where the wallet was left.

Lost property is personal property that was unintentionally left by its true owner; versus mislaid property that is personal property intentionally set down by its owner and then forgotten. In the wallet example above, if the same wallet were not intentionally left at the restaurant cash register but fell out of someone's pocket, on the way to the cash register; then the wallet is now lost not mislaid. Under common law, a person who has found lost personal property could keep it until and unless the original owner came forward to claim it. This applies to finding lost property in public places as well as finding lost property on one's property.

Many jurisdictions have statutes that modify the common law's treatment of lost property. Typically, these statutes require lost personal property to be turned over to a government official, or advertised as being found in a newspaper of general circulation. If the property is not claimed by the rightful owner within a set period of time, it goes to the finder and the original owner's rights to the property are terminated.

Abandoned Property

Property is generally deemed to have been **abandoned** if it is found in a place where the true owner likely intended to leave it, but is in such a condition and of such low value that it is apparent that the owner had no intention of returning to claim it back. For example, the guest that checked out that left half empty bottles of shampoo or conditioner, or a used razor blade. It is unlikely the guest expects to claim these in the future. Abandoned property generally becomes the property of whoever should find it and takes possession of it first. For example, housekeeping can make the decision to throw this abandoned personal property out.

Hotel and Motel Associations

American Hotel and Lodging Association

AHLA is the singular voice representing every segment of the hotel industry including major chains, independent hotels, management companies, REIT's, bed and breakfasts, industry partners and more.

www.ahla.com

American Hotel and Lodging Educational Institute

AHLEI is a nonprofit member benefit of the American Hotel and Lodging Association. It provides hospitality education, training and professional certification.

www.ahlei.org

Chapter Summary

The safety and security of their guests are of prime importance to the hospitality business. To properly address these issues, the hospitality business must use a duty of reasonable care in protecting their guests from injury.

The federal government's role with regard to innkeepers is one of regulation. The Civil Rights Act, Americans with Disabilities Act, and the Hotel and Motel Fire Safety Act must be followed by innkeepers.

The most important duty of a hotel is to receive guests. It is not an absolute right for a guest to be received, but a limited one based on lawful excuses that may be exercised by an innkeeper.

It is imperative that guests' personal information be kept private and that guests can expect privacy while in their room.

A guest reservation policy must be established. When a hotel overbooks, some states have adopted policies that an innkeeper must adhere to. Most large hotel chains have overbooking policies already in place.

There are circumstances when a transient hotel guest may be evicted, e.g., nonpayment, disorderly conduct, or using the property for unlawful purposes, etc. If there is nonpayment by a guest, many states have implemented innkeeper's liens.

Even if an individual is on a hotel property and is not a registered guest, the hotel still may have duties towards their safety and security.

Sometimes a hotel will be asked by a guest or a contractor to hold something for them, this is called a bailment. The category of bailment will determine the degree of care the hotel will have to exercise over the property being held.

It is important for an innkeeper to know the difference between mislaid, lost, and abandoned property. This difference in the status of the guests' personal possessions determines what the hotel can and cannot legally do with this property.

Key Terms

Innkeepers
Common law
Reasonable care
Negligence
Civil Rights Act of 1964
Americans with Disabilities Act

Hotel and Motel Fire Safety Act of 1990
Justice Department
ADA Standards for Accessible Design
Braille

Amicus curiae
ACLU
Eviction
Innkeeper's lien
Slip and fall
Invitee
Social guest
Licensee
Trespasser
Comparative fault

Proximate cause
Dram shop
Good Samaritan Acts
Personal property
Bailments
Bailor
Bailee
Mislaid property
Lost property
Abandoned property

Chapter Ten

Merchant Obligations as to Food, Beverages, and Alcohol

Chapter Objectives

How does the UCC regulate the service of food and beverages?

What does the Truth in Menu Law require a hospitality business to do?

How can a restaurant offer gluten-free foods?

What is required to accommodate patrons with food allergies?

What is a dram shop act?

Uniform Commercial Code Warranty of Merchantability

As a hospitality manager involved with the service of food, there is a legal obligation to only sell food that is wholesome and to deliver this food to a customer in a manner that is safe. This responsibility is mandated by the **Uniform Commercial Code** (UCC), as well as by specific state and local laws. When a foodservice operation sells food, there is an **implied warranty that the food is merchantable**. This means a foodservice manager is required to operate his or her facility in a manner that protects guests from the possibility of foodborne illness or any other injury that may be caused by consuming unwholesome food or beverages.

Sometimes food is served that contains something that the guest normally would not expect to find (for example, a small stone in a serving of refried beans). The question that must be answered in these cases is whether the food or beverage served was "fit" for consumption.

The courts usually apply one of two different tests to determine whether a foodservice establishment is liable to a guest for any damages suffered from eating the food. One test seeks to determine whether the object is *foreign* to the dish or a natural component of it.

If the object is foreign, then the implied warranty of merchantability (**fitness for consumption**) under the UCC has been breached, and the foodservice operator would be held liable. If it is a natural component of the food, the warranty would not have been breached.

For example, the stone in refried beans, although commonly found in large bags of raw beans, would be considered foreign, and thus the foodservice operator would probably be held responsible. If instead the guest had chocked on a fishbone while enjoying a bowl of fish chowder, the guest would probably not recover any damages under this test. The fishbone, as a natural component of fish, is also a natural component of fish chowder.

The foreign versus natural test is gradually being replaced by the "reasonable expectation" test. This test seeks to determine whether an item could be reasonably expected by a guest to be found in the food. The fishbone situation is a perfect example of why the law (and assessing liability) can be difficult at times. Bones are a natural part of fish, but are they really natural components of fish chowder? Put another way, would a guest reasonably expect to find a fishbone in a bowl of fish chowder? If a judge or jury decided that it was not reasonable to expect to find a bone in the chowder, then the foodservice operator would be held liable.[1]

UCC and Implied Warranty: Fitness for Particular Purpose

Restaurants can also be found liable if they serve wholesome food in an unsafe or negligent manner. Food cannot be served on dirty, chipped or cracked plates, cups, or bowls. Utensils must be properly washed. Serving food on a dirty or chipped plate can present just as much liability as serving spoiled or unwholesome food.

Raw meats and vegetables cannot be prepared on the same cutting board. Food must be cooked to a certain internal temperature. The **United States De-**

---

1. UCC §2-314: Merchantability; Usage of Trade.

partment of Agriculture (USDA) has recommended safe minimum internal temperatures:

- Cook all raw beef, pork, Lamb and veal steaks, chops, and roasts to a minimum internal temperature of 145 °F as measured with a food thermometer before removing meat from the heat source. For safety and quality, allow the meat to rest for at least three minutes before carving or consuming. For reasons of personal preference, consumers may choose to cook meat to higher temperatures.
- Cook all raw ground beef, pork, Lamb, and veal to an internal temperature of 160 °F as measured with a food thermometer.
- Cook all poultry to a safe minimum internal temperature of 165 °F as measured with a food thermometer.[2]

If a customer insists their oysters be served raw, it is imperative the customer be warned that there is a health hazard in eating uncooked shellfish. If a customer orders very rare meat, or if a restaurant serves **steak tartare** (a raw meat dish), again the customer needs to be warned of the potential dangers of eating undercooked meat. These warnings must be given every time a customer orders such a dish to establish a pattern.

Management should frequently review all food temperatures, serving containers, food production techniques, and delivery methods. In addition, restaurants should strive to accommodate guests who ask that dishes be prepared without a specific ingredient to which they are allergic. Food preparation of such dishes must be closely supervised.

If the restaurant cannot accommodate the guest's request for exclusion of a certain item, the restaurant must be honest in disclosing this or face legal consequences. If a guest asks if there is **monosodium glutamate (MSG)** in the food, the server cannot "guess" if it is or is not in the dish; they must know. Some people have a severe allergic response to MSG. If a diabetic asks if there is sugar in a dish, again, the server must accurately disclose whether there is or is not sugar in the food item.[3]

If an incident occurs, that involves how food was served, rather than what was served, the manager should complete an incident report at the earliest opportunity.

---

2. www.fsis.usda.gov.
3. UCC § 2-315: Implied Warranty; Fitness for a Particular Purpose.

Prevention of Foodborne Illness

To help foodservice operators prevent foodborne illnesses, local health departments conduct routine inspections of restaurants and other food production facilities and may hold training or certification classes for those who handle food. It is important to know the local health department requirements that relate to food handling and to work diligently to ensure that only safe food is served. The law in this area is very clear. Restaurants will be held responsible for the illnesses suffered by their guests if those illnesses are the direct result of consuming unwholesome food. Thus, managers must make every effort to comply with local ordinances, train staff in effective food handling and production techniques, and document their efforts. Documenting the restaurant's efforts at safe food preparation shows a pattern of compliance and thus reasonableness in the preparation of food at the restaurant.

Florida's law requires food managers to complete training and pass a certification exam within 30 days of employment. This law requires all public food service establishments to provide proof of food manager certification upon request, including, but not limited to, at the time of any division inspection of the establishment.[4]

Truth in Menu Laws

What is represented in restaurants' or bars' advertising, menu, and server's verbal description must be accurate. **Truth in Menu Laws** are designed to protect consumers from fraudulent food and beverage claims. These laws are in constant change—the key is to be honest with what is being represented to the customer.

The menu and representations made need to be accurate:

- On the price charged to the customer
- The food that is served
- The process by which the food is prepared
- Representing the ingredients in the item

---

4. Florida State Statutes § 509.039.

- The origin of the products
- If there are any health benefits associated with the food or beverage
- The size of the serving
- Whether there is a mandatory service charge included in or added to the price
- If there is a cover charge or minimum drink requirement
- If there is a **prix fixe** menu, then the customer needs to know what is included, and what entrees can be chosen

The National Restaurant Association® (NRA), as well as many state restaurant associations, produce educational materials designed to assist in compliance to these laws. The **Practical Guide to the Nutrition Labeling Laws** is a publication that is specifically written for the restaurant industry. This guide outlines all the nutrition claims that a hospitality manager can make for their various menu items.[5]

Laws Regulating Food Labeling and Advertising

1990/2000

The **Organic Foods Production Act** and the **National Organic Program (NOP)** are put into place to assure consumers that the organic foods they purchase are produced, processed, and certified to consistent organic standards. Foods that are sold, labeled or represented as organic will have to be produced and processed in accordance with the NOP standards.

2003

The **Department of Health and Human Services** announced that the FDA will require food labels to include **trans-fat** content. This is the first substantive change to the nutrition facts panel on foods since 1993.

2004

Passage of the **Food Allergen Labeling and Consumer Protection Act** requires the labeling of any food that contains a protein derived from any one of the following foods that, as a group, account for the vast majority of food

---

5. www.restaurant.org.; www.fda.gov.

allergies: peanuts, soybeans, cow's milk, eggs, fish, crustacean shellfish, tree nuts, and wheat.

Preparation Requirements

Under federal law, if an item or technique is included on a menu, the specific preparation requirements must be followed in a very precise way. The **Food and Drug Administration** and the *U.S. Department of Agriculture* have produced guidelines for accurately describing menu items.

Grilled

Items must be actually grilled, not just mechanically produced with "grill marks."

Homemade

The product must be prepared on the premises, not commercially prepared and then heated.

Fresh

The product cannot be frozen, canned, dried, or processed.

Breaded Shrimp

To qualify as breaded shrimp, the tail portion of the shrimp, of a commercial species, must comprise 50 percent of the total weight of a finished product labeled "breaded shrimp."

Kosher Style

A product flavored or seasoned in a particular manner; this description has no religious significance.

Kosher

These are products that have been prepared or processed to meet the requirements of the orthodox Jewish religion.

Baked Ham

A baked ham is one that has been heated in an oven for a specified period of time. Many brands of smoked ham are not oven-baked.

Ingredients in Food Served

Perhaps no area of menu accuracy is more important than the listing of ingredients that actually go into making a food item. While restaurants are not currently required to divulge their ingredient lists (recipes) to their guests, there are specific situations when the ingredients listed on a menu must precisely match those used to make the item.

If, for example, an operator offers Kahlua® and cream as a drink in a bar menu, the drink must be made with both the liqueur and the dairy product stated. Kahlua® is a specific brand of Mexican coffee liqueur, and cream is defined by the federal government as a product made from milk with a minimum fat content of eighteen percent.

Of course, a bar manager is free to offer a different, less expensive coffee liqueur to guests, and use half-and-half (which contains twelve percent milk fat) instead of cream, but the drink could not be called a Kahlua® and cream. To do so is unethical at best and unlawful in most areas.

Whenever a specific ingredient is listed on a menu, that item and that item alone should be served. For example, if the menu says maple syrup, then colored table syrup or maple-flavored syrup should not be served. This is especially important when listing brand-name products on a menu. If substitutions for the menu items must be made, the guest should be informed of those substitutions before ordering.

Origin of the Food Served

For many menu items, the origin of the product or its ingredients is very important. Many consumers prefer Colorado trout to generic trout; Washington's apples to those from other states, and Bluepoint (Long Island) oysters to those from other areas. It can be tempting to use these terms to describe similar menu items from other places, which may cost less to purchase. But to do so is unethical and fraudulent.

Size of the Food Served

Product size is, in many cases, the most important factor in determining how much a guest is willing to pay for a menu item. For example, a steakhouse could offer different cuts of beef and price them appropriately according to size. An 8-ounce steak might sell for $19.95, while a 12-ounce might sell for $23.95 and a 16-ounce for $25.95.

Other types of food products may be harder to associate with precise quantities. "Large" East Coast oysters must, by law, contain no more than 160 to 210 oysters per gallon, while "large" Pacific Coast oysters, by law, may contain no more than 64 oysters per gallon. Nevertheless, whether it is the size of eggs sold in a breakfast special, or the use of the term "jumbo" used to refer to shrimp, specifying size on a menu is an area that must be approached with the understanding that the law will expect the restaurant to deliver what is promised.[6]

Gluten Free

Gluten-free dining is here to stay. According to results from the *National Restaurant Association®'s* (NRA) annual chef survey, gluten free/food allergy requests represent major market growth.[7]

The FDA and Gluten Free

On August 2, 2013, the FDA issued a final rule defining "gluten free" for food labeling, which helps consumers, especially those living with **celiac disease**, be confident that items labeled "gluten free" meet a defined standard for gluten content. "Gluten free" is a voluntary claim that can be used by food manufacturers on food labels if they meet all the requirements of the regulations.

On August 12, 2020, the FDA issued a final rule on the gluten free labeling of fermented or hydrolyzed foods. It covers foods such as yogurt, sauerkraut, pickles, cheese, green olives, FDA-regulated beers and wines (e.g., generally those with less than 7 percent alcohol), and hydrolyzed plant proteins used to improve flavor or texture in processed foods, such as soups, sauces, and seasonings. The rule does not change the definition of "gluten free" but establishes compliance requirements for these hydrolyzed and fermented foods. It also includes a discussion of how the FDA will verify compliance for distilled foods such as vinegar.

Questions and Answers as to Gluten Free

What is celiac disease?

Celiac disease is a chronic inflammatory disorder of the small intestine in genetically susceptible individuals. It is triggered by ingesting certain proteins, commonly referred to as gluten, which are naturally present in some cereal grains.

---

6. www.fda.gov.
7. www.restaurant.org.

What is the estimated prevalence of celiac disease in the U.S.?

Experts estimate the percentage of the general population in the United States with celiac disease is as high as 1%.

Can celiac disease be cured?

No, but health care professionals state it can be managed with diet. Typically, individuals who have this disease are advised to avoid all sources of gluten in their diet. Over time, strictly avoiding consumption of all gluten sources can improve the symptoms and reduce the associated health risks of celiac disease.

What is "gluten"?

The term "gluten" technically refers to a specific complex of proteins that forms when wheat flour is mixed with a liquid and physically manipulated, such as in the kneading of bread.

How is the term "gluten" used in the context of celiac disease?

In the context of celiac disease, the term "gluten" is used to collectively refer to gluten in wheat, and to the proteins in other grains that have been demonstrated to cause harmful health effects in individuals who have celiac disease. These grains are wheat (including different varieties such as spelt and kamut), rye, barley, cross-bred hybrids (e.g., triticale, which is a cross between wheat and rye), and possibly oats.

What is the FDA's definition of the term "gluten free"?

The FDA defines the term "gluten free" to mean food bearing the "gluten free" claim, is either naturally "gluten free," or does not contain an ingredient that is derived from a gluten-containing grain (e.g., wheat). Unless that gluten-containing food has been processed to a level of 20 parts per million (ppm) or less of gluten. Any food that bears the claim "no gluten," "free of gluten," or "without gluten" in its labeling and does not meet the requirements for a "gluten free" claim will be deemed misbranded.

Will foods that meet the definition for "gluten free" be required to bear a "gluten free" claim?

No. "Gluten free" is a voluntary claim that can be used by food manufacturers on food labels if they meet all the requirements of the regulations.

What are examples of food products that are naturally gluten free?

The following are examples of, **but are not limited to,** foods that are naturally, gluten free:
- Milk; nonfat dry milk
- 100 percent fruit or vegetable juices
- Fresh fruits and vegetables that are not coated with wax or resin that contains gluten
- A variety of single ingredient foods: butter; eggs; lentils; peanuts; seeds like flax; tree nuts like almonds; non-gluten containing grains like corn; fresh fish like cod; fresh shellfish like clams; honey; and water.

*Why did the FDA not include oats as one of the "**prohibited grains**" in its definition of the term "gluten free"?*

- There is no consensus among nutrition experts or authorities on the unconditional exclusion of oats from the diet of individuals with celiac disease. For example, the following celiac disease experts/ authorities do not support the unconditional exclusion of oats: The **National Institutes of Health**, the **American Dietetic Association**, and some celiac disease research/treatment centers.
- Research data suggests that the majority of individuals with celiac disease can tolerate a daily intake of a limited amount (e.g., 50 grams) of oats that are free of gluten from wheat, rye, barley, or their crossbred hybrids.
- Oats are reported to add variety, taste, satiety, dietary fiber, and other essential nutrients in the diet of individuals with celiac disease, and may make their diet more appealing.
- Allowing oats free of gluten from wheat, rye, barley or their crossbred hybrids, to bear a "gluten-free" labeling claim would make it easier for consumers to identify such oats in the marketplace and may serve as an incentive for more manufacturers to produce such oats.

Why did the FDA include less than 20 ppm of gluten as a criterion in its definition of "gluten free"?

The level is based on the available analytical methods. Data from peer-reviewed scientific literature demonstrates that current analytical technology can reliably and consistently detect gluten in wheat, rye, and barley at levels of 20 ppm and more in a variety of food matrices.

How does the FDA enforce "gluten-free" label claims?

In the enforcement of FDA-regulated food labeling claims, the agency would deem the product to be misbranded on the basis of the result of one of the following:

- Review of labels
- On-site inspections of food manufacturers
- Analysis of food samples

What are the benefits for consumers of having a standardized definition for the term "gluten free"?

A standardized definition for the term "gluten free" serves to protect the public's health by providing consumers with celiac disease, and others who must avoid gluten in their diet, the assurance that the foods bearing this labeling meet a clear standard established and enforced by the FDA as to the meaning of "gluten free."

What is the gluten threshold level that other countries use to define the term GF and what gluten detection analytical methods do they use?

The **Codex Alimentarius Commission** "gluten-free" standard, is at 20 ppm or less gluten, and recommends using the "**ELISA R5 Mendez Method**" for determining the gluten content of foods. This standard was adopted in 2009, in regulations by 27 countries currently comprising the **Commission of European Communities**.[8]

Serving Customers with Food Allergies and Celiac Disease

People with food allergies or celiac disease are extremely loyal customers. Having a food allergy or celiac disease usually means a person is restricted to eating at home, or at very few restaurants. So, when people with food allergies find a restaurant that can safely accommodate their needs, not only do they become regular and frequent customers, but they also make it the place to take their families and friends when eating out. Therefore, just by creating and ensuring that at least one dish and dessert is free from one or more allergens or from gluten, a restaurant can become a regular dining place for allergic and celiac customers, as well as their friends and families.

Remember though, if a gluten-free, nut and peanut-free, egg-free or any other allergen-free dish is promoted and served, the statement that the food

---

8. www.fda.gov.

is free from a specific allergen must be true. Some individuals could suffer fatal consequences if the allergen is found in their food. There must be procedures in place to always ensure that there is no allergen cross-contamination from other dishes, working surfaces and kitchen utensils are kept apart from the allergen; there are no hidden sources of allergens in the food supplied to the restaurant; and all the staff are aware of all procedures that need to be followed in serving customers with food allergies. Below is a suggestion list of the main procedures that should be followed to ensure a safe meal is being served to customers with food allergies and celiac disease.

Gluten-Free and Allergy-Free Ingredients

1. **Be familiar with the common terms for allergens**, such as "whey" or "casein" for milk, "albumin" for egg, or *Arachis* for peanuts.

2. **Train staff to identify hidden sources of at least the most common allergens** (such as gluten, wheat, eggs, fish, milk, peanuts, shellfish and tree nuts; including almonds, Brazil nuts, cashews, chestnuts, hazelnuts, hickory nuts, macadamia nuts, pecans, pine nuts, pistachios and walnuts). Ingredients that can cause severe allergic reactions that can be present in products where they are not expected to be.

3. **Always consider all ingredients**, not only those used directly in the dish, but also those used as a garnish, as a topping, or as a salad dressing. It is ideal to have a list of all the ingredients that go into a dish.

4. **Always check the ingredients of ready-made and processed food**. Check if the supplier is the same and if there were no ingredient changes, as manufacturers sometimes change ingredients. "**May contain**" warnings means it is possible the product has come into contact with a potential allergen. If ingredient information is missing, inaccurate or hard to read, call the supplier. If there is any doubt, don't advertise it as allergy free.

5. **Do not make product substitutions without warning serving staff and reflecting the change in the menu**. Specifically, avoid all changes that include adding a potential allergen to the food. A regular customer will not ask whether the recipe has been changed.

6. **Keep a copy of the ingredient information on the labels of any ready-made foods** so they can be checked if a customer requests them.

7. **Always store foods separately — in closed containers**, especially peanuts, nuts, seeds, milk powder, and flour.

Allergy-Free Food Preparation and Cooking

It is important for the chef, and all kitchen staff, to know even a minuscule amount of an allergen in food can trigger a severe allergic reaction. It is not enough to simply remove the allergen food from a prepared dish.

Here are some procedures that should be followed to prevent contamination from other dishes:

1. **Do not share any utensils.** All preparation tables, utensils, chopping boards, knives and other cutlery, containers, trays, pans, bowls, and grills should be carefully cleaned with hot, soapy water before being used to prepare a dish for a food-allergic or celiac diner.

2. **Hands should be washed before preparation of the meal, and clean aprons and kitchen towels should be used.**

3. **Do not use oils that have been used to cook or fry other foods.** Even if there are separate fryers and separate oils for different ingredients, they may be contaminated if oils are filtered through a single filtration system.

4. **Do not place the dish in the same oven, tray, or grill; or next to other dishes containing the allergen.**

5. **If any allergen-free alternatives are offered, prepare them first** and wrap them to prevent contamination from other dishes.

6. **If possible, keep separate areas for the preparation of allergen-free dishes.**

7. **Keep the safe meal separate from other dishes before serving it** to the customer, and have a procedure to make sure that orders are not mixed up. Many restaurants will use special toothpicks or other such devices to differentiate the meals.

8. **Make sure the kitchen staff always tells the serving staff about any recipe changes,** particularly if foods that can cause severe allergic reactions are now being used in a dish.

Menus and Allergy-Free

1. **If a dish contains one of the main foods that can cause an allergic reaction, make sure to reflect it in the name of the dish or its description** (for example: "chocolate mousse with almonds" instead of "chocolate mousse").

2. **Always update the menu when recipes change.**

3. **If the names of the dishes, or their description, contain words in a language other than the country's official language, provide a full translation.**

4. **Do not state on the menu a dish does not contain a particular food if this may not be true.**

5. Have a note on the menu encouraging food-allergic and celiac customers to inform the staff about their dietary restrictions.

Alerting Staff How to Accommodate Food-Allergy Customers

1. **Make sure the restaurant staff pays close attention when guests say they have a food allergy or celiac disease.** The staff must understand these conditions must be taken seriously. Ideally, they should write down all the recommendations made by the customer instead of relying on their memory.

2. **The chef and the kitchen staff should always be informed of any food allergies or restrictions communicated by the customer.**

3. **Servers should be able to describe a menu item and its ingredients and where to find this information upon request. Ideally, there should always be at least one person on staff who can answer questions about ingredients.** On some occasions, it may be helpful to show customers the labels of the product so they can judge whether the food is safe for them or not.

4. **The most important message to be given to all serving staff is to always *tell the truth and never guess*.** If the wait staff is not sure whether a dish contains the allergen, if ingredient information is not available, or if the server is not sure that procedures to prevent cross-contamination were followed, they should say so.

5. **Servers should always double-check with the kitchen staff every time someone asks for a meal free from a certain food** as ingredients may have changed.

6. **Servers should wash their hands before serving the safe food** to prevent cross-contamination.

7. **Make sure the serving staff knows they should *never* simply remove the allergen food from a prepared dish** as trace amounts—enough to cause a severe reaction may be present.

8. **Staff should be aware that foods in buffets, self-service areas, and sweet trolleys may not be safe** (even if they do not contain the offending food) due to the possibility of cross-contamination. If one runs a buffet-type restaurant, warnings should be posted at the beginning of the buffet line.

9. Although other conditions can have similar symptoms, **if the staff realize that a customer is having difficulty breathing, their lips or mouth are swollen, or if the customer becomes unconscious, the wait staff should call an ambulance immediately**. They should describe the symptoms and stay with the customer until help arrives.

10. **All staff must be trained about allergens before they start to work**, regardless of whether they are going to work in the kitchen or serving customers.

The Serving of Alcohol

The **Twenty-first Amendment** to the Constitution of the United States repealed the **Eighteenth Amendment**. This ended **Prohibition**.[9] For the 21st Amendment to pass it had to give a great deal of power to each state to control the sale of liquor, the granting of liquor licenses, and the distribution of liquor to the public.

The repeal of the 18th Amendment did not totally deprive the U.S. Congress of the power to legislate liquor,[10] but Congress is constrained to the regulation of intrastate activities, in liquor, that potentially affect interstate commerce.[11]

On June 26, 2019, the U.S. Supreme Court, by a 7–2 decision, in *Tennessee Wine and Spirits Retailers Assn. v. Thomas, Executive Director of the Tennessee Alcoholic Beverage Commission, et al.,* 139 S. Ct. 2449 (2019), chipped away at some of the state's control over alcohol. Tennessee's law imposes durational-residency requirements on persons and companies wishing to operate retail liquor stores, requiring applicants for an initial license to reside in the state for the prior two years; requiring an applicant for renewal of a license to reside in the state for 10 consecutive years; and providing that a corporation cannot obtain a license unless all of its stockholders are residents. Following the state attorney general's opinion that the residency requirements discriminated against out-of-state economic interests in violation of the Commerce Clause, the Tennessee Alcoholic Beverage Commission (TABC) declined to enforce the residency requirements.

This is when the Tennessee Wine and Spirits Retailers Association (TWSRA) appealed to the U.S. Supreme Court, saying that the 2-year residency requirement was enforceable. Tennessee is one of 35 states with a residency requirement for selling liquor. The TWSRA said the law is protected by the second section of the 21st Amendment, which overturned prohibition. This section giving states the option to stop the import of liquor across state lines.

The U.S. Supreme Court held:

---

9. *Massey v. United States* (1934) 291 U.S. 608, 78 L Ed 1019, 54 S Ct 532.

10. *Old Monastery Co. v. United States* (1945, CA4 SC) 147 F2d 905, cert den (1945) 326 U.S. 734, 90 L Ed 437, 66 S Ct 44.

11. *Hanf v. United States* (1956, CA8 Minn) 235 F2d 710, cert den (1956) 352 U.S. 880, 1 L Ed 2d 81, 77 S Ct 102.

Tennessee's 2-year durational-residency requirement applicable to retail liquor store license applicants violates the Commerce Clause and is not saved by the Twenty-first Amendment.

(a) The Commerce Clause by its own force restricts state protectionism. Removing state trade barriers was a principal reason for the adoption of the Constitution, and at this point, no provision other than the Commerce Clause could easily do that job. The Court has long emphasized the connection between the trade barriers that prompted the call for a new Constitution and its dormant Commerce Clause jurisprudence. See *Guy v. Baltimore*; *Granholm v. Heald*.[12]

(b) Under the dormant Commerce Clause cases, a state law that discriminates against out-of-state goods or nonresident economic actors can be sustained only upon a showing that it is narrowly tailored to "advanc[e] a legitimate local purpose." *Department of Revenue of Ky. v. Davis*.[13]

Tennessee's 2-year residency requirement plainly favors Tennesseans over nonresidents.

(c) Because the 2-year residency requirement applies to the sale of alcohol, however, it must be evaluated in light of §2 of the Twenty-first Amendment. (1) Section 2's broad text—the "transportation or importation into any State, Territory, or possession of the United States for delivery or use therein of intoxicating liquors, in violation of the laws thereof, is hereby prohibited"—could be read to prohibit the transportation or importation of alcoholic beverages in violation of any state law. But the Court has declined to adopt that reading, instead interpreting §2 as one part of a unified constitutional scheme and in light of the provision's history. History teaches that §2's thrust is to "constitutionaliz[e]" the basic structure of federal-state alcohol regulatory authority that prevailed prior to the Eighteenth Amendment's adoption. *Craig v. Boren*.[14]

Age Restrictions for Alcohol

The United States has the highest age requirement, worldwide, for the legal purchase of alcohol—21. In other countries, the average age for purchase of alcohol is 18.

In 1984, Congress enacted the **National Minimum Drinking Age Law**, which requires that states—as a condition of receiving state highway funds—

---

12. 100 U.S. 434, 440; 544 U.S. 460, 472.
13. 553 U.S. 328, 338.
14. 429 U.S. 190, 206.

prohibit persons under the age of 21 from purchasing or publicly possessing alcohol. By 1988, every state had passed legislation to meet the federal funding requirements.

Training Employees for the Service of Alcohol

A good example of how to train an employee in the service of alcohol is the Washington State law as to the certification of the servers of alcohol.

The Washington Responsible Alcohol Sales Training Course for bartenders, sellers, and servers goes over all the required information for learning how to sell and serve alcohol in Washington and provides state-specific certification. The Washington course covers such topics as:

1. How to spot someone who has been drinking too much.
2. How to properly check IDs.
3. The responsibilities/liabilities of the server.

The Washington Responsible Alcohol Sales Training Course features interactive learning through audio, videos, and text. Each lesson of the course deals with different areas that a bartender, seller, or server in Washington needs to be familiar with. At the end of each lesson, interactive flashcards help with retention of the important details, and the lesson quizzes test for knowledge of the area.[15]

Liability and Alcohol Service

Many states hold commercial vendors of alcohol (bars, taverns, and package stores) responsible for injuries caused by drunken patrons. This is called the dram shop act. In Texas, *minors* can sue a drinking establishment for their own injuries sustained while intoxicated. In other states, dram shop liability extends to serving the "habitually intoxicated."

Laws in most states require the injured person suing a commercial alcohol vendor to prove that the serving of alcohol was a "**proximate cause**" of their injury. In other words, they must show a provable connection between the injury and the drunk person's act of drinking at that particular bar or tavern.

Laws vary widely by state. In Nevada, commercial vendors won't be held responsible for injuries caused by drunken patrons, probably because of the devastating impact this would have on the visitor industry. In some states, commercial vendors will only be held responsible for serving alcohol to minors.

---

15. www.lcb.wa.gov.

In other states, the amount of damages that can be collected from a commercial vendor is capped at a specific amount under the theory that the major share of blame for the injury should be placed on the drunken person.

Most states hold a commercial vendor liable where:

- Alcohol was served to a minor
- The vendor was reckless in serving, or should have realized the extent of the patron's intoxication
- The vendor sold liquor without a liquor license
- The vendor sold liquor after hours

The burden of proof to prove liability is lower when a bar or tavern has served a minor, as it's illegal.

The test for deciding whether a bar employee should have realized the extent of a patron's intoxication is not clear. Courts look at the condition of the drunken person, and whether it should have been "**foreseeable**" to a bar employee serving him or her that the person was already "**visibly intoxicated**" and shouldn't be served any more alcohol. It's not a matter of how many drinks the person has had, but how the alcohol has affected them.

How to Prove Excess Intoxication

Some states have tried to clarify this vague test by requiring proof that the drunken person demonstrated "significantly uncoordinated physical action or significant physical dysfunction." In other states, it must be proven that the bar patron was so obviously intoxicated that he or she presented a "clear danger to himself and others."[16]

Missouri's Dram Shop Act

Sale of alcoholic beverages may be a proximate cause of personal injuries or death, requirements (dram shop law).

537.053. 1. Since the repeal of the Missouri Dram Shop Act in 1934 (Laws of 1933–34, extra session, page 77), it has been and continues to be the policy of this state to follow the common law of England, as declared in section 1.010, to prohibit dram shop liability and to follow the common law rule that furnishing alcoholic beverages is *not* the proximate cause of injuries inflicted by intoxicated persons.

2. Notwithstanding subsection 1 of this section, a cause of action may be brought by on or behalf of any person who has suffered personal injury or

16. 30 Am. Jur. 573, §607.

death against any person licensed to sell intoxicating liquor by the drink, for consumption on the premises, when it is proven by clear and convincing evidence that the seller knew or should have known that intoxicating liquor was served to a person under the age of twenty-one years, or knowingly served intoxicating liquor to a visibly intoxicated person.

3. For purposes of this section, a person is "visibly intoxicated" when inebriated to such an extent that the impairment is shown by significantly uncoordinated physical action or significant physical dysfunction. A person's blood alcohol content does *not* constitute prima facie evidence to establish that a person is visibly intoxicated within the meaning of this section, but may be admissible as relevant evidence of the person's intoxication.

4. Nothing in this section shall be interpreted to provide a right of recovery to a person who suffers injury or death proximately caused by the person's voluntary intoxication unless the person is under the age of twenty-one years. No person over the age of twenty-one years or their dependents, personal representative, and heirs may assert a claim for damages for personal injury or death against a seller of intoxicating liquor by the drink, for consumption on the premises, arising out of the person's voluntary intoxication.

5. In an action brought pursuant to subsection 2 of this section, alleging the sale of intoxicating liquor by the drink for consumption on the premises, to a person under the age of twenty-one years, proof that the seller or the seller's agent or employee demanded and was shown a driver's license or official state or federal personal identification card, appearing to be genuine and showing that the minor was at least twenty-one years of age, shall be relevant in determining the relative fault of the seller or seller's agent or employee in the action.

6. No employer may discharge his or her employee for refusing service to a visibly intoxicated person.[17]

Chapter Summary

As a hospitality manager, there is a legal obligation to only serve food that is wholesome and safe. Under the UCC, there is an implied warranty that the food served is merchantable.

The UCC requires wholesome food to be served in a manner that is not negligent. Dishes and utensils must be clean and free from defects such as chips

---

17. www.revisor.mo.gov.

and cracks. Local ordinances must also be complied with in regard to food safety and sanitation.

Truth in Menu laws are designed to protect consumers from fraudulent food and beverage claims. An item must be honestly represented on a menu. This includes the preparation style, the ingredients, size of the portion, and the origin of the food served.

An area of concern for many diners is "gluten free." If a restaurant wishes to offer "gluten-free" food, there are preparation, presentation, and serving issues that must be addressed. The staff must be thoroughly trained in the preparation and service of these menu items.

Food allergies are additional issues that must be addressed by a vendor of food or beverages. If a patron communicates to the staff they have a food allergy, and the staff assures them their food allergy can be accommodated, this adjustment to the food must be made. If this is not done, the restaurant could face serious legal consequences.

The service of alcohol is, for the most part, covered under state laws as per the 21st Amendment to the U.S. Constitution. In the U.S. it is imperative no one under the age of 21 be served alcohol. If a vendor of alcohol allows underage drinking, legal sanctions will be imposed against that business.

Dram shop acts hold commercial vendors of alcohol responsible for injuries caused by drunken patrons. Laws vary from state to state, but the state law where the business is located must be scrupulously followed, or else the business can face significant liability.

Key Terms

Uniform Commercial Code
Implied warranty that the food is
     merchantable
Fitness for consumption
United States Department of Agri-
     culture
Steak tartare
Monosodium glutamate
Truth in Menu Laws
Prix fixe
The National Restaurant Association

Practical Guide to the Nutrition
     Labeling Laws
Organic Foods Production Act
National Organic Program
Department of Health and Human
     Services
Trans-fat
Food Allergen Labeling and Con-
     sumer Protection Act
Preparation requirements
Food and Drug Administration

Chapter Eleven

Crisis Management/Ethics

Chapter Objectives

What should be done before a potential crisis?

What should be done during a crisis?

What should be done after a crisis?

How can a hospitality business prepare for a terrorist attack?

What ethical responsibilities does a hospitality business have to its patrons; to the company; to itself?

Crisis Management

In the hospitality industry, it is inevitable that sooner or later the hospitality manager will be faced with a crisis. This could be a hurricane, an ice storm, the tainting of food, or a terrorist attack.

Planning, training, conducting drills, testing procedures, and providing additional external resources are important functions in the preparation for a crisis.

The following "components" are required in order to handle any crisis situation effectively:

1. Leadership (crisis coordination).
2. Adequate emergency response (ambulance/paramedics/medical support).
3. Victim identification.
4. Media relations.

5. Family assistance.
6. Information dissemination.
7. Internal and external communications.

Each manager must:

- Develop written plans that direct the staff in how to handle the crisis
- Train the initial crisis responders
- Conduct regular rehearsals prior to the crisis happening (the equivalent of mustering onboard a ship upon sailing)

Stage 1 — Before the Crisis

It must be determined:

- What will constitute a true crisis as opposed to the normal day-to-day hospitality operations?
- How to assess the potential crisis issues.
- What are the crisis teams' responsibilities?
- How to set up an emergency communication protocol.

Stage 2 — During and After the Crisis

- There must be some center or person in charge of crisis communication.
- There needs to be the preparation of "**talking points**."
- There needs to be guidelines in place as to interviews given post-crisis.
- The story must be controlled in favor of the hospitality business.
- What are the plans to get "back to normal" after the crisis?

Crisis Response

In almost every instance of a successful response to a crisis, there are management and response activities. These consist of sound operations execution coupled with superior communications.

Operational response (how the staff responds and how the business responds) is essential. It is this response that saves lives, property, and other assets. The ability to communicate effectively is imperative; this saves the business. The simple fact is, perception is reality, and public perception of a company's reaction to a crisis is as important as the operating response.

There are no clear boundaries with any crisis. There is rarely a single moment when one can say an incident or issue has transformed into a crisis. Crisis management experts recommend adopting a low threshold when defining a crisis; err on the side of caution, and assume a small episode can escalate into a crisis quickly.

Check data backup systems: Are they all onsite or are copies of data, systems, and staff records kept elsewhere? Is the safe fireproof or just a box with a key? Online backup systems work well, and data storage is very cheap, but they don't work if they are not in place prior to the crisis.

Is insurance coverage complete? Will the business's insurance cover situations like floods, hurricanes, or tsunamis? Does the business's insurance cover intangible items, such as "**goodwill**" as well as equipment? What about the loss of profits and staff wages while rebuilding happens?

Is the staff trained for fire and first-aid emergencies? This is a type of training that's usually regarded as "nice to have" rather than essential. Does the staff know how to handle grease or electrical fires? What about the elderly customer who faints or collapses, or **tsunami** waters coming near electrical connections?

How will customers and staff be kept informed? It is more effective if email and business alerts are already in place and used daily. If the business is active on Facebook® or Twitter® these can be used to communicate with the staff, customers, and the public.

Have a crisis management plan: Which staff member is responsible for what duties? Have a backup for that person as well. The key person may be on vacation or out sick the day of the crisis.[1]

Ten Steps of Crisis Communications

Identify the Crisis Communications Team

A small team of senior executives should be identified to serve as the organization's **Crisis Communications Team**. Ideally, the team would be led by the organization's CEO, with the firm's top public relations executive and legal counsel as his or her chief advisers. If the in-house public relations executive does not have sufficient crisis communications expertise, he or she may choose to retain an agency or independent consultant with that specialty. Other team

---

1. www.training.fema.gov.

members should be the heads of major organizational divisions, including finance, personnel, and operations.

Identify Spokespersons

Within each team, there should be individuals who are the only ones authorized to speak for the organization in times of crisis. The CEO should be one of those spokespersons, but not necessarily the primary spokesperson. The pool of potential spokespersons should be identified and trained in advance.

Not only are spokespersons needed for media communications, but for all types and forms of communications: internal and external, including on camera; public meetings, employee meetings, and so on. Don't wait to make decisions about choosing spokespersons. Do this in advance, so this is not being done while "under fire."

Spokesperson Training

It is management's responsibility to prepare a well-thought-out response to a crisis situation. Spokesperson training teaches everyone to be prepared and to be ready to respond in a way that optimizes the response of all.

Establish Notification Systems

It is absolutely essential to establish notification systems pre-crisis that will allow everyone to rapidly reach all that are affected by the crisis. The best plan is to have multiple forms of communication used — email, phone, text, fax, or Social Media. If more than one form of communication is used, the chances are much greater that the message will go through and be received by the parties involved.

Identify and Know Who Needs to Be Informed and What They Should Hear

Everyone on the contact list will be talking about the hospitality business to others (even those not on the contact list). It is imperative, prior to the crisis, to ensure the message received is one that the business wants to be disseminated and repeated.

Anticipate Crises

It is important to gather the Crisis Communications Team for long brainstorming sessions on all the potential crises which can occur at the hospitality organization.

There are at least two immediate benefits to this exercise:

- It may be realized that some situations are preventable by simply modifying existing methods of operation.
- The organization can begin to think about possible responses, best case/worst case scenarios, and so on. Better now than when under the pressure of an actual crisis.

Develop Holding Statements

Although full message development must await the outbreak of an actual crisis, "**holding statements**" — messages designed for use immediately after a crisis breaks — can be developed in advance to be used for a wide variety of scenarios in which the organization is perceived to be vulnerable.

Examples of "holding statements" would be:

"We have implemented our crisis response plan which places the highest priority on the health and safety of our guests and staff."
"Our hearts and minds are with those who are in harm's way, and we hope that they are well."
"We will be supplying additional information when it is available and will be posting this information on our website."

The organization's Crisis Communications Team should regularly review holding statements to determine if they require revision and/or whether statements for other scenarios should be developed.

Assess the Crisis Situation

Reacting without adequate information is a classic "shoot first and ask questions afterwards." This is not the way to handle a crisis. It is imperative to prepare in advance to ensure the right type of information is being provided to the staff in a timely manner, so all can proceed with determining the appropriate response.

Although the assessment of a crisis cannot be planned for in advance, with the use of advanced planning, reaction time to the crisis will be much shorter and more informed.

Identify Key Messages

With holding statements available as a starting point, the Crisis Communications Team must continue developing the crisis-specific messages required for any given situation. The team already knows what type of information is being sought. The Crisis Communications Team needs to assess what everyone should know about this crisis. Messages need to be kept simple. Keep it to three main messages for each group — staff, guests, and the media/public.

Riding Out the Storm

No matter what the nature of a crisis, no matter whether it's good news or bad; no matter how carefully the organization has prepared and responded; some individuals are not going to react the way they were expected to react.

What to do?

- Take a deep breath.
- Take an objective look at the reaction(s) in question. Is it the company's fault, or the individual's (stakeholder's) unique interpretation?
- Decide if another communication to those stakeholders is likely to change their impression for the better.
- Decide if another communication to those stakeholders could make the situation worse.

Post Crisis

A psychological study of the effects of reconstructive memory after a crisis points the way in how to deal with the damage done to a business's reputation. This study contradicts the commonly held myth that it is best to avoid communicating for a time, and let consumers "forget" an unfortunate incident. Instead, given what is now known, the crisis situation can be used as a means to re-establish a relationship with consumers. The study proposes that post-crisis communication efforts should be focused on building positive emotional connections with the business's customers.

An example would be the **Wendy's®** crisis — when in 2005, a customer in Las Vegas, Nevada, accused Wendy's® of serving her a bowl of chili with a finger as one of the ingredients. Wendy's® was very hesitant to refute this; even after it was found that the woman had purposely placed the finger in the chili herself. Wendy's® sales dropped. What did Wendy's® do, post-crisis? They offered customers a free "Frosty®" during the weekend of May 13–15, 2005. Customers did not "warm-up" to this attempt to lure them back.

A better approach, based on the study of reconstructive memory, would have been to invoke a poignant connection to Wendy's®. They could have discussed founder Dave Thomas and his daughter Melinda (Wendy, for short), and the history behind the chain. This would then have re-established customer emotional bonds to the Wendy's® brand.[2]

Crisis Management in Saint Lucia

The **National Emergency Management Organization** (NEMO) is the state-appointed agency charged with the responsibility of preparing the nation and mobilizing the populace in response to disasters, natural and man-made. Given Saint Lucia's geographical location, the most frequent threat from disasters are mainly hurricane related.

Despite NEMO's best efforts, it is recognized that the hospitality industry has special needs in the management of disasters or crises based on the following factors:

- Large numbers of visitors, many of whom do not speak English, are housed in the most vulnerable and disaster prone areas of **Saint Lucia**, i.e., along the coast.
- The Saint Lucia tourist industry has collective responsibility for the safety and welfare of visiting tourists.
- Tour operators, travel organizers, visitors, and relatives at home need to be informed and apprised of the situation/status of the crisis.

The management of crises within the hospitality industry poses some different challenges peculiar to the sector. One important difference relates to the option of evacuating guests to nearby islands or to their countries of origin. Although such actions can help to considerably lessen the problem, their implementation requires the availability of all information in a timely and accurate basis and the cooperation of all relevant actors. These are, therefore, the key factors upon which this plan is based.[3]

Terrorism

Terrorist attacks and threats against the hospitality industry, whether large international chains or individual properties, have grown alarmingly since 9/11. This trend, unfortunately, may continue to grow in terms of numbers and level of sophistication.

---

2. *Is That a Finger in My Chili?* By Kathryn A. Braun-Latour, Michael S. Latour, and Elizabeth F. Loftus, 2006.

3. www.nemo.gov.lc.

Modern day **terrorism,** which until the second half of the 20th century was mainly focused on targeted attacks, but has since been increasingly directed against soft targets (targets that are not major public or government centers or sites). By attacking soft targets, because of their relative ease of access, terrorists have improved their chances of achieving their objectives, which include inflicting higher numbers of casualties, causing extensive property damage, and undermining the well-being and public morale of local, as well as national populations.

The hospitality and tourism industries are certainly natural targets. The effects of attacks on such sites are devastating and far-reaching. Even with this new awareness, it appears that only the airline and cruise industries have adopted stronger measures in light of the 9/11 attacks. One has just to look around and compare the investment in security measures between airports, cruise lines, and hotels. Are hotels that different from airplanes or cruise ships?

A professional security assessment should be conducted on each individual site by a qualified security company. The company should have experience and expertise in the hospitality industry. Evidence seems to indicate that hospitality and related industries are still not prepared to take appropriate action. Hotel and resort management's reluctance to invest accordingly is dangerous, especially for high-risk situations or locations.

Ethics and the Hospitality Industry

Many times, hospitality managers are confused about legality and **ethics.** They think to themselves, "If I follow the law, I will be ethical as well." This is only partially true. To follow the law and do things legally is the bare minimum of being ethical. Ethics, although beginning with law, presents a much higher standard to adhere to.

For example, a resort offers its guests a free midnight pizza party. While making the pizzas, the resort uses all the ingredients required for the pizza, but decides to use, instead of fresh and firm tomatoes, some tomatoes in the kitchen that are just beginning to rot. Although these old tomatoes will probably not make the resort guests sick, and thus it would not be unlawful to use, is this ethical?

Another scenario: a wedding planner is paid to order Mumm's® champagne for a wedding reception. But, the wedding planner thinks, "Hmm I could make some extra money and order a cheaper brand." This borders on fraud and it is definitely not ethical.

In the hospitality industry, one's reputation and goodwill are critical to staying in business. Although it is tempting to try to save a few dollars by "cutting corners," if this were exposed to the public the business would have a very difficult job of recreating the favorable goodwill they had prior to the public knowing of their indiscretions. Ethics comes down to three questions:

- Is it legal?
- Would you, as a customer, want this done to you?
- Would you want the world to know what you had done?

If the answer to any of these three questions is no — don't proceed, it is not ethical.

Ethical Responsibilities in the Hospitality Industry

- It is imperative that a hospitality manager provides factual and accurate information about their services and the services of any firm they represent.
- It is only ethical to provide complete details about the cost, restrictions, and other terms and conditions, of any hospitality service sold, including cancellation and service fee policies.
- Always promptly respond to customer concerns.
- Always remit any undisputed funds under the hospitality business's control within the specified time limit to return them. If there are any reasons for delay in returning such funds, these reasons must be provided to the customer promptly.
- Every customer's transaction must be treated confidentially. No information should be disclosed about the customer without their permission, unless it is required by law.
- If there are any changes in fees, services, or itinerary, the customer is to be notified promptly. If there is a need to provide alternate accommodations or services, these must be of equal or greater value. If something of lesser value is given, the customer must be given appropriate compensation for the difference.

Chapter Summary

It is inevitable that a crisis will strike the hospitality business. It could be a natural disaster, a food recall, or a terrorist attack. The key is to be prepared in advance; handle the crisis intelligently; and keep the potential legal consequences in mind during and after the crisis. Always do a post-crisis analysis of how the situation could have been handled better.

Legality and ethics are not the same. To be legal and follow the law is the bare minimum of being ethical; being ethical is a much higher standard. Ethics can be remembered as doing what is "right or wrong."

Key Terms

Talking points
Goodwill
Tsunami
Crisis Communications Team
Holding statements
Wendy's®

National Emergency Management
    Organization
Saint Lucia
Terrorism
Ethics

Chapter Twelve

Insurance

Chapter Objectives

What is the difference between a property and a casualty insurance policy?

What is workers' compensation?

What is business interruption insurance?

Who is affected by the Affordable Care Act?

What does life and disability insurance do for a business?

Who should buy product liability insurance?

Who needs errors and omissions insurance?

What should a dram shop policy cover?

What is an umbrella policy?

What does the term endorsement mean in an insurance policy?

Property/Casualty

"Business insurance" can be broken down into a list of various types of insurance policies.

Property Insurance

Property insurance insures against loss or damage to the physical structure and contents of the hospitality business. Property insurance can cover multiple losses or be for a specific risk. For example, a fire insurance policy insures only against a fire loss to the location. A tornado is not a fire and, therefore, that loss would not be covered under fire insurance. Each risk that is to be covered must be listed in the insurance policy. The amount of maximum monetary coverage must be stated, and the premiums for this policy must be paid on time for the policy to be effective. Property insurance can be purchased if one rents, leases, or owns the structure and contents of the business.

Insurance policies come in two basic forms — **all-risk policies** covering a wide-range of incidents and perils, or **peril-specific policies**, which cover losses from only those perils listed. Examples of peril-specific policies include fire, flood, crime, and **business interruption insurance** (discussed below).

All-risk policies cover risks faced by the average small business. Peril-specific policies are usually purchased when there is a high risk of peril in a certain area, for example, if a business is located in a flood zone. It is best to consult an insurance agent in the business's locale to determine what policies are suggested or required.

Casualty Insurance

Casualty insurance is a broad area of insurance. It includes vehicle insurance, liability insurance, and workers' compensation. (All discussed below.)

Liability Insurance

Liability insurance insures against liability legally imposed upon the business due to the negligence of the business or its employees. It protects the business when the business is sued for this tort.

Commercial Auto

A personal automobile policy does *not* cover vehicles used by businesses. If the business uses vehicles or anything that is required to be titled, then **commercial auto** policies are needed. Commercial auto coverage insures against property damage to vehicles and damage caused to others by those vehicles.

Workers' Compensation

It is required, by state law (with the exception of Texas), to insure employees against on-the-job injuries. **Workers' compensation insurance** is a system whereby the employee is not allowed, by state statute, to sue their employer for on-the-job injuries; but, in return, the employer must participate in a system that provides nearly automatic payment to the employee in case of injury. This must include medical bills and damages.

There are many options for workers' compensation coverage. Some states allow an employer to opt-out of the system if the employer is self-insured; some states run the system through private insurers, and others use state agencies.

Alabama's Workers' Compensation Law

In Alabama, any business that has five (5) or more employees, other than contractors, is required by law to have workers' compensation coverage. The term employee includes all full or part-time employees, officers of a corporation or members of an LLC.

In Alabama, an employer may opt to self-insure. The requirements are: A net worth of $5 million; current assets to current liabilities ratio of 1 or greater, and a positive net income for the past three years.

There's no security required except that the self-insured employer must belong to the Alabama Workers' Compensation Self-Insurers Guaranty Association. Further, a self-insured employer must have and maintain specific excess insurance coverage with a retention amount of $250,000 or greater.[1]

Hawaii's Workers' Compensation Law

The employees' safety and well-being on the job are important to employers. However, accidents and illnesses can arise from work, and when they do, employees are covered under the WC law. The Hawaii WC law was enacted in 1915, and its purpose was to provide wage loss compensation and medical care to those employees who suffer a work-related injury. The WC law, in essence, requires the employer to provide certain benefits without regard to the fault from the employer and generally prohibits an employee from filing civil action against the employer for work-related injuries or illnesses.

Any employer, other than those excluded (section 386-1), having one or more employees, full-time or part-time, permanent or temporary, is required to provide WC coverage for its employees.

The statutory "presumption" places on the employer the burden of producing substantial evidence to the contrary to rebut a claim for a covered work injury [emphasis added].

---

1. www.labor.alabama.gov.

In the event of a work injury, the employee should immediately report the injury to their supervisor/employer. The employer should then file an "Employer's Report of Industrial Injury" (WC-1) to the WC Division within seven (7) working days. The employer can also file a report if the employer believes the injury is not work-related.

Because of the potential costs of a WC claim, most employers purchase insurance from insurance carriers authorized to transact WC in Hawaii. An employer is prohibited from requiring the employee to contribute towards the WC insurance premiums. The alternative would be for the employer to become self-insured and pay statutory benefits directly to the injured employee. Self-insured employers must furnish proof of financial solvency and the ability to pay benefits, and this must be approved by the WC director.

Each employer shall post and maintain in places readily accessible to employees a printed statement concerning benefit rights, claims for benefits, and such other matters relating to administration of the workers' compensation law. Each employer shall furnish within three (3) working days of notice of injury a copy of the brochure — Hawaii Workers' Compensation Law to each injured employee.

Benefits for injured employees include the following:

- Medical benefits — all medical treatment which includes surgical and hospital services and supplies related to the injury. The injured employee is entitled to choose the treating physician.
- Temporary total disability benefits — wage loss benefits paid as long as the employee is certified disabled from work by a treating physician.
- Permanent partial disability benefits — payments due to an employee when an injury results in a percentage loss of use of specified portions or functions of the body.
- Permanent total disability benefits — payments due to an employee if the injured employee cannot return to work because of the injury.
- Disfigurement — payments due to an employee for scars, as a result of laceration or surgery, including deformity and discoloration.
- Death payments due to a surviving spouse and dependent children in work-related death cases.
- Vocational rehabilitation — if the employee is unable to return to their usual occupation. The injured employee may receive career counseling, testing, training, and job placement.

If an employer does not have WC coverage for its employees, the injured employee may contact the Investigation Section in Honolulu, or the closest neighbor island's Department of Labor and Industrial Relations District Office for assistance.[2]

Business Interruption Insurance

Business interruption insurance insures against loss or damage to the cash flow and profit of a business due to the business not being able to operate. This could be because of a breakdown of a piece of equipment; damage from a storm; or loss of an essential service, such as power. If the business can't run — there can be no profit.

Health Insurance

To get the best employees, most businesses need to offer their workers' health insurance. This coverage is usually a group policy where the employer pays some or all of the premiums for the employee, and possibly their family.

In 2010, Congress passed the **Affordable Care Act** (ACA), also known as "Obama Care." This Act calls for every individual in the United States to be covered under a healthcare policy. It does not matter whether the individual is covered under their employer's health plan, Medicaid, Medicare, or if they purchase an individual policy.

If the individual does not have such insurance, there is a monetary amount assessed against them for their non-compliance. This is called the "**individual mandate**." This aspect of the ACA was challenged on Constitutional grounds by those opposing the ACA and was taken to the federal courts for resolution of this issue.

On June 28, 2012, the U.S. Supreme Court, by a vote of 5–4, upheld the "individual mandate" provision of the ACA. Chief Justice Roberts cast the deciding fifth vote in this decision. In the majority opinion, the five justices voting to uphold this provision of the ACA found the requirement that all citizens purchase health insurance (the individual mandate) or pay a monetary amount to be a tax. It was held by the Court, "The mandate may be upheld as within Congress's power to 'lay and collect Taxes.'" Art. I § 8, cl. 1.[3]

---

2. www.hawaii.gov.

3. *National Federation of Independent Business v. Sebelius*, 183 L. Ed. 2d 450 (2012), Argued March 26, 27, 28, 2012 — Decided June 28, 2012.

In 2017, both houses of Congress voted to repeal the Affordable Care Act's (ACA) individual shared responsibility penalty (individual mandate penalty), effective for 2019, as part of the 2017 tax reconciliation act. The long title to this action is — an *Act to provide for reconciliation pursuant to titles II and V of the concurrent resolution on the budget for fiscal year 2018, Public Law 115-97,* was originally introduced in Congress as the ***Tax Cuts and Jobs Act** (TCJA)*. This tax cut act does not repeal the individual mandate, what it does do is zeros out both the dollar amount and percentage of income penalties imposed by the mandate. Section 5000A remains in the statute and still provides:

> An applicable individual shall for each month beginning after 2013 ensure that the individual, and any dependent of the individual who is an applicable individual, is covered under minimum essential coverage for such month.

As a result of this "zeroing" out of the penalty for not having insurance, the State of Texas stated that since there was no longer any penalty for not complying with the "individual mandate," under the ACA, the entire law should be struck down.

In February 2018, Texas led 19 other states in a federal lawsuit in the United States District Court for the Northern District of Texas challenging the constitutionality of the ACA following the removal of the individual mandate penalty in the Tax Cuts and Jobs Act of 2017. (see above) The suit, *Texas v. Azar*, established that since the individual mandate was seen as a core provision of the ACA as determined by the Supreme Court in *Sebelius*, (see above) then with its removal, the entire law became an unconstitutional exercise of Congressional taxing power.

On December 14, 2018, District Judge Reed O'Connor released his opinion in that case, affirming that, without the individual mandate, the whole of the ACA was unconstitutional. O'Connor wrote, the "Individual Mandate can no longer be fairly read as an exercise of Congress's Tax Power and is still impermissible under the Interstate Commerce Clause — meaning the Individual Mandate is unconstitutional." He then further reasoned that the individual mandate is an essential part of the entire law, and thus was not severable, making the entire law unconstitutional. The reaction to this decision was California and several other states, vowed to lead a challenge to this ruling.

By early January 2019, 17 states led by California filed an appeal of O'Connor's decision in *California, et al. vs. Texas, et al.* (19-10011) in the United States Court of Appeals for the Fifth Circuit. The Fifth Circuit issued its ruling on December 18, 2019. The 2–1 decision, joined by Judges Elrod and Engelhardt, upheld in principle District Judge O'Connor's decision that with the elimination of the individual mandate, parts of the ACA were potentially unconstitutional.

The California-led group filed a petition for a *writ of certiorari* to the Supreme Court by January 3, 2020, in response to the Fifth Circuit's decision. The filing asked for the case to be heard on an expedited schedule, "because of the practical importance of the questions presented for review and the pressing need for their swift resolution by this Court." Texas and the other states also filed a petition in February 2020 to the Supreme Court, asking them to deny the expedited review of the case. The U.S. Supreme Court refused to hear the case on an expedited review schedule but did agree to hear the case. The case to be heard during the 2020–2021 term. The Court consolidated both California's and Texas' petitions (Dockets 19-840 and 19-1019, respectively) under *California v. Texas*.

Oral arguments were heard on November 10, 2020. Observers of the arguments believed that Chief Justice John Roberts and Justice Brett Kavanaugh, along with the three more liberal justices, appeared to accept the severability arguments of the individual mandate that would leave the rest of the ACA in place.

On June 17th, 2021, the USSC dismissed the challenge to the Affordable Care Act, leaving the law intact. Justice Stephen Breyer wrote the Court's 7–2 opinion. Justices Samuel Alito and Neil Gorsuch dissented.

The U.S. Supreme Court's majority opinion stated that plaintiffs do not have standing to challenge the "minimum essential coverage provision [codified at 26 U. S.C. § 5000A(a)] because they have not shown a past or future injury fairly traceable to defendants' conduct enforcing the specific statutory provision they attack as unconstitutional." *California et al. v. Texas et al.* No. 19-840. Argued November 10, 2020 — Decided June 17, 2021 (www.supremecourt.gov /opinions/20pdf/19-840_6jfm.pdf).

Small Businesses and the Affordable Care Act (ACA)

The **Small Business Health Options Program** (SHOP) is for small employers who want to provide health and/or dental insurance to their employees — affordably, flexibly, and conveniently. To purchase SHOP insurance, a business or non-profit organization generally must have 1 to 50 employees. If eligible, the business does not have to wait for an Open Enrollment Period. A business can start offering SHOP coverage to employees at any time of year. SHOP insurance gives small businesses choice and flexibility. Employees can be offered one plan, or they can choose from multiple plans. The small business can offer only health coverage, or only dental coverage, or some plans offer health and dental. Small businesses can choose how much to pay toward their employees' premiums and whether to offer coverage to their dependents. The business can decide how long new employees must wait before enrolling. Small businesses are encouraged to work with an agent or broker to help enroll in coverage.

The business may be eligible for the **Small Business Health Care Tax Credit**. The business may qualify for the tax credit if the business has fewer than 25 full-time equivalent (FTE) employees, if the average employee salary is about $50,000 per year or less, if the employer pays at least 50% for the full-time employees' premium costs, and if the business offers SHOP coverage to all full-time employees. (The business does not have to offer it to dependents or employees working fewer than 30 hours per week to qualify for the tax credit.)[4]

Dental Insurance

Dental insurance is insurance coverage for individuals to protect them against dental costs. It insures against the expense of treatment and care of dental diseases and accidents to teeth. The most common types of *private* dental insurance plans are **preferred provider organizations** (PPOs) or **dental health maintenance organizations** (DHMOs). Both types are considered managed care.

Preferred Provider Organizations

A preferred provider organization (PPO) plan allows a particular group of patients to receive dental care from a defined panel of dentists. The participating dentist agrees to charge less than usual fees to this specific patient base, providing savings for the plan purchaser. If the patient chooses to see a dentist, who is not designated as a "preferred provider," that patient may be required to pay a greater share of the fee-for-service. Unlike the more restrictive DHMO, however, the employee can go out-of-network and still receive some benefits.

Dental HMOs

These insurance plans operate like their medical HMO cousins. This type of dental plan provides comprehensive dental care to enrolled patients through a designated provider office (dentist). The dentist is paid on a per capita (per person) basis rather than for actual treatment provided. Partici-

---

4. www.healthcare.gov.

pating dentists receive a fixed monthly fee based on the number of patients assigned to the office. In addition to premiums, client co-payments may be required for each visit.

Vision Insurance

Vision insurance helps to cover the cost of eye exams, contact lenses, and glasses. Some vision plans will also pay for corrective procedures such as laser eye surgery. Most plans will cover one pair of glasses or a supply of contacts for a year.

Pet Insurance

Many animal medical procedures, such as surgeries and sickness, are very expensive to treat. To help with these costs, a pet owner can buy a policy of **pet insurance**. The cost and coverage of this insurance changes with which policy the employee gets, and for what type of animal they are insuring. Recently, fewer employers are offering this insurance option to their employees.

Life and Disability Insurance

Life and disability insurance protects the business against the death or disability of key employees. For example, one partner carries a life insurance policy naming the partnership as a beneficiary. If that partner dies, and the business has planned properly, the proceeds of the policy can be used by the business to buy out the share of the decedent's partnership interest from the estate. This prevents the situation when the entire business must be sold to pay the deceased partners' heirs.

Product Liability Insurance

Companies that manufacture, wholesale, distribute, and retail products may be liable for their safety. **Product liability insurance** protects the business against financial loss stemming from a defective product causing injury or bodily harm. The amount of insurance that should be purchased depends on the products that are sold or manufactured. A gift shop would have far less risk for a product's sale than a manufacturer of a food item.

Professional Liability Insurance

Business owners providing services, such as realtors, attorneys, and account-ants should consider having professional liability insurance (also known as **er-rors and omissions insurance**). This type of liability coverage protects the business against malpractice, errors, and negligence.

Depending on the profession, a business may be required by state law to carry such a policy. For example, in certain states, physicians are required to purchase malpractice insurance as a condition of practicing.

Home-Based Business Insurance

Contrary to popular belief, homeowners' insurance policies do *not* generally cover home-based business losses. To cover these potential losses, **home-based business insurance riders** may be added to the homeowner's policy to cover normal business risks such as property damage. However, homeowners' policies only go so far in covering home-based businesses. There may be a need to purchase additional policies to cover other risks, such as general and professional liability (see above).[5]

Dram Shop Insurance

Dram shop or liquor liability insurance is business insurance that protects the business against losses or damages claimed as a result of a patron of the business becoming intoxicated and injuring themselves or others.

Liquor liability coverage may be sold as an add-on to a commercial liability policy, or as a separate liability policy. This insurance must be purchased in addition to the standard liability coverage. A standard policy does *not* protect against liquor liability.

This coverage is expensive — depending on one's business location. If the state where the business is located has a "dram shop liability" statute, and the business is in the business of manufacturing, selling, serving, or facilitating the use of alcohol, this insurance is important.

---

5. www.sba.gov.

What to Look For/Ask For in a Liquor Liability Policy

Assault and Battery Coverage

Most claims against bars and restaurants are the result of fights. The liquor liability policy should include coverage for assault and battery. If not, the policy has a much lower real value.

Defense Costs Included

The biggest cost facing the business in liquor liability claims is the cost of retaining a lawyer; insurers know this. That is why they sell policies where "defense costs" are deducted from the total coverage. For example, a $500,000 policy will be reduced to $400,000 in coverage because $100,000 was paid out by the insurance company in attorneys' fees.

Pass on a liquor liability policy that does not include providing the business skilled legal counsel.

Employees Included

If liquor is served, employees will drink, regardless of the rules. Insurers know this and sometimes exclude employees from coverage. Make sure employees are covered as are patrons.

Damage Definition Includes Mental Damages

Claimants may claim they were damaged in non-physical ways — stress, mental anguish, or psychological damage. Some policies exclude these types of damages. Don't purchase a policy with limited damages definitions.

Reduced Premiums Based on Safety and Claims

Market leaders in bar and restaurant insurance will offer free liquor safety training to their clients' employees. These companies may offer up to a 15–20% discount on premiums if all employees complete such trainings. Further, if there is no liquor liability claim history against the insured business, there may be additional premium reductions.

Remember, liquor liability insurance will *not* cover sales that are contrary to state law or if sales are being made to minors.

Umbrella Policies

What Does an Umbrella Insurance Policy Mean?

Umbrella insurance provides an additional layer of security for those who are at risk of being sued for property or personal injury damages. An umbrella insurance policy is very helpful when the insurance owner is sued and the dollar limit of the original policy has been exhausted. It protects the assets and future income of the policyholder above and beyond the standard limits on their primary policies. The added coverage provided by umbrella insurance is most useful to individuals who own a lot of assets, or face liability exposure in running a business.

Typically, an umbrella policy is pure liability coverage over and above the coverage afforded by the regular policy and is sold in increments of one million dollars. The term "umbrella" is used because it covers liability claims from all policies underneath it, such as auto insurance, business insurance policies, and homeowners' insurance.

For example, if the insured carries an auto insurance policy with liability limits of $500,000, and a homeowners' insurance policy with a limit of $300,000, then with a million-dollar umbrella policy, the insured's limits become, in effect, $1,500,000 on an auto liability claim and $1,300,000 on a homeowners' liability claim.

How to Read an Insurance Policy

It's important to remember each section of an insurance policy must be considered to determine what is and is not covered. Here are the major sections of an insurance policy and what to look for:

Declarations

While a large portion of the insurance policy is **boilerplate**, the **declarations** section of the policy is customized to one's individual business.

Specific values for the building, personal property, business interruption, payroll, sales, fleet list, and so forth, appear in this section. The declaration section is easy to identify, because it is the only portion of the policy where information is manually typed in.

When reviewing the declarations page, make sure the information shown is accurate and includes what items were supposedly covered in the policy. Check that the primary insurance company's name is correct and any additional business/corporate entities are listed.

Coverage Form or Insuring Agreement

This section outlines which losses are covered and which are excluded. For example, a standard general liability policy promises the company, "Will pay those sums that the insured becomes legally obligated to pay as damages because of 'bodily injury' or 'property damage' to which the insurance applies." With an insurance policy, it is easier to determine what is covered by reading what is not covered.

When reviewing the coverage form, read the **exclusions** (what is not covered). The coverage form is generally boilerplate, but if there are concerns with any of the exclusions, insurance companies can often modify the exclusion by attaching an **endorsement** (a written document that modifies the policy by changing the insurance coverage) to the policy. Speak with one's insurance agent if there are concerns as to what is covered.

Definitions

The **definitions** section defines the terms used in the coverage form of the policy. This section is often overlooked, because many people feel a commonly used word has the same definition as it would in normal use. That may not be the case.

For instance, a liability policy may define property damage to include "tangible property only." This serves to exclude damage to electronic data, which is intangible. When reviewing the definitions, be sure to read and understand everything listed. This will further clarify the coverage established by the coverage form.

Endorsements

Endorsements may offer additional coverage or may limit or eliminate coverage in certain areas. Often, endorsements, which limit coverage, are in response to large, unpredictable claims the company feels cannot be accurately underwritten (charged for).

For example, after 9/11, insurance companies endorsed policies to exclude terrorism coverage. This coverage can now be brought back for a small charge.

But many policy owners may not be aware of this exclusion and the current ability to reinstate this coverage. Often times, endorsements are added without notice to the policyholder as part of a **policy modification**.

When reviewing the endorsements, determine if any of them will reduce coverage in a way that is unacceptable. Ask the insurance agent for his or her opinion and agree on an action plan if the endorsement can be negotiated.

Conditions

The **conditions section** outlines the responsibilities the insured must fulfill to qualify for coverage if a loss occurs.

A typical condition is one requiring the insured to report any loss in a "timely manner." For example, if a visitor breaks his or her arm after tripping over the worn rug in the lobby, and this incident was not reported until the hotel received a letter from the plaintiff's attorney the day before the **statute of limitations** runs out, two years later; it's a safe bet the insurance company will determine the condition for timely reporting has *not* been met.

Other typical conditions include cooperating with the insurance company during the investigation of any claim; allowing inspections by the insurance company; and notifying the company of significant changes in one's business operations.

It is important when reviewing the insurance conditions to read them carefully. Claims which could otherwise have been covered are often denied due to failure to meet the policy conditions.

Chapter Summary

Property insurance insures against loss or damage to the physical structure and the contents of the business. Liability insurance insures against liability imposed upon the business based on the negligence of the business or its employees.

Workers' compensation insurance is required by state law (with the exception of Texas) to insure employees as to on-the-job injuries. Having this insurance protects the employer from being sued by the injured employee for his/her injuries.

Business interruption insurance covers the business for losses to the cash flow and profits of the business due to an event that prevents a business from operating.

Product liability insurance should be purchased by any company that manufactures, wholesales, distributes, or retails products. This insurance protects against financial loss due to injury caused by a defective product.

In the hospitality industry, any business that serves alcohol should have dram shop insurance. These policies protect a business against loss or damages claimed as a result of a patron of the business becoming intoxicated and injuring themselves or others.

Umbrella insurance policies provide an additional level of security for a business. This type of policy provides coverage over and above the coverage afforded by the standard insurance policies in place under the "umbrella" policy.

Although it is best to have one's attorney review an insurance policy before signing it, basic knowledge of how to read a policy is a valuable skill for a hospitality business owner to have.

Key Terms

Property insurance
All-risk policies
Peril-specific policies
Business interruption insurance
Casualty insurance
Liability insurance
Commercial auto
Workers' compensation insurance
Health insurance
Affordable Care Act
Individual mandate
Tax Cuts and Jobs Act
Small Business Health Options
    Program
Small Business Health Care Tax
    Credit
Dental insurance
Preferred provider organizations
Dental health maintenance organizations

Vision insurance
Pet insurance
Life and disability insurance
Product liability insurance
Errors and omissions insurance
Home-based business insurance
    riders
Dram shop or liquor liability insurance
Umbrella insurance
Boilerplate
Declarations
Exclusions
Endorsement
Definitions
Policy modification
Conditions section
Statute of limitations

Index